Migration, Diasporas and Citizenship Series

Series Editors: **Robin Cohen**, Director of the Int
Professor of Development Studies, University of (
Professor of Politics, University of Warwick, UK.

Editorial Board: **Rainer Baubock**, European University Institute, Italy; **James F. Hollifield**, Southern Methodist University, USA; **Jan Rath**, University of Amsterdam, The Netherlands

The Migration, Diasporas and Citizenship series covers three important aspects of the migration progress. Firstly, the determinants, dynamics and characteristics of international migration. Secondly, the continuing attachment of many contemporary migrants to their places of origin, signified by the word 'diaspora', and thirdly the attempt, by contrast, to belong and gain acceptance in places of settlement, signified by the word 'citizenship'. The series publishes work that shows engagement with and a lively appreciation of the wider social and political issues that are influenced by international migration.

Also published in Migration Studies by Palgrave Macmillan

Rutvica Andrijasevic
MIGRATION, AGENCY AND CITIZENSHIP IN SEX TRAFFICKING

Claudine Attias-Donfut, Joanne Cook, Jaco Hoffman and Louise Waite (*editors*)
CITIZENSHIP, BELONGING AND INTERGENERATIONAL RELATIONS IN AFRICAN MIGRATION

Grete Brochmann, Anniken Hagelund (*authors*) with – Karin Borevi, Heidi Vad Jønsson, Klaus Petersen
IMMIGRATION POLICY AND THE SCANDINAVIAN WELFARE STATE 1945–2010

Gideon Calder, Phillip Cole and Jonathan Seglow
CITIZENSHIP ACQUISITION AND NATIONAL BELONGING
Migration, Membership and the Liberal Democratic State

Enzo Colombo and Paola Rebughini (*authors*)
CHILDREN OF IMMIGRANTS IN A GLOBALIZED WORLD
A Generational Experience

Huub Dijstelbloem and Albert Meijer (*editors*)
MIGRATION AND THE NEW TECHNOLOGICAL BORDERS OF EUROPE

Thomas Faist and Andreas Ette (*editors*)
THE EUROPEANIZATION OF NATIONAL POLICIES AND POLITICS OF IMMIGRATION
Between Autonomy and the European Union

Thomas Faist and Peter Kivisto (*editors*)
DUAL CITIZENSHIP IN GLOBAL PERSPECTIVE
From Unitary to Multiple Citizenship

Katrine Fangen, Thomas Johansson and Nils Hammarén (*editors*)
YOUNG MIGRANTS
Exclusion and Belonging in Europe

Martin Geiger and Antoine Pécoud (*editors*)
THE POLITICS OF INTERNATIONAL MIGRATION MANAGEMENT

John R. Hinnells (*editor*)
RELIGIOUS RECONSTRUCTION IN THE SOUTH ASIAN DIASPORAS
From One Generation to Another

Ronit Lentin and Elena Moreo (*editors*)
MIGRANT ACTIVISM AND INTEGRATION FROM BELOW IN IRELAND

Ayhan Kaya
ISLAM, MIGRATION AND INTEGRATION
The Age of Securitization

Marie Macy and Alan H. Carling
ETHNIC, RACIAL AND RELIGIOUS INEQUALITIES
The Perils of Subjectivity

George Menz and Alexander Caviedes (*editors*)
LABOUR MIGRATION IN EUROPE

Laura Morales and Marco Giugni (*editors*)
SOCIAL CAPITAL, POLITICAL PARTICIPATION AND MIGRATION IN EUROPE
Making Multicultural Democracy Work?

Eric Morier-Genoud
IMPERIAL MIGRATIONS
Colonial Communities and Diaspora in the Portuguese World

Aspasia Papadopoulou-Kourkoula
TRANSIT MIGRATION
The Missing Link Between Emigration and Settlement

Ludger Pries and Zeynep Sezgin (*editors*)
CROSS BORDER MIGRANT ORGANIZATIONS IN COMPARATIVE PERSPECTIVE

Prodromos Panayiotopoulos
ETHNICITY, MIGRATION AND ENTERPRISE

Vicky Squire
THE EXCLUSIONARY POLITICS OF ASYLUM
Anna Triandafyllidou and Thanos Maroukis (*editors*)
MIGRANT SMUGGLING
Irregular Migration from Asia and Africa to Europe

Vron Ware
MILITARY MIGRANTS
Fighting for YOUR Country

Lucy Williams
GLOBAL MARRIAGE
Cross-Border Marriage Migration in Global Context

Migration, Diasporas and Citizenship
Series Standing Order ISBN 978–0–230–30078–1 (hardback) and
978–0–230–30079–8 (paperback)
(outside North America only)

You can receive future titles in this series as they are published by placing a stand-ing order. Please contact your bookseller or, in case of difficulty, write to us at the address below with your name and address, the title of the series and the ISBN quoted above.

Customer Services Department, Macmillan Distribution Ltd, Houndmills, Basingstoke, Hampshire RG21 6XS, England

---

Children of Immigrants in a Globalized World

A Generational Experience

Enzo Colombo and Paola Rebughini
University of Milan, Italy

First published 2012 by
PALGRAVE MACMILLAN

Palgrave Macmillan in the UK is an imprint of Macmillan Publishers Limited, registered in England, company number 785998, of Houndmills, Basingstoke, Hampshire RG21 6XS.

Palgrave Macmillan in the US is a division of St Martin's Press LLC, 175 Fifth Avenue, New York, NY 10010.

Palgrave Macmillan is the global academic imprint of the above companies and has companies and representatives throughout the world.

Palgrave® and Macmillan® are registered trademarks in the United States, the United Kingdom, Europe and other countries.

ISBN 978-1-349-43470-1   ISBN 978-1-137-00529-8 (eBook)
DOI 10.1057/9781137005298

This book is printed on paper suitable for recycling and made from fully managed and sustained forest sources. Logging, pulping and manufacturing processes are expected to conform to the environmental regulations of the country of origin.

A catalogue record for this book is available from the British Library.

A catalog record for this book is available from the Library of Congress.

10   9   8   7   6   5   4   3   2   1
21 20 19 18 17 16 15 14 13 12

Transferred to Digital Printing in 2013

Contents

Acknowledgements

This book is based on seven years of qualitative research and many people helped along the way. We especially wish to acknowledge Luisa Leonini, who participated in several parts of the research and whose thoughts and comments were invaluable. Roberta Bosisio, Paola Bonizzoni, Lorenzo Domaneschi and Chiara Marchetti also played an important and active part in the project; we wish to thank them for their work, for sharing ideas and offering helpful advice. Maurizio Ambrosini, Luca Queirolo Palmas, Chantal Saint-Blancat and Antonella Spanò also gave us suggestions and empirical insights.

The research received financial support from the Italian Ministry of Education, Universities and Research (Ministero dell'Istruzione, dell'Università e della Ricerca, MIUR) for the projects PRIN 2001-04, 'Socialization and inclusion/exclusion processes in a multicultural context: The case of Milan'. PRIN 2005-07, 'Second-generation youths in Italy: values, group-identifications, consumptions, projects. A confrontation on the inclusion/exclusion paths of the "new second generation" among different theoretical perspectives'. PRIN 2005-07, 'Family Network and Second Generation: Between Consumption and Solidarity'.

As the manuscript evolved through several drafts, a number of readers helped us to improve it. In particular, our sincere thanks go to Melissa Butcher, Michael Eve, Anita Harris, Bruno Riccio and Giovanni Semi, who read and commented on the manuscript and gave us important insights and suggestions.

Parts of the research findings were presented at different meetings and congresses both in Italy and abroad, and many colleagues, generously, gave us important feedback and noteworthy observations. They are too numerous to mention individually, but their suggestions and comments inspired us to refine our arguments.

A special thanks to Danièle Joly who actively supported the book proposal; without her help this book could never have seen the light of day. We are grateful to the Series Editors and the Editorial Board who trusted in our project. Mary Alba gave us essential support and transformed our faulty English into a readable language with keen precision. Finally, our editorial team at Palgrave Macmillan provided all the support we could ask for. We especially thank Philippa Grand and Andrew James.

Introduction

In sociological literature, the life pathways of children of immigrants have always been a controversial topic, at least when compared to the comprehension of the social pathways of first-migrants. Rooted for the most part in ambivalence, the situation of immigrants' descendants is more complex to analyse: for them, difference is simultaneously both a resource and a constraint, identifications deal with reification and relativism, belonging with differentiation and adaptation, and behaviours with contingent rules related to the context and normative patterns linked to cultural roots.

From the empirical point of view, many differentiated situations exist depending on local and national contexts, laws, ethnic relations, historic heritage and colonial past. However, the way in which immigrants' descendants find their path to being part of the society in which they live cannot be reduced to either their economic position or a reified idea of their ethnic identity. Hence, sociological studies of children of immigrants have explored the theoretical and empirical aspect of the constitutive ambivalence of their situation by offering different interpretative frames: some studies leaning towards the ubiquitous pathways of integration, some towards ethnic distinction, others interested in the ability of these children to keep together plural references and habits.

The aim of this book is to show how children of immigrants, living in a globalized world, deal with the specific situations in which they are involved and with opportunities and constraints when tracing their biographical pathways; how they cope with the necessity to use, avoid or struggle against reification of difference and with the need to make their identifications credible and accountable. The goal is to recognize the generational characteristics of these experiences, and to understand how specific they are to our time.

In a globalized world – characterized by pluralism and complex connectivity and in which locality no longer refers to being born or residing in a particular place – coping with ambivalence and change become a mundane necessity. This is particularly true for young people from an immigrant background, who often experience different contexts, languages, rules and expectations which require the capacity to mediate, translate and use the right codes fitting the situation. The relation between structural factors and personal capacities becomes more complex and, from a sociological perspective, it becomes necessary to understand the intersection between historical changes and the situated experiences of the individual actors.

To pursue this understanding of these intersections we refer to specific analytical concepts that constitute the theoretical backbone of our analysis and that continue through the presentation of our research. The historical scenario is conceptualized by means of the analytical tool of *generation*, drawn mainly from Karl Mannheim. The initial hypotheses are that young people nowadays are encountering new specific historical experiences, and that the central characteristics of the new unity of generation deriving from such experiences are particularly evident when looking at the daily lives of children of immigrants. Focusing on the idea of a shared historical experience helps us to shed light on the opportunities and threats the children of immigrants have in common with others of the same age group, and avoids an over-reified reference to their difference or ethnic identity. The concept of generation highlights what is new and original for the cohort of young people living today in Western countries, and what is in fact specific to the situation of immigrants' descendants.

The contextualized evaluation not only of what is common and what is specific to the children of immigrants, but also of the opportunities and threats that concern them, is developed in the description of our empirical work. In this vein, the concepts of *tactical ethnicity* and *justness* are introduced in order to focus on contingent situations to understand how adolescent descendants of immigrants concretely deal with ambivalence in daily life. The objective is to show to what extent these young people are able to navigate between different references according to the situations and the interlocutors, eschewing a definitive choice between *being in* or *being out*. This means investigating how children of immigrants fit into their contexts of living – which are not homogeneous cultural environments – claiming their rights and justifying their choices. Hence, the aim is to verify how they choose and coordinate different options and values in different situations, managing the uncertainties and the risks involved.

To better investigate such capabilities we have focused our attention on a selected group of immigrants' children. The research we present in this book deals mainly with young people having a high level of education and cultural capital, as well as positive relationships with their autochthonous[1] peers – characteristics which are relatively independent of their economic status. We argue that educational resources have to be considered crucial in the ability to deal with the constant construction of self and with the never-ending requisite of playing one's cards right in individualized and globalized societies. As difference can be either an advantage or a constraint, a source of fascination or humiliation, personal capacity to interpret the situation can minimize constraints and open up opportunities. For this reason, our empirical research has been mainly focused on young people who do not want to be merely 'integrated' into a cultural system, but who ask for participation in a process of social change.

Our theoretical references are intentionally hybrid. We set up our theoretical framework not only by discussing and drawing from the recent and more classical specialized literature on the children of immigrants, on their assimilation or transnationalism, but also from sociological studies on globalization and cosmopolitanism, on community and locality, on contemporary social theory on agency and personal capacity, and on debates on justice and equality. To understand how the children of immigrants deal with the ambivalence of difference and with the contradictions of the situations in which they are involved, it was necessary to refer to a broader theoretical scenario able to give us more insightful analytical tools.

Our aim was to understand the choices made by immigrants' descendants and the meaning they give to these choices, rather than analysing the structural position immigrants' descendants occupy within a specific society. Thus, our starting point was to consider them as subjects who are at the forefront of social change in pluralist societies. For this reason, we believe that the study of the children of immigrants is a sociological topic that does not exhaust its interest in itself, and in its specific research literature. On the contrary, insights into immigrants' descendants can offer a privileged perspective for the observation of broader social changes, such as the characteristics of individualization processes in globalized societies, the importance of contingency and practices to understand how social actors interpret situations, their necessity to learn how to navigate between different references, opportunities and constraints, surviving structural uncertainty.

Investigation into the lives of immigrants' children may shed light on the fact that, in a globally interconnected and rapidly changing world, making 'the right choices' is more than ever a vital skill.

Outline of chapters

The first chapter is a theoretical introduction to the concepts we discuss in the book from an empirical point of view. We take into consideration the principal views of the current theoretical debate on the children of immigrants: the ideas of inclusion, integration and assimilation; the segmented assimilation theory; and the perspective of transnationalism. We focus on the historic and cultural contexts in which these frameworks have been developed; we then add theoretical insights by focusing on the concept of generation. On the one hand, the generational perspective – and the idea of generational experience – is a way of reducing widespread insistence on the specificities of immigrants' descendants, without erasing the importance attributed to cultural differences. On the other hand, it is a way of highlighting the characteristics of the globalized and pluralist environment in which children of immigrants – as well as their autochthonous peers – live today.

In this first chapter we also justify our interest in a specific avantgarde of children of immigrants: those who can rely on a high cultural capital and have decided to invest in their education beyond the compulsory level. These are the children of immigrants whose personal skills in finding their own way of managing cultural codes, identifications and belonging are more visible.

The second chapter is mainly dedicated to the description of our methodology and the fieldwork of our research. This was carried out in Italy, in the city of Milan. However, our aim was not to describe a national or local case, but to connect specific contexts with subjective interpretations. Moreover, new theoretical insights can be developed from observation of the present generation of children of immigrants growing up in Southern European countries, where migration processes have a history rooted directly in the globalized post-industrial era. In this chapter we explain how we matched our method and the selection of the panel – based on 7 years of qualitative research (2003–9) and 266 narrative interviews – to our interest in the more educated avant-garde of immigrants' descendants. We then briefly describe the characteristics of the Italian context as well as the situation of primo-migrants and children of immigrants in Italy.

In the third chapter we begin our empirical analysis by investigating the way in which the adolescent children of immigrants we interviewed make sense of their uncertain and mobile social location. We point out their capacity to manage the ambivalence of continuity and change, respect for parents' teaching and achievement of personal autonomy. They show a dual competence which allows them to deal with the reified aspects of difference as well as with the necessity of using this difference in a relative and flexible way, in order to adapt themselves to diverse and rapidly changing situations. As the interviewees reveal, the identifications and self-images of young people are not necessarily consistent and stable, but are related rather to specific contexts, and are multifaceted with varying levels and potentials.

In the fourth chapter our focus is citizenship and belonging and the way in which children of immigrants claim new forms of inclusion and participation. First of all, we analyse the concept of belonging, pointing out how the idea of feeling part of a specific community no longer derives from an idea of destiny; it is instead made up of a never-ending series of choices and achievements which necessitate the ability to mix one's commitments. The interviews highlight explicitly how the feeling of belonging is a continuous process of positioning and negotiation of boundaries, rather than simply being the mechanical effect of ascribed characteristics. Claiming different forms of belonging in different situations has to do with the capacity to choose and negotiate inclusion.

The fifth chapter is dedicated to the discussion of plural and mobile identifications, in particular to the analysis of hyphenated identifications. In our interviews the hyphen represents a transformation of the idea of identification: avoiding definitive choices, accepting ambivalence, adding rather than subtracting. Again, we refer to a process rather than a category: like locality and belonging, hyphenated identifications have to be brought into play in different ways in different contexts, managing multiplicity and ambivalence. In this case, the hyphen does not simply refer to being *in-between*, kept between two different worlds; it refers to the fact of being, here and now, fully part of *both* worlds.

This has led us to introduce the idea of *tactical ethnicity*, a concept that encapsulates the ability of children of immigrants to manage difference according to situations, adapting what they have learned from different people and from different experiences and contexts, as well as the persistence of structural restraints. By referring to tactical ethnicity it is possible to point out that ethnicity is neither a completely self-determined feat nor a totally imposed injunction.

In the final chapter we present our concluding observations. We argue that it is possible to synthesize our empirical findings and our theoretical investigation by referring to the idea of *justness* which offers a grid of intelligibility to the behaviours and identifications of the present generation of children of immigrants. If, on the one hand, the concept of generation represents a diachronic analytical tool to shed light on the historical changes in which the children of immigrants live today, on the other hand, the concept of justness represents the synchronic analytical tool to point out the way in which these children claim their rights, manage their identifications and justify them according to the context. The children of immigrants are in search of justness because they do not simply seek some kind of adaptation and integration, nor do they want to choose the alternative of an ethnic identity. Justness means bringing together the feeling of appropriateness to the contingent situation, the ability to justify one's decisions, belonging and identifications, and the claim of equality considered as important as the recognition of difference. Consequently, the search for justness is the mark of a globalized and individualized society in which members are obliged to face contradictory choices, ambivalent identifications and different registers of accountability, learning the art of shifting codes.

We have attempted to point out the existence of new and ambivalent processes of identification and belonging among the children of immigrants, who may also be thought of as distinctive actors in broader social changes involving us all.

1
The Future of Immigrants' Children in a Globalized World

The social fate of the descendants of immigrants is almost certainly a central concern of migration studies. While migration flows and the adult first migrants have been studied mainly to assess the impact of cultural difference in western societies, to evaluate social policies or to study subjective capacity to adapt, the fate of immigrants' children has become a wider theoretical test bed. Assimilation, integration, cosmopolitanism, hybridity, ethnicity are all possible interpretations of the various pathways the descendants of immigrants might follow in coming to terms with their family origins – that frequently means different names, different phenotypes, complex family trees and children's memories, sometimes different values and religious references. However, the principal sociological challenge seems to be represented by the necessity to reconsider what *being part* of a society means for people with immigrant origins. Belonging, memberships, citizenship, recognition of rights, recognition of identity claims, are all components of a feeling – and practical status – of inclusion; their extension and composition define the force and the quality of such inclusion.

In this chapter we analyse the main theoretical perspectives currently used to study the situation of immigrants' children. After presenting the classical assimilation theories – mainly used in Fordist industrial contexts to show the inevitable assimilation of the off-spring of immigrants into the mainstream of the host society – we critically discuss more recent theoretical perspectives: new assimilation theory, segmented assimilation and transnationalism. Here we pose the question of how, if at all, the analytical tools developed to study and understand the old immigration flows into countries experiencing a phase of huge industrial growth are still useful in trying to analyse a new form of immigration in more fluid and global contexts.

We start with a discussion of the mainstream literature on the children of immigrants, then we introduce the concept of *generation* as a diachronic analytical tool useful to shed light on the historic changes in which the children of immigrants live today, the structural specificities – in terms of opportunities and constraints – which characterize this generation of young people. To better analyse their characteristics, we have focused our attention on a specific category of immigrants' children, identified as a sort of potential *avant-garde* or *active minority*: the children of immigrants who frequent high schools, come from families with significant cultural capital and are more motivated towards their social mobility. This selection was necessary since the specificities we were interested in are more visible and predictable in this category of immigrants' children, even though it is more than likely that they extend throughout this entire generation of young people.

Taken as a whole this chapter can be considered as a theoretical introduction to those that follow in which these concepts are taken up again and analysed from an empirical point of view.

On inclusion

The first generation of migrants, as well as their descendants, have long been the objects of sociological studies interested in assessing their degree of *integration* into the societies in which they lived, both in Europe and the US. This idea of integration did not overlap exclusively with a functionalist framework but it was largely inspired by it. Nonetheless, the reference to integration remains ambiguous in the sociology of migration; sometimes considered as too close to a determinist concept of assimilation, intrinsically ideological: a person has to be integrated into a superior and already existing entity (Wieviorka 2008); in other cases it has been considered as inevitably partial, in terms of collective blocks: here integration refers to constructed but always plural identities, such as the ethnic group and the nation-state, or to more partial realties – for example, the neighbourhood, the school, or the work group (Eve 2010).

This intrinsic ambiguity of the concept of integration may explain the diffidence with which it has been approached by scholars – they themselves, mostly of immigrant origin – more inclined to point out the relationships of domination concealed in the integration processes. Since Franz Fanon's research (1963, 1966) integration has been regarded with suspicion, as a form of 'violent unconscious' of the white world, the determination to delete difference in a society which is expected to be homogeneous. Later on, the studies on racism and discrimination, on the representation of immigrants and the post-colonial studies on the speeches and constructions of otherness (Bhabha 1994; Spivak 1999; Said 2001) have also brought about a critical reconsideration of a naive concept of integration, as simple social or economic processes.

Overall, the idea of integration remains controversial: considered as too generic or unable to detect dominations and injustices. This is why we prefer to adopt in this work the concept of *inclusion*, with a reference to the idea of being part of a society, in the sense of participation – to participate and to feel concern with one's specificities – and not of simple assimilation. In this vein, the idea of participation can be related also to the contingency of inclusion – in a specific situational frame – or with the opportunity to keep together a plurality of references, rather than with an idea of being part of a systemic framework of values and identities.

Certainly, assimilation is a more theoretically developed concept than those of integration or inclusion, and not surprisingly – even if reassessed – it continues to be at the forefront of research on the descendants of immigrants. Thus, it is interesting to illustrate the changing declinations of the theoretical idea of assimilation – whose core arguments remain however the same, in spite of all deviations that can be observed in empirical studies in existing globalized societies. Then it is possible to show how, in the last two decades, new concepts, such as those of transnationalism, have traced a third way in the radical antithesis of assimilation and ethnic distinction.

The predicament of assimilation

Assimilation was for a long time considered the forgone conclusion of the process that immigrants and their descendants have to follow to avoid falling into deviance and marginality. This idea implicitly took for granted that assimilation of the newcomers would occur gradually, differentially but inevitably, because the only alternative was expulsion from a regulated social system. Even though uneven or controversial, the process of assimilation seemed the 'only highway': 'customs regulations, immigration restrictions and racial barriers may slacken the tempo of the movement; may perhaps halt it altogether for a time but cannot change its direction, cannot at any rate, reverse it', said Park (1950: 149).

The United States has been the central reference for empirical theories of assimilation, even though these concepts have been important in French literature on immigration too. Concerning prominent American literature, this position is evident in the classical studies of Robert Park, and later in those of Milton Gordon. In particular, this takes shape in the studies of Park as a sort of general law: observing immigration fluxes in Chicago, Park refers to a four-phase process in which contact, conflict and accommodation are considered as the predecessors of a final process of assimilation. The societies in which immigrants lived were supposed to be homogeneous and monolithically stable in order to face the arrival of newcomers, and these societies overlapped with the nation-state considered as an assimilating social system.

Inevitably, this position was typical of a phase in which the western model, represented by wealthy and industrialized nations, was considered as an undisputed value and a unique standard of living. This idea of assimilation was necessarily deterministic, because newcomers were bound to become simply Americans (not yet hyphenated Americans), which was also part of the melting pot theories of that time (Kivisto 2006).

In the 1960s Gordon (1966) proposed a more analytical definition of assimilation, classifying it in different positions and stages: acculturation, structural, economic and institutional assimilation, marital assimilation, civic assimilation and so on. Assimilation, as a differentiated process, was no longer conceptualized as a monolithic and determinist path. Despite this, however, in those years the idea of assimilation had already lost its hegemony in the US and was being challenged by the theories of pluralism and by criticisms of the melting pot. In the following two decades, assimilation lost its appeal in the American literature, even though it did not disappear completely. Only in the 1990s, with the works of Herbert Gans,

Richard Alba, Alejandro Portes and other scholars, did the concept of assimilation return to the centre of the debate, with a new heuristic and theoretical role.

Herbert Gans has tried to restore the concept of assimilation by avoiding determinism – assimilation is not a normative precept – and searching for a feasible combination with the idea of pluralism (Gans 1997); in his opinion assimilation is clearly supported by empirical evidence and has to be distinguished from the idea of acculturation. Assimilation 'refers to the newcomers' move out of formal and informal ethnic associations and other social institutions into the nonethnic equivalents accessible to them in the same host society' (1997: 877). Gans affirms that such a distinction was already present in the Park analysis; however he insists on a fundamental new point: assimilation also means *participation* in American public life (i.e. in terms of political and economic positions). Assimilation, as a structural process, is slower than acculturation. With acculturation ethnic practices and identities become purely symbolic (i.e. food, rituals, celebrations); assimilation on the other hand involves not only personal attitudes and decisions but a wider process of social integration too. Hence, assimilation is not a straight-line process, rather a combination of agency and structural contexts.

In a similar manner – within 'new assimilation theory', developed more recently and primarily in response to 'segmented assimilation theory' – the concept of assimilation remains sociologically relevant in the theoretical positions taken by other scholars. Alba and Nee (1997) as well as Brubaker (2001) – although they try to avoid any association of the word assimilation with a normative programme, imposed by the nation-state and oriented to eradicate minority cultures – affirm that contesting the idea of assimilation is a mistake. On the contrary, the idea of assimilation can be used in an effective way, as an analytical tool, in order to indicate spontaneous and often unintentional social processes characterizing all prolonged contacts between the majority and minority groups. Hence, assimilation continues to be a useful reference to record the fate of the descendants of immigrants in western societies.

These scholars support the concept of assimilation because it is in contrast with an excessively positive appraisal of difference and because it can account for processes which do not take place on an individual level (transformation of identity, values, and personal behaviour), but on a collective level, involving several generations or the society as a whole. Again, these scholars are mainly interested in the social context, and in its influence on economic changes in the life of immigrant families. Economic factors are considered relevant and connected to the processes of social inclusion, which, in this case, are conceived as an important aspect of assimilation. Social inclusion by virtue of economic factors means first of all social mobility, the abandonment of formal and informal ethnic associations in favour of equivalent non-ethnic social institutions concerning family and labour interests, work and professional life, with a parallel laicization of religious beliefs and values.

In this vein, assimilation is no longer a process that dissolves difference and imposes a sort of national universalism – without which the only alternative would be that of deviance and social exclusion – it is instead, a process spread over different sectors of social life and based on the opportunity of social integration, in professional life and spending patterns. The focus on social position and social mobility valorizes the capacity of immigrants to gather economic, educational and social capital. Thus, assimilation is considered mainly as a process connected to historic contexts and economic cycles. Conversely, the role of difference is not investigated in depth: there are varying degrees of ethnicity, but little attention is dedicated to their contextual uses and mediations.

Overall, we notice that, although at least in the US, reference to assimilation has returned to the centre of the debate on the basis of empirical research on immigrants, it is only with the 'segmented assimilation theory' that immigrants' children became the real focus of the theoretical debate on assimilation.

The segmented assimilation theory

The concept of assimilation is still central to the widespread theoretical frame of 'segmented assimilation', put forward by American scholars such as Alejandro Portes, Ruben Rumbaut, Min Zhou and others. The idea of assimilation is broken down into three separate results characterizing the integration paths of the children of immigrants in post-Fordist societies – the 'new second generation' – and it is presented as an articulated process with potentially differing results.

The idea of segmentation has been used both to indicate that the assimilation process is all but taken for granted, smooth, unavoidably oriented toward an upward economic and social mobility, as well as to accentuate once again the idea that economic and social inclusion can be disconnected from the acculturation process (Portes 1996; Portes et al. 2009). Moreover, this assimilation means integration into different subcultures of the host society; different trajectories mean different forms of assimilation, but without necessarily cultural 'amalgamation'.

On the other hand, the ability to maintain strong ties with the ethnic network and a fluent bilingualism usually amount to the premise for upward mobility. A second generation who can rely on a consistent and pluralistic ethnic network have more opportunity for educational and professional achievement (Portes and Rumbaut 2001); while the young people of the second generation living without the support of a strong ethnic network may experience processes of downward assimilation, pushing them to associate with the urban underclass. Again, cultural heritage is not considered in its content, but as a strategic resource, connected to being able to rely on communitarian support.

This theoretical model has been constructed by focusing mainly on the American situation, which is not quite the same as the European, and with particular attention to socio-economic positions and residential locations, more than to cultural and racial perceptions. According to its authors such an analytical model aims to offer a complete overview of the various paths of inclusion or difficulties of inclusion by means of the three-way renowned typology.

The first possible path is that of assimilation into the middle class of the majority. Cultural differences are likely to fade following full socio-economic integration. Hence, successful integration into the mainstream of the autochthon society – and relinquishing completely any public claim of difference – seems to be the premise for upward social mobility. The second path leads to downward assimilation, towards permanent poverty with a parallel acculturation to spending patterns that will never be affordable. Downward mobility is also due to anachronistic self-recognition with the traditions and networks of the parents, displaying a difference which is hostile towards the dominant culture. The third path links economic integration into the middle class with the preservation of strong community solidarity and networks. In this case, cultural ties with the ethnic community are considered an alternative to the acculturation into mainstream western habits to obtain the same results of economic integration. This is the typical case of segmented assimilation, in which the retention of strong ties with the parents' ethnic network and culture functions as a resource for upward social mobility.

As maintained by this interpretation, the principal reason to cultivate ethnic ties remains linked to job opportunities and community protection. However, we cannot overlook the fact that community and family ties are cultivated in a widespread and geographically transnational way for symbolic, emotional and identity reasons too. These family, friendship and sentimental networks can be a transnational symbolic space transcending national boundaries, embedded in specific cultural and personal relationships. For the second generation the reference to this symbolic space may be situated and personal, and not necessarily perceived as a binding structure.

Overall, in the different versions of assimilation theories, assimilation remains a useful analytical tool to assess the capacities of integration of the state or to evaluate, with the help of longitudinal studies, the intergenerational trajectories of social mobility. In particular, segmented assimilation has been useful in documenting the differential pathways taken by different groups and cohorts of immigrants' children. However, such perspectives seem less effective when investigating the subjective evaluations of difference and otherness, the feelings of discrimination, the dynamics of identifications according to the contexts, or the impact of technologies, media and networked communication on the very ideas of assimilation or multiculturalism.

The transnational turn

This attention towards the singularity of social actors and the impact of media technologies in a globalized society has been mainly developed by another theoretical perspective, that of transnationalism.

The transnationalist perspective places the inclusion path of children of immigrants into the wider present-day context of globalization. In contrast with previous theories – more focused on intergenerational legacies – in such a theoretical framework the changes brought on by the globalized fluxes of people, jobs, images and information technologies is considered as paramount. According to the foremost scholars of transnationalism, migration processes create new social fields connecting spatially separated places and groups as well as a new category of social actors – *transmigrants* (Levitt and Glick Schiller 2004) – who maintain strong instrumental and affective ties over national boundaries (Glick Schiller et al. 1992; Smith and Guarnizo 1998).

The experience of transnationalism is not that of migration, it does not mean living in two different countries and being permanent migrants; rather, technology and media are the main vehicles of the awareness of concrete and lasting ties – based on exchange, reciprocity and solidarity – between different places and social contexts. This awareness leads to the creation of social cohesion and collective symbolic representations (Kivisto 2001; Faist 2000; Vertovec 1999). Thus, transnationalism has to do with a space of imagination (Appadurai 1996), communicative and affective fluxes, the movement of goods, news and information, rather than with specific and long-term spatial collocation.

While assimilation theories assume the nation-state remains an appropriate conceptual unit to assess the inclusion or exclusion of immigrants and their descendants, this idea is explicitly challenged by transnationalist approaches. In this respect, inclusion cannot be evaluated solely from the perspective of the host society – the nation-state – on the contrary inclusion is related also to exchanges, reciprocities, solidarities and networks which connect groups and communities in a transnational perspective.

In a globalized world, the space people experience as personal and unique is made meaningful by relational and imaginative dimensions, rather than by the spatial dimension. This meaningful space is constructed by a dynamic synthesis that links together the local and territorial dimensions with the routines of everyday life – such as habits and consumer patterns – personal relationships, expectations and projects. In this context, children of immigrants negotiate and create collective identities. They take their symbols and references for identification wherever they can, from the global cultural fluxes as well as from local specificities and habits, both from the country of their parents and the country where they live (Baumann 1996; Hannerz 1996).

Emphasis on these transnational dimensions can vary according to the interpretations. The more radical interpretations of transnationalism tend to overestimate the individual freedom and creativity of the transmigrant actor. They transform the idea of difference into a never-ending process: a mere exercise of aesthetic construction oriented toward personal gratification, a desirable condition for a wider consciousness and a stronger warranty for freedom and justice. However, this means underestimating constraints, risks, struggles and power relationships. The exclusive emphasis on the mixing processes risks slipping into a normative dimension, which hides power relationships by presenting the possibility of hybridity always in a positive fashion (Anthias 2001). The tendency to overemphasize individual freedom – in adapting contexts in order to obtain the greatest personal advantages – also risks representing identification as a pure contingency without structural consequences, such as conflict and exclusion related to identity claims.

Having said that, in its weaker version – a version that does not assume difference as a solipsistic and purely contingent construction – the transnational approach can stress some important processes of globalized societies. Specifically, the transnational dimension underlines how immigrants' children learn to put themselves into relational and cognitive horizons which transcend the national dimension to bind the local and the global in an innovative way. This multiplies the opportunities of identification and belonging as well as helping to reassess the weight of cultural claims, for the reason that the new generations of immigrant children seem to be no different from any other youngsters growing up in a globalized context and having an adequate set of cultural and social resources.

More generally, among the topics emphasized by the transnational perspective, there is that of a reflection on globalization and its consequences on the fate of immigrant children. Globalization has at the same time been an economic, political and cultural phenomenon, which has affected the destiny of immigrant families in its entirety (Kivisto 2006; Suárez-Orozco 2001). More than ever before, globalized capitalism and neo-liberalism have intensified migration fluxes in which a cheap labour force moves from the peripheries of the world – the countryside and the poorest regions – towards globalized cities or other areas in need of the low-cost global working class (Sassen 1998). If, on the one hand this has encouraged ethnic enclaves and the *ethnicization* of the job market, on the other hand, it has also enhanced new opportunities and forms of transnational entrepreneurship, especially among the more educated children of immigrants, and those able to use ethnic networks without being controlled by or confined to them.

On the political side, globalization and transnationalism have moved discussion of citizenship to the top of the agenda for immigrant people and their children. Citizenship is no longer associated with the exclusive belonging to a nation-state, but remains a fundamental right, necessary to develop full participation, on an equal basis, in the societies in which ones lives. In transnational and globalized societies, citizenship is a crucial point of tension: it can be the grounds for exclusion and discrimination, as well as the multiplier of memberships, belonging, identifications and self-fulfilment. This is why rules and laws about citizenship are always a sensitive topic for the children of immigrants.

Finally, from the cultural point of view, transnationalism is firmly entrenched in the cultural dimension of globalization, for which social and national spaces become transnationalized, giving people the opportunity to choose, developing translations, syncretism and hybridization (Faist 2000). People are no longer obliged to belong to just one culture, conceived as a closed system, they live instead in a situation of simultaneity of different cultural references. Cultural incorporation into the host society is no longer inevitable, the alternative to permanent exclusion; social inclusion does not mean losing one's difference and specificity, it means having the opportunity to move towards more personalized and context-related pathways of inclusion.

Overall, we could say that the weak points of the transnational perspective are for the most part related to an excessive focus on contingency and difference, as an exclusive pivotal reference in the identification and integration patterns, and to an underestimation of the constraints – both contingent and structural – in which transmigrants and transnationalized actors make their choices. Starting from these weak points, we now move towards a further analytical position, developed during our research in Italy: the *generational perspective*. In particular, insight into the generational characteristics may help to reassess the role of cultural difference in the identification patterns, to analyse hybridity as a product of both agency and contexts, which means both opportunities and constraints, and to consider some attitudes of the children of immigrants, such as cultural code-switching, as a typical generational skill.

Looking beyond assimilation and transnationalism

The children of immigrants have become an increasingly important part of migration studies over the last three decades. This interest concerns the social and educational mobility, the evaluation of the integration process of these young people, as well as their lifestyles, identification patterns, family relationships and consumer tastes. Since the 1980s a considerable amount of research on the children of immigrants has been published not only in the US, where investigations focus on the 'new second generation', whose parents were migrants mainly from Latin America and Asia (Portes and Rumbaut 2001), but in Europe too.

This means that in both Europe and the US, the children of immigrants have become an important social topic in the same period of history: that of the progressive crisis of the industrial era and its Fordist model of production, characterized as well by the passage to a globalized economic system, no longer based on national media, but on an interconnected framework, centred on globalized communication networks (Castells 2009). It is during this period that the children of immigrants began to be considered as a generation, and the idea of 'second generation' became a central topic for research on immigration, a focal point to understand the more general transformations of western societies.

Indeed, before the 1980s, the life of the children of immigrants was rarely investigated as a specific sociological issue; the future of immigrants and their children was instead understood as a process of progressive social and cultural assimilation, or – on the other hand – as a pathway towards the construction of some sort of claimed ethnicity, or as the descent into some kind of deviance and marginality. The late 1970s inaugurated a phase in which it becomes progressively more evident that the children of immigrants are not necessarily destined to succumb to the only alternatives of assimilation/auto-referential ethnicity/marginalization. On the contrary, their participation in the society in which they live can follow different and more complex paths: the new generation of immigrants' children (the majority of non-European origin and born after the western economic boom) did not seem so keen to abandon any reference to the culture of their parents, nor to be completely tied to them. It is also in this period that the topic of cultural difference became a fundamental political issue for western democracies, for which the descendants of immigrants represent social actors who might be involved to a great extent in synthesis and mediation (Benhabib 2002).

On this topic, the theoretical traditions behind European and American research differ, as do the interpretations and the specificities of the phenomenon. However, since these interpretations have been elaborated in the same historical time frame – mainly the two decades of the 1980s and 1990s – we can consider the generational features of the children of immigrants, analysed by these theories, as relevant.

In the interpretation elaborated in the 1980s, the mounting and inexorable crisis of the industrial model of society is the main background for the core of the research on: the collapse of working-class community life, of which immigrants were an important part; the worsening of the quality of life in the urban areas in which immigrant families live; growing unemployment especially in traditionally industrial towns; the expansion of mass consumption, and the rise of spending capacities as the thermometer of social inequalities; the difficulties of relevant quotas of the children of immigrants at school. This analysis of the socio-economic context – focused mainly on social inequalities – is explicitly visible in the French and British studies on immigrants' offspring around the 1980s (Dubet and Lapeyronnie 1992; Gilroy 1987; Solomos and Beyon 1987; Hall et al. 1978; Rex 1996). However, particularly since the 1990s, other interpretations have been put forward: new research focuses attention on the social mobility of some groups of immigrants' children – for example fresh job opportunities for the better educated in modern service sectors – while other studies analyse their claims of difference, as well as the redefinition of ethnic networks and ethnic relationships, towards more individualized and situated approaches to ethnicity (Kasinitz et al. 2008; Yuval-Davis et al. 2006; Purkayastha 2005; Levitt and Waters 2002).

We could say on the one hand, that the framework of analysis remains that of the transformations of the socio-economic system, with consequences concerning the practical integration opportunities, strategies or difficulties of immigrants' children. On the other hand, we find other analyses focused more on cultural topics: on the transformations of ethnicities and ethnic identities towards new forms of ethnic claims, hybrid identities or transnational and personalized cultural references.

Certainly, in spite of the global tendency of such changes, some differences depending on national context have been observed. Some specificities are evident in the histories and memories of colonization and the management of decolonization and post-colonial relationships, particularly in Europe – for instance in the United Kingdom and France – as well as between countries with strong relations with former colonies and countries with a weaker and shorter colonial history.

Social policies and integration paths: Britain and France

Until the 1970s none of the European countries – as destinations of large-scale immigration flows – had elaborated any specific policies in favour of immigrants' children, who as members of working-class families were still the concern of general welfare policies. As a matter of fact, the children of immigrants were not recognized as a specific category, even in the countries in which migration issues were already at the centre of the national political debate. Only in the 1980s, especially in the United Kingdom and in France – following the statistical data showing the growing number of children of immigrants in schools and high drop-out rates from education – were specific school policies inaugurated (Crul and Vermeulen 2003; Crul and Schneider 2009).

We can briefly be reminded here of the main characteristics of the two French and British paradigmatic cases, pointing out how the children of immigrants have emerged, in Europe, as a political and sociological topic during a period in which migrants themselves could no longer be considered as temporary unconventional elements, and their subaltern role could no longer be accepted as inevitable.

In France the situation has been characterized by the cultural tradition of universalism, secularism and centralized republicanism. The social integration of immigrants and their families was considered as the corollary of the social equality formally guaranteed by the Republic. Cultural and religious differences were supposed to be confined to the private space, in order not to disturb the integration process (Wieviorka 2008). Since the Third Republic, that is since the nineteenth century, the Republican school has been the main institution with the responsibility of integrating working-class children of both French and immigrant origins. However, despite the historical role of guardian of social stability, the Republican school has often been accused of betraying its formal commitment to social integration. It has in fact been accused by many scholars as being responsible for the social exclusion of many children of immigrants in France, as the producer of social inequality (Payet 2002; Dubet 2004).

The banlieue riots in the 1980s, and the marches and demonstrations against racism in the same years, were the first important signals of the difficulties of the 'French model' of integration. The children of immigrants – living in the urban suburbs during the transition from an industrial and expanding economy to the post-Fordist spread of unemployment – were the first generation to discuss and to argue against the French assimilation model (Touraine 1997).

The institutional answers to these protests and unrest were focused on the solution of the 'urban question'. The troubles of the children of immigrants – and the complementary political reactions to the rise of the right-wing xenophobic *Front National* party – were considered social problems of economic integration and urban marginalization. Hence, the bulk of the financial resources and social projects were allocated to the urban 'rehabilitation' of the banlieue areas and to the reinforcement of social services (Rebughini 1999; Boubeker 2003). Until the end of the 1990s, this financial commitment was not accompanied by public debate on the French model of integration; the claims of cultural difference put forward by the children of immigrants, as well as the more general topic of multiculturalism, continued to be neglected by the French institutions or considered as a potential vehicle of social disaggregation. Even the so-called *beurgeoisie* – the first middle class to be made up of the offspring of immigrants from the former North African colonies, the *Beurs*, made up of bureaucrats, white-collar workers and academics – failed in its attempt to mediate the claims of recognition of cultural specificities and the request of social equality as the basis of French universalism (Body-Gendrot and Withol de Wenden 2007).

Thus, since the 1990s, and even more so in the following decade, the immigrant population living in the urban banlieue areas – people from the first, second and even third cohort of immigrants – became the 'bad consciousness' of the French model of integration and, according to some French sociologists, 'social garbage', a French version of the American ghetto (Lapeyronnie 2008; Boucher and Lapeyronnie 2010).

This means that the French sociological analysis of the offspring of immigrants has been far more concentrated on the failures and troubles of integration, than on the meanings and transformations of integration itself. The approach remains primarily associated with the consequences of structural economic and social transformations, and less concerned with cultural changes concerning identifications and ethnic relationships. Certainly, more 'culture-oriented' research and theoretical approaches exist, and they have for the most part been developed to find the cultural and symbolic reasons behind such social malaise (Wieviorka 1996, 1999). However, they have been mainly perceived as a discussion or an interpretation of debates elaborated elsewhere, first of all in the United Kingdom and in the US.

In the international debate it is taken for granted that France and the UK have developed different approaches to ethnicity, and the French universalist approach appears as a national exception. However, if we turn to the British case, we can verify that, despite a very different political approach to immigration issues, the growing visibility of a generation of immigrants' children since the 1980s has also been a turning point in the perception and interpretation of inclusion/exclusion issues.

In Britain, the situation of immigrants has been characterized by a long history of immigration from Commonwealth countries and by the early onset of racial tension and conflicts, especially in working-class areas. For example, episodes of 'race riots' in Nottingham and London's Notting Hill in 1958. This racial tension was not ignored by the media and the institutions; on the contrary, the problem was immediately treated as dangerous, following a tradition of government concern for 'racial harmony' begun in colonial times (Rich 1986). Moreover, important anti-racist demonstrations since the 1970s obliged public institutions to consider ethnic and cultural difference as a political topic of relevance (Anthias and Lloyd 2002). The institutional answer, attempting to prevent social and racial conflict, was the British government's approval of the 'Race Relations Act' and the 'Commission For Racial Equality' (1976) openly admitting the existence of racist discrimination within British society and encouraging the idea of living in a multicultural country (Keith and Cross 1993; Solomos and Back 1995).

As for education, important enquiries followed by social programmes were set up by the government, such as the Youth Training

Scheme and the Swan Committee. The Urban Programme, to improve the condition of working-class areas and to prevent urban segregation, completes the welfare backdrop of this historic phase, in which universalistic policies were still predominant. Some years later the free-market turn, imposed by the Thatcher government, brought about a different attitude, based on negotiations with single minorities and communities, in an attempt to avoid a solid front of social complaints (Keith and Cross 1993). Thus, in the United Kingdom the children of immigrants grew up in a context in which cultural differences matter and are clearly of political significance.

Furthermore, between the 1970s and the 1990s, with more visible, explicit and successful strategies than in the French context, this generation of immigrants' children in the UK was at the forefront of social struggle for the recognition of difference. They claimed the need to politicize ethnicity, to build up ethnic lobbies and to negotiate with the government, while at the same time initiating the processes of cultural hybridization that would be further developed by the following generation. Meanwhile British sociological cultural studies had already begun to analyse the lifestyles and consumer cultures of these young people, pointing out their forms of multiculturalism and hybridization of languages (Back 1996; Baumann 1996). Daily life, cultural products, local contexts, symbolic meanings and personal relationships are considered as relevant as structural features in understanding the role of cultural difference.

Nevertheless, at least until the early 1990s, the children of immigrants growing up in the 'Thatcher era' lived in a context in which the nation-state was still important, industrial relations and social classes were still relevant – in spite of their evident crisis – and racial discrimination was often associated with social hierarchies or urban segregation, as pointed out in the 'race and class' and 'colour line' interpretation. In the decades from the 1970s to the 1990s, social networks were not yet influenced by internet or communication technologies and claims of recognition were for the national government and local institutions.

It is only towards the end of the 1990s and above all in the following decade that new generational characteristics started to be developed in the whole of Europe: complex connectivity and communication technologies blurred the boundaries between local and global, nation and world, consumer patterns were changing and were hybridized, identifications became more flexible, situated and no longer linked to the place of living or exclusively to ethnic origins. Hence, also the struggle for recognition was no longer related to a precise spatial and cultural idea of belonging.

Certainly, this does not mean that individuals have been released from any form of constraint. For instance, the French context continues to be involved in a relatively 'technocratic' approach to the topics of discrimination and social integration, while the descendants of immigrants still ask for a less bureaucratic and nationalist approach to their needs for recognition (Boubeker 2003). The British context remains deeply involved with the topic of race – for linguistic, historical and political reasons – even though this has been discussed in various forms. The opportunity to choose ethnic identification remains constrained inside a social framework characterized by a reference to race relations (Song 2003). Hence, despite the growing importance of agency and individual choice, racial labelling and ethnic identities still remain an obstacle to a free and individualized negotiation of ethnicity.

Overall, the literature elaborated to analyse the situation of the children of immigrants from the 1970s to the 1990s has taught us a great deal about that generation and their way of life. This literature has focused specifically on the social integration of the children of immigrants, their social mobility, their family relationships and ethnic networks. Fresh and revised analysis of this type continues in the more recent literature towards the new formulation of concepts of assimilation or integration. In the last decade or so, though, the situation of the children of immigrants has been analysed even more from the point of view of their cultural identifications and new emphasis has been put on their capacity to cope with different contexts and cultural references.

Changing contexts and personal capacities

More recent analyses of the situation of immigrants' descendants have tried to focus on the changes brought about by globalization processes and the widespread use of new communication technologies. In the more recent literature, the children of immigrants are no longer classified as either melting into the society in which they live, abandoning every reference to a cultural difference, nor following a destiny of separation, in an ethnic culture or even a deviant subculture.

Despite such general awareness of the changing context, the transnational approaches are certainly more convincing in relation to the influence of transformations on the lives of the new generation of migrants, even though these approaches tend to associate changes with the centrality of cultural difference, emphasizing the peculiarity of biographies and migration trajectories. Indeed, the capacity to mix up and contextualize the references to cultural difference does not seem necessarily related to a biography of migration or to an obvious cultural distinction. Instead, the capability to switch from one context to another, from a cultural code to another, translating what has been acquired in one context to the constraints and opportunities of a new context, can be considered as a generational skill of 'late modernity', more than a competence related to a cultural difference.

In this case, the starting point of observation should be the globalization processes, rather than a specific predictable cultural difference. Although the capability to mediate, the coexistence of different cultural codes, choosing from them according to the situation, is probably an indispensable skill for immigrants and their children, these are also skills necessary for everyone in order to move and to adapt to a globalized environment. The need to articulate a plurality of belonging is not an imperative restricted to the descendants of immigrants, who on this point are no different from their native peers without family experiences of migration. Consequently, an excessive emphasis on cultural difference underestimates those generational features that help us to understand the more general aspects of the daily life and fate of immigrants' children. As some scholars have pointed out, living in complex, dynamic and transnational fluxes of information and experiences is predominately a generational experience, deeply rooted in the day-to-day routines of young people (Appadurai 1996; Hannerz 1996).

Certainly, the capabilities to deal with and to take advantage of such information and experiences are not equally distributed. More than emphasizing a neutral meeting of cultural differences, it is important to point out the differences and inequalities of economic and technological resources, social capital and relationships, and individual and personal skills. On this point, theoretical approaches on transnationalism have often underestimated the role of social positions and above all of the specificity of personal capacity. Counting on differentiated cultural references, managing symbolic codes, translating competences and skills from one situation to another – these are not the automatic outcome of being children of immigrants born into a transnational family. The ability to build a hyphenated identity is neither a spontaneous product of socialization into two different cultural constellations, nor is it a simple question of putting two parts together (Levitt 2009; Colombo 2010a).

Although these capabilities are immediately more visible and strategic for the children of immigrants, they are first of all a generational feature, whose existence and development are more connected to the opportunity and constraints of social situations than to the simple presence of cultural differences. Power relationships, social inequalities in the access to information, and lack of opportunities in developing personal capabilities to manage difference and ambivalent contexts are always determinant, also when they are not related to more explicit forms of discrimination. Hence, social positions, and cultural and economic capitals of the family still matter, both for children of immigrants and natives, even though they cannot be considered on simple economic grounds (Nussbaum and Sen 1993). In a post-industrial and neo-liberal scenario, individual self-entrepreneurship, flexibility, creativity and improvisation also become part of an indispensable personal capital. More generally, structural resources are increasingly related to symbolic personal capacity to adjust and mediate, which is becoming a fundamental agent of inclusion in a situation in which inclusion itself has a plurality of dimensions. A subaltern economic position is not necessarily associated to a marginal social position, to a form of passive acculturation or to feelings of frustration. In many situations, this subordinate economic position can be associated with the presence of personal skills for which the social actors are engaged in a never-ending process of mediation, to deal in a tactical way with the constraints of the context, in order to avoid or reduce exclusion and discrimination (de Certeau 1990).

In the case of the children of immigrants, what is at stake is the capacity to go beyond the feeling of a 'double absence' (Sayad 1999) moving towards the development of a 'double competence' (Baumann 1999): on the one hand, the capacity to manage inevitable reified – or racialized – hetero-identifications – or other kinds of constraints related to the social position – and, on the other hand, the capacity to manage contingent identifications, demotic discourses, and temporary negotiations to fit to the context.

Such capacities are encouraged and became necessary in the specificity of our time. Regardless of their national origins, these young people belong to a generation which grew up with cheap transnational phone calls and airfares, email, the exchange of family videos and frequent communications, and download of films and music. Even though it is difficult to evaluate the influence of these technological tools on pluralism and transnationalism, they offer different options and can be used to maintain meaningful connections, as well as to explore identifications and references. This new historic and technological framework allows the present generation of immigrants' children to shift and to select among different cultural practices: ethnicity can be valorized or hidden, presented as fashionable or claimed as a right. Hence, constructing a hyphenated identification in a non-neutral operation: 'hyphenated identities are formed of complex sets of layers that do not always converge or overlap and often remain fragmented' (Purkayastha 2005: 76).

That's why these capacities to fit into changing contexts, to manage the complexity of an interconnected world, and to overcome subordinate positions with the help of mediations and tactics can be considered a generational capacity, the mark of contemporary youth as a *generation location*[1] – to use the term of Karl Mannheim (1952) – whose characteristics are shared, even though in different ways and situations, by both the children of immigrants and their native peers, regardless of any national belonging. Indeed, a focus on the generational perspective can help us to reduce the widespread insistence on the 'particularity' of the children of immigrants, without erasing the value attributed to cultural differences. Now, in order to clarify the heuristic force of such a reference to generation, it is necessary to explain its meaning.

A generational experience

The children of immigrants and their native peers share the same generational experience: they share at least some of the major significant changes – social, technological, environmental, organizational – which characterized the same milieu in a specific time period. The concept of generation introduces an essential *historic* and *diachronic* reference: generations are held together by their common experiences. The immigrants' children and their peers, who are now adolescents and young adults living in a globalized and post-industrial society, represent a *generation location*: they share similar competences in using communication technologies, they are all rooted in transnational and intercultural frameworks of imagination, they are involved in the same economic crisis and changes of labour market, they share the same individualization processes. Certainly, a generation is not a simple cohort of people who are born at the same time; it is composed of people who have experienced the same key events and who develop a collective consciousness, similar identifications, that can lead to common agency patterns and common roles in social change.

More generally, the concept of *generation* can shed light on some specificities of the children of immigrants, which are less visible if we use exclusively the concepts of identity, ethnicity or cultural difference. Moreover, the idea of generation can point out common features without applying the ubiquitous references of integration or assimilation, avoiding the risk of a crypto-ideological approach. Thus, when researching the children of immigrants, it is interesting to point out not only a *unity of space* – the context of a European country, a specific town or urban area – but also a *unity of time*, whose characteristics are – at least partially – not the same as the lifetime of the descendants of the previous generation of immigrants.

Despite such analytical advantages, the concept of generation has been relatively neglected by present and previous research on the children of immigrants, while the temporal issue is considered only if related to the vicissitudes of integration processes.[2] Usually, the emphasis has been on individual or communitarian features – identity, ethnicity, race or gender differences – which cross-cut daily lives and the historic context in which people live, thus ignoring the possibility of a *temporal* common frame, which is not necessarily that of a common *cultural* frame.

Certainly, the analytical difference between temporal and cultural similarities can be considered inadequate to avoid the risk of ideological assimilation into a given cultural frame. For instance, deconstructionism and post-modernism – particularly in the works of Derrida and Lyotard – have directly or indirectly challenged, and spread mistrust, towards comprehensive interpretative models such as the idea of belonging to a common generation. However, it is possible to avoid a meta-narrative emphasis when using the concept of generation, and to combine it with the attention to difference; the sensitivity towards difference itself can be considered as a historic product. In this respect, the generational outlook can be useful to point out not only what is common in a given time frame, but also to provide an insight into the contextual, personal and differentiated manners with which people react and deal with this common frame of reference. For instance, from a historical point of view, young generations have often been considered critical components of social and cultural change.

Generational marks

According to Karl Mannheim – probably the foremost sociological reference on this topic – a generation can be defined as such if people belonging to it share some important historical events; moreover, the sensation of being part of the same generation is stronger if such events have been experienced during their youth and in the time of their reaching maturity. Crucial for Mannheim is also the rapidity of social change (*tempo* of change): periods of accelerated social change tend to produce more cohesive and distinctive generations.

To belong to the same 'generation location' means sharing the same events which shape life and personality, which cannot however be considered as a form of common consciousness: class, gender, ethnicity and other forms of social stratifications are also important; we could say though that the way of belonging to the same generation can change according to the variability of social positions (Pilcher 1994).

Following Mannheim, we find it useful to make a distinction between the concepts of *generation location* and *generation unit*. The idea of generation location points out the importance of the historic context and the common experience of people who live and who are born in the same historic period without having chosen it. Hence, young people who are born in the globalized era share a common generation location, characterized by the experience of pluralism and ambivalence, regardless of their ethnic origins. On the other hand the idea of *generation unit* points out the relevance of belonging to a more specific social group, sharing common problems, and a common way of thinking, knowing and of representing reality.[3] Hence, in our research we were particularly interested in the generation unit represented by the children of immigrants who share, more specifically, the ambivalence of being at the same time *in* and *out*, the experience of multiple belonging, the need to fit into the context as well as the need to claim recognition and equal opportunities.

However, in sociological literature, the concept of generation is generally used with the meaning of generation location, to point out the characteristics of a cohort of people in a specific historic context. Pierre Bourdieu (1980) suggested considering a generation as a cohort rooted in social positions, social classes, tastes, expectations and aesthetics, as well as potentially rooted in past traumas such as warfare, migrations and diasporas. Bourdieu in particular seems to consider generation as an analytical alternative to the concept of class in explanations of social change, especially among intellectuals and artists, where antagonism between generations is expressed by 'clashes between systems of aspirations'. Only some of them can become innovative agents, a generation in their capacity to create cultural and social change.

More recently, two other scholars – Edmunds and Turner (2002) – have pointed out the analytical centrality of the concept of generation, following the intuition of Bourdieu: 'the erosion of a strong class theory has provided an opportunity to reconsider generations, especially in relation to politics and cultural change ... and has provided greater opportunities for exploring generation as a further collective identity' (Edmunds and Turner 2002: 3). In this interpretation, the notion of generation has become more central in the rise of globalization and in the growing possibilities of cross-national contacts and exchanges among people belonging to the same 'technological generation'. This is particularly evident in recent research concerning online social networks, in which the majority of young people are involved nowadays (Elias and Lemish 2009).

It is interesting to reconsider the idea of generation also compared to previous cohorts of young people, at least from the recent past. In the 1950s, the work of Eisenstadt (1956) on the transition from generation to generation pointed out the innovative central role of younger generations in the post-war industrial world. At that time young people were the protagonists of social change and the promoters of innovative forms of social ties. On the other hand, in both Europe and the US, the generations born after the 1960s have often been defined more by their absence – Generation X – than by their characteristics. This definition was based on the comparison with the previous generations, such as the protagonists of World War II and the conscientious objectors, or the protagonists of social movements and cultural changes of the 1960s.

After the flames of these events had died down, young people seemed to no longer be at the centre of social conflict and rarely have they been considered as the agents of social change. On the one hand, young people continue to be studied as actors of deviant behaviour; on the other hand, sociologists point out their need for protection in the private and domestic space, in intimacy and with friends, in consumption styles, in the more protracted permanence in the family home. Rebel and eccentric attitudes concern some minorities, but public discourse and the mass media seem interested mainly in the predictable deviance of young people belonging to marginal classes and segregated urban areas, in which the children of immigrants play a central role. Thus, growing unemployment, precarious jobs, disillusion, absence of 'conflicts that matter' have put the generations of the 1980s and 1990s in the shade, sporadically on stage, mainly as negative or defeated protagonists, never as a generation of protagonists of a fundamental change.

However, if the cohort born after the 1960s has not experienced significant traumas or upheavals of social organization – so it is more difficult to identify them as a generation – the cohort born after the 1980s has been involved since their initial socialization in at least two major changes: the technological shift towards a global and interconnected world and the spread of relentless migration fluxes for which cultural difference became a permanent element of daily life. The growing importance of media, ICT and migration have implied a paramount turning point in late modernity and in the work of subjectivity. Although these changes have certainly involved every age group, they are recognized as more relevant in the socialization of the younger generations (Livingstone 2002).

Overall, the children of immigrants have already been protagonists of important social changes: since the 1960s they have challenged the hegemonic national consciousness and they play a critical role in transforming it, introducing the notions of difference, hybridity and hyphenated identities. For example, in the United Kingdom the political activism of immigrants' children from the working class was supported by a generation of intellectual minorities who transformed popular thinking about what it meant to be British (Werbner and Anwar 1991). Black intellectuals in particular challenged English nationalism by emphasizing the issue of minorities as the centre of the political agenda, they were involved in leftist movements against Thatcherism, and presented themselves as a post-colonial intelligentsia. Many other migrant intellectuals have helped to reinvent the idea of diaspora, transforming it into a positive and cosmopolitan identity, or have challenged the idea of social integration revealing its authoritarian implications. Certainly, these intellectual minorities are a restricted avant-garde of 'global citizens' who can easily move beyond national identities and belonging. However, they had a fundamental role in constructing the possibility of hyphenated references for the younger generation.

Another important legacy from that time is the focus on personal imagination and creativity as both a resource for social change and for personal achievement. In the past such youthful imagination was, without doubt, linked to both the desire to break away from the previous generations – their values, projects for the future or family patterns – as well as to a situation of economic growth and to the national welfare state, which encouraged hedonism and a self-centred search for authenticity (Boltanski and Chiapello 2005).

Today, generational conflicts and confidence in the future are weaker; the role of imagination is more connected to technological changes and to the daily contact with difference, than to a political horizon. However, imagination still leads to agency driven by collective and generational aspirations: the capacity to imagine and to aspire as a counter-tendency is still considered a typical resource of younger and more active generations (Appadurai 1996). The world of electronic media, international messages and images has been part of the childhood and adolescence of the present generation of immigrants' children, offering them new resources and new disciplines for the construction of their imagined selves. Such characteristics are clearly collective and generational, and they do not concern just single or privileged individuals. The processes of globalization have altered the relationships between subjectivity, location, political identification, and notions such as 'diasporic public spheres' or 'translocal communities' are now often taken for granted in sociological analysis.

Finally, imagination and the opportunity to navigate through plural cultural fragments can also be considered as typical features of the present generational experience. Discontinuity in space and time is certainly an enduring legacy of modernity, for which historical identities and communities have lost their solidity and authenticity (Zukin 2010). Since the days of Walter Benjamin's prophetic observations about technical reproduction, in the early decades of the twentieth century, individualized modern subjects have learned to navigate through fragments of memories and identities, looking beyond reproductive logic and routines.

However, today this ability to navigate growing plural references seems to have become an element of social selection: the capacity to compose different references and to move among them is not an automatic skill and this navigation is not a mapped and coherent route. There is not a 'right' or appropriate direction, and to navigate doesn't mean to be free to move without constraints: some rules have to be respected to avoid going adrift, and it is necessary to find tactics to go forward. If in the past such uncertainty was compensated for by stable references to class, political ideologies, religious faith, national identities and, for immigrants, ethnic cultural traditions, today such references have lost their stability: they are debatable, questionable, they have mobile and blurred boundaries. Hence, even though living inside a frame of plural references is a generational experience, there is always a sort of social selection between those able to gather, to waken and to re-establish different cultural fragments, giving them new meanings, and those unable to move among identities and communities, thus destined to be part of just one of them.

Hence, we find it useful to refer here to the concept of *generation unit*, to point out the reference to a more specific social group, that of the children of immigrants who not only share with their native peers more general characteristics related to belonging to the same historic context (the generation location), but who are characterized by the necessity to deal with more specific forms of ambivalence. The children of immigrants we studied in our research are a generation unit aware that ethnic difference can be a constraint or an opportunity, a negative label or a source of fascination, that refusing a definitive choice between being *in* or *out* requires the capacity to manage ambivalence. The main characteristic of this generation unit is the choice to stay in-between, to avoid definitive positions, looking to personal and contextualized forms of justness.

To be part of a generation unit does not mean sharing the same destiny or considered as uniform in respect to a given cultural frame. Differences remain relevant within the common characteristics and potential skills, regarded as generational references. The capacity to articulate plural references and belonging is becoming a crucial competence of some of the more selected segments of the present generation of the children of immigrants. This is why we have concentrated our in-depth analysis on the children of immigrants whom we can define as a type of potential *avant-garde*, or even as an *active minority*.

We may say that the concepts of generation unit and avant-garde partially overlap. The children of immigrants we interviewed represent an active minority and an avant-garde because they are able to use their experience to look beyond the context. They are able to elaborate representations and practices that can be applied by other young people in other contexts. Hence, they are an avant-garde not for economic or hierarchical reasons, but mainly for their specific capacity to manage the ambivalence typical of globalized and pluralist societies.

A generational avant-garde

During our research on the children of immigrants we were particularly interested to understand *how* they are able to use different codes in different situations, in order to achieve different goals and justify them as right and legitimized. It was immediately evident that, in both the literature and empirical research these characteristics are more visible and present in some specific sections of immigrant children: those with higher cultural capital, attending high school and living in broad-minded families. Consequently, such characteristics and capacities are typical of what we can call the avant-gardes or the active minorities of the present generation of immigrants' children. It is among such young people that the generational potential we described above is more widespread.

As we prefer to use the concept of inclusion instead of that of integration – to avoid an overused sociological term – for the same reason we prefer to use here the concepts of avant-garde and active minority instead of that of elite. Elite is too narrow a definition, deeply associated with an idea of a privileged social and economic position. Indeed, the capacities in which we are more interested are not necessarily linked to elitist positions, for the added reason that in many situations the children of immigrants live in families with a subaltern social position. On the other hand, the ideas of avant-garde and that of active minority suggest that this specific sector of immigrants' children can rely more on their cultural and relational competences than on a favourable social position in terms of family income. Moreover, such concepts suggest the presence of a desire of involvement and participation, as well as of the capacity to act and to speak in an innovative way. A marginal or subaltern position is not incompatible with the will and the capacity of participation.

Overall, we can define these potential avant-gardes by the presence of some specific characteristics such as: a serious investment in higher education usually – but not systematically – with the support of families with a solid educational and cultural capital; an ability to develop intense and steady relationships with native peers as friends, schoolmates or neighbours, to avoid isolation or exclusive ethnic relationships, and the opportunity to live in families where parents promote the autonomy of their children. These parents do not limit themselves to supporting their children's education, pushing them towards social mobility; they also support their autonomous choices, their wider social relationships, and they encourage them to take their own responsibilities. Hence, these young people show valid personal skills in investing in themselves, finding a personal way of managing cultural codes, identifications and belonging, and perceiving themselves as cosmopolitan citizens.

Again, these competences are not the reserve of a privileged social elite of immigrant families – these skills are potentially available as generational references, as consequences of the processes of individualization and familiarization with differences and otherness. At the same time, they are also necessary resources that one must have to avoid the risk of marginalization and discrimination.

A potential active minority

The notion of 'active minority' was first theoretically conceptualized by the social psychologist Serge Moscovici in his influential book *Psychologie des minorités actives* (1979). In his anti-functionalist approach Moscovici argues that cultural change and cultural *influence* can be developed by small innovative groups. Despite their clear position as a minority and their small number, these groups are able to set up an original and exemplary action and to offer different interpretations of the social world. Their position is neither that of deviance nor of rebellion, subversion or disobedience, because it is not immediately related to a dominant majority. According to Moscovici, the innovative creativity of the active minorities is persuasive, avoiding open conflict by the force of their example and arguments. In this reference to exemplarity Moscovici tries to go beyond the dichotomies of acculturation and emancipation, of passive assimilation and explicit resistance. Active minorities do not limit themselves to resistance but they offer a new way by the example of their choices and lifestyle.

The concept of active minorities has been fundamental for the theories of social movements. The theoretical framework of 'new social movements', mainly developed by Alain Touraine (1984) and Alberto Melucci (1996a), has particularly insisted on the centrality of symbolic action expressed by active minorities. In late modernity and the information age, change is frequent and extremely rapid: not all the capacity for change can be translated and transformed into political and institutional innovations and organizations. Hence, active minorities show the hidden potential for change, they produce imaginative skills and they open the door for the 'capacity to aspire' (Appadurai 2004). In this vein, that of active minorities can be considered mainly as a symbolic action:

Symbolic action cannot be assessed using the standards applied to other forms of action. Symbolic resources do not operate with the same logic as material or physical resources. The critical mass has lost the weight it may have had in the past, as often the big changes are produced by small symbolic multipliers, through action carried by active minorities evolving into major issues [...] The effects of what is mainly such action of small active minorities on a larger audience which could have been considered apathetic have at times been surprising; what actually happens is that these minorities prove capable of bringing about a change in the way people's experiences have been perceived and named.

(Melucci 1996a: 185)

We believe that this interpretation can be useful also to understand the position and the role played in our society by the active minorities among the children of immigrants.

Our interviewees – that we have defined as an avant-garde of active minorities – are probably going to follow positive paths of inclusion and they represent an exemplary case. They are a potential active minority also because they are more often involved in associations and social activism. Beyond formal associations, the informal networks of these young people (online as well as traditionally offline) are able to facilitate each individual to promote their personal version of ethnicity. They provide a public space away from family interpretations and traditions and they create affirmative narratives of belonging in which ethnic boundaries can be negotiated. This more specific section of the present generation of immigrants' children does not demand to have their claims incorporated into the political system, but instead they introduce new ways to combine identifications and moral concerns into the public culture. They do not want to be 'integrated' in a cultural system already there, but they ask for participation and they wish to take part in a process of change.

Certainly, we must not forget that to be an active minority also means to be exposed to risks. As Appadurai himself admitted in his book *Fear of small numbers* (2006), the potential of active minorities – especially when represented by immigrants and their descendants – can be challenged by new forms of nationalism, regional identities and a general growing fear of cultural difference. The fear of minorities – especially if they are active and visible – is well rooted in classical liberal thought and in the democratic dynamics between majorities and minorities. In spite of the positive procedural values ascribed to minorities – they bring dissent and debate – democracies are often reluctant to recognize the value of minorities as carriers of difference and multiple forms of belonging.

For these reasons, the potential represented by being part of a generational avant-garde and an active minority is not a guarantee for successful social inclusion. The pathway towards full social participation does not depend solely on personal will and capacities. Hence, there is always the risk of frustration. If personal potential is ignored and fails, the effect can be even more tragic than in the past. Since we live in a hyper-individualized society, where trials and situations tend to be personalized, failures tend to be personalized too. Thus, the sense of frustration and the need for revenge can lead to depression and passivity or to radicalization of self-referential collective identities.

Ambivalences of inclusion

The results of many years of international research have shown that the children of immigrants run a greater risk of discrimination and of belonging to the less privileged social strata; however, this has not prevented most of them from achieving upward social mobility or demonstrating motivation towards complete social participation (Alba and Nee 2003). Indeed, social mobility is not only an economic issue. Hence, the idea of inclusion does not seem a simple structural process – even though it continues to be a socio-economic process – particular identification tactics and the ability to fit into the contexts are not a simple contingent and fading attitude, but they are a relevant part of the opportunity for inclusion and social mobility.

Certainly, there are specific and contradictory patterns towards such inclusion. For example, graduating or becoming middle class do not totally solve discrimination issues and stereotypes. Again, the research literature shows that economic integration and a high level of education do not diminish or delete the perception of differences. The children of immigrants, like their parents, are often concerned by invisible daily struggles against discrimination and stereotypes which devalue their talents, facilitate pay iniquities, and justify a range of legal and social barriers. Theoretical positions around the concept of assimilation focus mainly on economic integration, and consider an ethnic group integrated – by professional and urban standards – when it is integrated into a white middle-class social stratum. However, other research (Purkayastha 2005; Kibria 2002) argues that ethnic groups become even more discriminated against when they integrate with native middle classes.

These kinds of discrimination are variable according to the contexts, however, the persistency of a sentiment of *foreignness* in the life of immigrants' children cannot be totally avoided. This is often linked to the feeling of being part of a hetero-defined 'ethnic group', due to physical appearance. Especially for youngsters with Asian, African and in many cases also Latin American origins, it is more difficult to hide immigrant backgrounds, because their difference is obvious. Indeed, young people with families migrated from Eastern or Southern Europe can also have similar problems, because of the social stigma that considers them 'unreliable' (Perry 2001; Aparicio 2007). At school – from junior to high school – and sometimes in other public spaces, the episodes of some sort of racialization make the children of immigrants aware of their difference. Such 'incidents' can be simple jokes or become subtle and sometimes explicit forms of discrimination. Moreover, such forms of exclusion can be added to others related to more universalist aesthetic parameters such as skin colour, weight, body shape and so on. Implicit racialization can also force the use of essential cultural references and to construct ethnic boundaries (Back 1996). The sentiment of foreignness can force immigrants' children to avoid being drawn into racially inferior positions by proving to be 'like' their peers, thus adopting mimetic attitudes. At the same time the stereotypes and the general attitude towards their culture or religion can encourage them to be more conscious of their traditions, making them more significant, especially when such traditions have to be explained to their friends and peers (Baumann 1996).

Overall, the topic of inclusion of immigrants and their children cannot be interpreted in a univocal way. As Rogers Brubaker noted a decade ago (Brubaker 2001), the differentialist change in social sciences had already reached its peak at that time, and effectively at least since that very year, naive attitudes towards difference and multiculturalism have changed (Benhabib 2002). This has encouraged a reassessment of the topics of assimilation, universalism, and more generally, social cohesion. Such oscillations from the political valorization of differentiation, to new attention to unifying features, certainly characterize a change in terms of values; claims of cultural recognition remain important, but socio-economic equality returns as a core topic (Fraser 2009).

However, despite such changes in terms of priorities and evaluations, what we define as the significant turning point towards a deep familiarity with globalization issues, communication technologies, transnational ties, and daily experience of multiform differences remains paramount to understanding the present generation of immigrants' children. Increasingly, social life takes place across symbolic, national and cultural boundaries, and belonging is no longer an automatic result connected to specific social places: the younger generation have been completely socialized in such a transnational environment.

Today, in order to understand how the processes of inclusion works, it is necessary to understand how the descendants of immigrants are able to refer to this plurality of belonging – that is also a plurality of participation and inclusions – how they keep up mediated relationships and use different codes in different situations in order to achieve different goals. In a globalized, and inevitably culturally differentiated, society – regardless of the evaluation of this differentiation – social inclusion cannot be considered simply as the result of material assimilation, that is, towards consumption or qualified professions. Participation, social justice and equality of opportunities are even more interconnected too with cultural competences, such as the capacity to fit into the context, to mediate and to avoid polarities or self-exclusive identifications.

Certainly, people cannot always use belonging and differences at will – constraints, risks, power relationships and discriminating attitudes can be part of the frame in which the children of immigrants live. However, even in the case of restricted spaces for autonomy, the fact of living in a world accustomed to difference can give them the opportunity to use difference in a plural and contextual way, without using it as an external label. Hence, such capabilities must not be considered as a subjective 'gift'; they are instead, first of all generational opportunities, relatively independent from ethnic and national belonging.

2
Framing Contexts and Actors

Introduction

Theoretical insights into the children of immigrants are inevitably inspired by the empirical contexts in which they are elaborated: local, national, political, historic and linguistic features frame the way in which individuals and groups act and make their choices, but these empirical features influence theoretical interpretations too.

Certainly, consideration for the empirical context and its specificities does not mean that theories are simply anchored to localized, rigid perspectives, from which it is impossible to generalize; on the contrary, in a globalized and interconnected world, local situations are always interwoven with broader changes. However, we cannot ignore or underestimate the connections between specific, situated 'facts' – such as the history, typology and timing of migrations, the general characteristics of social stratification of migrants, the role of the nation-state or the welfare state in dealing with them – and the analytical interpretations of their characteristics and evolutions. These interpretations are not only inspired by a 'theoretical taste' – for example preferential attention to the social positions of actors, rather than sensibility towards individual symbolic capacity for identification – but also by the evidence of empirical contexts and the making of situations (Lamont et al. 2011).

Hence, following the previous discussion on the main theoretical perspectives currently used in interpreting the situation of the children of immigrants in Western societies, in this chapter we introduce, on the one hand, the methodology of the research that constitutes the empirical base of our argumentation and, on the other hand, we briefly present the main social characteristics of the Italian context in which our fieldwork took place. The aim of this presentation is not solely descriptive; we wish to underscore how the contexts in which actors live are framed according to broader historic and generational transformations. New theoretical insight can be developed from the observation of the present generation of immigrants' children growing up in Southern European countries and in a globalized post-industrial era. Thus, the Italian context in which our research has been carried out must not be considered as just one national case among many others. The social space in which the children of immigrants live is not constituted only within the framework of a nation-state nor is it constituted only by geographical or political locations but also by mental spaces framed both by context-related situations and more global references. Hence, our aim is not to describe the situation of immigrants' children in Italy. Starting from specific fieldwork, the aim is to acquire more extensive insight into the connections between characteristics of the contexts, subjective interpretations, and theoretical analysis.

Since the last decade, the children of immigrants have become, in Italy as in many other Western societies, an important demographic component of the youngest cohort of people, with whom they share many generational characteristics and contexts of daily life. Adolescents and young adults have become accustomed to a world increasingly characterized by a growing fluidity of people, goods, images and information, which contributes to the blurring of national boundaries and to posing new questions concerning the principles of inclusion and exclusion. In some cases young people are able to deal with this environment by seizing the best opportunities; in other cases circumstances oblige them to take defensive attitudes. Understanding such ambivalence also means investigating how it is interwoven with the contexts in which these young people live.

The children of immigrants in Italy currently number approximately one million people, and this figure has quadrupled in the last decade. As a result of this growing visibility, Italian research on second-generation immigrants has developed rapidly in the last ten years and is now becoming well established.

Italian scholars have concentrated their research mainly on educational trajectories and scholastic success or failure, on changes to teaching models or school organization in order to best fit an multicultural education, and on the role schools can play in the dynamics of social inclusion or exclusion (Favaro and Omenetto 1998; Queirolo Palmas 2006; Besozzi et al. 2009). A second important field of research is represented by the study of the more general paths of inclusion or exclusion of the children of immigrants, on a national or local level. On the local scale there are already numerous pieces of qualitative research which look in depth into the daily and situated relationships, lifestyles and identification patterns of the children of immigrants (Bosisio et al. 2005; Riccio 2008; Valtolina and Marrazzi 2006; Colombo et al. 2011; Leonini and Rebughini 2010; Spanò 2011). Numerous and periodical surveys have also been dedicated to the study of more general quantitative tendencies in the patterns of inclusion, and to the analysis of the risks of exclusion (Della Zuanna et al. 2009; periodical national surveys of specialized institutions such as *Ismu* and *Caritas* are also published on a yearly basis).

Other researchers have been oriented towards specific ethnic groups, stressing the continuities and fractures with parents and peers (Saint-Blancat 2004), religious attitudes (Frisina 2010), racist and ethnic discrimination (Andall 2002), transnational activity and networking (Ambrosini and Queirolo Palmas 2005), and the challenges these 'new Italians' are posing to Italian society as a whole. Overall, we can say that sociological knowledge of the children of immigrants in Italy covers now almost all the issues and all the regions of the country. Certainly, the situation is evolving rapidly, and the differences and specificities on the local level remain important, especially in a highly differentiated country such as Italy; thus it is necessary to update frequently both quantitative surveys and ethnographical material.

Panel and methodology

The empirical research on which we base our analysis and argumentations in this book is based on seven years of qualitative national research (2003–9) on the teenage children of immigrants living in the urban area of Milan. During these years we have monitored the evolution of the situation of these children with a longitudinal series of qualitative studies.[1] We have tried to focus our attention not only on descriptive parameters, but especially on the social locations and the identification patterns of a generation of immigrants' children living in a differentiated and ever changing environment, in which the ability to manage multiple belonging and to fit into the context became paramount resources (Bosisio et al. 2005; Colombo et al. 2009; Leonini and Rebughini, 2010).

During these 7 years of research we collected a total of 266 narrative interviews with children of immigrants of different national origins (from Asia (21.8 per cent), Eastern Europe (14.3 per cent), sub-Saharan Africa (7.1 per cent) and North Africa (21.1 per cent), and Latin America (35.7 per cent)), all aged from 16 to 21; 143 girls (53.8 per cent) and 123 boys (46.2 per cent). Among them, given the recent history of migration fluxes in Italy, only a relatively small percentage (around 21.1 per cent) actually belonged to the 'second generation' as they were born in Italy, while most of them came to Italy during childhood.[2] The aim of gathering young people to interview from such a wide national spectrum is related to the extremely diversified presence of nationalities on Italian soil, and particularly in Milan where we carried out our fieldwork. Even though some immigrant groups are more substantial, the daily experience of immigrants' children – at school and in the neighbourhood – is probably centred on meeting other young people of different nationalities, besides their Italian peers of course.

During our research we used mainly qualitative methods, particularly in-depth interviews and focus groups. We also asked 12 of the teenagers we interviewed to take pictures of their homes, friends, consumer goods and typical situations of their daily lives. We then asked them to comment on their photographs, to explain the choice of the subjects and the meaning of those choices. The aim of this visual methodology was primarily a form of complementary information – above and beyond the traditional interview – to explore the meanings that these young people give to their identifications in different contexts of their daily lives (Domaneschi and Rebughini 2009).

The seven focus groups we put together were also conceived as a complementary method to analyse and discuss specific subjects already covered during the individual interviews: national identifications, relationships within the peer group, consumer behaviour and free time, gender relationships and gender identities, and stereotypes and racism. Each focus group involved between 7 and 12 students, both male and female, and of different national origins. However two focus groups involved respectively only young people whose parents had North African nationalities and young people whose parents had Asian national origins.

Concerning the in-depth interviews, the schedule (average duration of 90 minutes) and the key questions proposed in the focus groups dealt also with various aspects of everyday life (school integration, relationships with parents, friends, boyfriends and girlfriends, likes and dislikes, consumer habits and ways of life, use of languages and social networks). The aim of such a broader set of questions was to investigate and collect information about the connections between identifications and contexts, identity claims and social relationships.

Special emphasis was placed on personal narrations about the individuals themselves and about the groups each respondent identified with. The overall aim of the research was to detect the self-identifications used by the interviewees to make sense of their actions and their biographies, rather than their presumed identities. Special attention was paid to identifications in order to appreciate their constitutive process and the possibility that – although the reifications are constructed on a macro scale – they are structured within local and biographical specificities, thus enabling distinctions, dissent and innovation. Our attention was focused on the capacity to manage the ambivalences of situation and the multiplicity of identifications as a generational skill, certainly more evident among the children of immigrants, and especially among the more educated sectors of these youngsters.

When selecting the site of the interviews, we tried to give a faithful representation of the various ethnic and national origins, and the different trajectories of immigration – born in Italy or joining the family – characterizing the current picture of Milanese schools where our research took place. However, the choice of selecting such a variegated panel was not only to reflect a situation of very highly diversified immigration fluxes towards Italy and the absence of strong ethnic communities; our objective was also to focus on the three specific core topics of our analysis:

1. a *generational perspective* rather than an ethnic perspective: we decided to avoid an ethnic focus on specific nationalities or religious traditions;

2. a focus on a *potential avant-garde* of children of immigrants: the aim was to direct the analysis towards a more selected group of descendants of immigrants born into families with high cultural and social capital;
3. a *situated focus on a more specific context*, in this case the city of Milan: Italy is a highly diversified country in terms of economic and cultural regional differences. We concentrated our attention on Milan – the most multicultural and economically prominent city in Italy – to detect fundamental features characterizing the way of life of our interviewees.

A generational perspective

Following the pathway we have traced in the previous chapter, we constructed our panel of interviewees bearing the generational perspective in mind. Consequently, we focus our analysis on a specific cohort of teenagers and young adults (aged 16–21), without distinction of ethnic origin. We were interested in investigating a generational perspective in which the children of immigrants share a similar 'generation location' with their Italian peers. The aim was to investigate to what extent they share specific historical and biographical experiences, regardless of any particular ethnic and national belonging. Hence, in order to point out common generational characteristics it was necessary to gather narratives from children of immigrants from different ethnic backgrounds.

This generation location is that of young people born into a postindustrial and globalized context, in which it became paramount to be able to manage experiences of multi-location, recognizing the rules of each specific and separate context. This is also a generation that seems particularly close to what Appadurai (1996) calls the *work of imagination* – as a constitutive feature of subjectivity – enhanced by frequent encounters with differences. Such characteristics are collective and generational; they do not concern single individuals, groups or nationalities. Young people belonging to this generation feel similar sentiments of partial and overlapping belonging, with attachments and aspirations that increasingly cross-cut national and cultural identities.

In this respect, during the research we were interested in investigating in which way those generational characteristics are neither purely 'emancipatory' (compared to previous generations) nor entirely disciplined; they constitute instead a space of practices and identifications modulated according to context and situation. Certainly, even though such abilities can be considered a generational resource, they are not equally widespread among the children of immigrants. This is why we were paying particular attention to a more specific avant-garde of these young people, not only from the point of view of their generation location, but as a *generation unit* too. The specificities of this generation unit are those of being accustomed to the complexity and switching of languages and lifestyles, of the ability to move between contexts characterized by different rules and practices and the capacity to translate behaviour, identifications and skills accordingly.

A potential avant-garde and the self-selection of the panel

The second characteristic of our research is the specificity of the panel. This panel over-represents the children of immigrants with the potential abilities we described above. Even though we gathered our interviews from children of immigrants with different educational and family backgrounds, those brought up in families with a high cultural and social capital represent the majority of the interviewees.[3] This was not only a planned choice but also the result of a form of self-selection of the panel itself.

As a matter of fact, the selection of the interviewees was an important part of our methodology. The young people to interview were contacted mainly through high schools, following a presentation of our research programme to the students and the teachers. However, only a selected and motivated number of students agreed to participate in the research. Hence, participation meant more than being keen to be interviewed; as the greater part of the interviews and all of the focus groups took place in the rooms of the University of Milan the students who participated were motivated enough to come, of their own free will, to the university to answer our questions.

This form of spontaneous self-selection of the panel reinforces the specificity of our interviewees and demonstrates, on the one hand, their reflexive interest in research on their generation and their need to speak about themselves in order to improve the knowledge of their specificities; on the other hand the self-selection showed the importance of the cultural capital of their families. The majority of the students who came spontaneously to the university to be interviewed were from families with educated and open-minded parents. In contrast, such motivation to take part in the research was generally weaker among the students from families with lower cultural capital.

The potential avant-garde has been defined in our research as the children of immigrants whose main features can be summarized as a serious investment in higher education, usually supported by parents with a high educational and cultural capital. Generally speaking, this high cultural capital lays the groundwork for the development of an elevated level of reflexivity, applied to judge the society of settlement. Usually, such judgement is neither a complete acritical acceptance nor a radical rejection. The high cultural capital is also related to the ability to develop steady and constant relationships with autochthons as friends, schoolmates or neighbours, in order to avoid isolation or exclusive ethnic relationships. This can also be considered as the capacity to set up solid social capital; these resources ensure a thorough understanding of the cultural world of their parents as well as of the society in which they are planning their future.

Thus, the children of immigrants we interviewed – thanks to this self-selection – are likely to live in families in which parents promote autonomy and responsibility. This allows immigrants to pass on valid knowledge of the culture of their country of origin, so that their children can be proud of their family history and value their roots. Moreover, this promotes a deeper awareness of the reason for their parents' migration, stressing the social, economic and cultural deficiencies that allegedly characterize their countries of origin.

More generally, these young people show *personal capacities*. We can define them as: 'a formal and processual capacity which enables the individual to assume a situational identity without a loss of a deeper sense of continuity with her/his personal existence' (Melucci 1996b: 52). Hence, personal capacities are the skills to invest in oneself, to find a personal way of managing cultural codes, identifications and belonging, to avoid the risk of marginality and to be able to react to the risks of discrimination. As already noted, such competences are not necessarily reserved to a socially privileged elite – made up of immigrant families of a high social class – on the contrary, such abilities are potentially available as generational resources. The point is that such resources concern not only the children of immigrants, but they are a potential for the entire generation of young people living in this specific historical moment of globalization and they are associated with contextual support, such as media and communication technologies.

In this respect, it is important to remember that this potential avant-garde is not automatically related to economic status and upward mobility. Social mobility is certainly among their desires, but these young people can be considered a privileged avant-garde more for their relational and cultural competences than for their economic objectives. Their ability is in tracing elaborate, articulated and innovative paths for integration, rather than in pursuing patterns of economic assimilation. From the point of view of their economic status, the social position of their families is often that of a sort of 'marginal middle class'[4] developing high cultural and relational capacities, but with a fragile perspective of a better economic status. The immigrants' children we interviewed come from families with a subaltern position in Italian society, which they aim to overcome. However, to accomplish this, they rely more on their cultural, reflexive and relational competences than on a better wage or higher consumer standards. In the situation we have analysed, in particular, subalternity is not necessarily associated to a form of passive acculturation, with feelings of economic frustration or potentially deviant attitudes. Instead, diversity in the country of origins of immigrants and an Italian welfare system for the most part inclusive – despite its evident and mounting inadequacies – seem to support the creation of a marginal middle class, characterized by subaltern integration (Ambrosini 2001, 2011) at the economic level (marginal jobs with low wages and low status), as well as by daily interaction with autochthons, in never-ending engagement in order to avoid or reduce exclusion and discrimination.

Certainly, potential opportunities of inclusion and participation are not a forgone conclusion. The pathway towards personal abilities of multiple belonging and identifications is just one possibility. If this fails, there is always the risk of disappointment and rage, of selfish forms of opportunism, or of depressive reactions because failure is more likely to be felt as a personal mistake (Beck 2002; Martuccelli 2010).

The focus on a multicultural urban context

Since we were mainly interested in investigating a generational avant-garde, the children of immigrants interviewed in our research do not represent a statistically significant sample of teenage children of immigrants in Italy. This is not only the result of the self-selection of the panel, but this is also associated with the place in which we held most of our interviews. Our research was conducted in the urban area of Milan, which is neither representative of the Italian situation, nor of Northern Italy. Milan was the country's most important industrial city and it is now at the centre of the most economically active and wealthiest region of Italy, specialized in highly developed services, such as soft-technology, fashion and finance.

In the last 20 years, Milan has attracted around 220,000 immigrants (18 per cent of the population) offering jobs mainly in the complementary lower-skill service sectors such as health and family care, construction, food manufacturing, and domestic services. Most of the children of immigrants we interviewed have parents who work in such services. In spite of their position in a sort of marginal middle class, most of them seem quite confident about their future and their chance of mobility – both social and geographical mobility. Despite difficulties, most of our interviewees preferred to valorize the opportunity of living in a multicultural and dynamic context – at least when compared to other Italian regions – where it is easier to improve their capacity to manage different situations.

Certainly, among immigrant families living in Milan we do find very different situations, in terms of social conditions, educational and cultural resources, or structure of family ties. However, downward assimilation with passive acculturation – typical of the American black underclass as segmented assimilation theory has pointed out – does not seem a probable, or inevitable scenario for the children of immigrants in Milan. It seems unlikely even among the youngsters who arrived recently and who live in problematic families, or among the large number of children of immigrants enrolled in vocational schools and without any real expectations of social mobility. A general prospect of downward assimilation is unlikely mainly because the social stratification is different from that of the US. Social stratification is less visible on an urban scale with very few cases of explicit urban segregation of the underclass (both of immigrant or Italian origin). Also compared to other European countries, such as France or the UK, social stratification is less associated with housing and racial matters. At least in the case of Milan, the lower social strata are spread over different urban areas, without noticeable effects of negative labelling.

Generally speaking, Milan can be considered as the Italian context where it is easiest to become accustomed to pluralism. Again, this is an opportunity, a possibility, not an objective data concerning everyone; that is why we insist on the fact that our interviewees do not represent a significant sample of teenage children of immigrants living in Milan. Instead they are a specific segment of the population of Milanese children of immigrants: those who decided or had the resources and the ability to engage in continuing their education beyond compulsory schooling, and who, having acquired a broader and stronger cultural capital, will probably play a key role in defining patterns of living together in Italian society.

The Italian context

When compared to other European nations with a longer history of immigration, the Italian context presents some specific characteristics, which need to be identified, albeit concisely, to understand the historic and cultural environment in which the children of immigrants live today. Certainly, such a national perspective must not be conceptualized as a form of 'methodological nationalism', considering the nation as a unified system in order to comprehend social life (Beck 2006; Levitt and Glick Schiller 2004). On the contrary, the Italian study is mainly an empirical standpoint to observe some wider historic changes in immigrant generational changes, and to put to the test some of the mainstream sociological theories on the integration of immigrants' children.

In the Mediterranean countries – where immigration flows are more recent and where the descendants of immigrants are still regarded as a relatively historical novelty – the present generation of immigrants' children is demonstrating how complex the ties between quests for inclusion and plural identifications have become in contemporary global societies. Thus, their contextual identifications and lifestyles are a strategic viewpoint from which to observe how the passage from a class-bound Fordist society to a less class-bound and globalized society has transformed the attitudes towards assimilation, ethnicity or social integration, the risks of racism and exclusion as well as the potential for new forms of flexible identifications.

Concerning the Italian study we can briefly focus our attention on the differences between the first generation of migrants and their children.

An overview of the 'First' generation

The Italian peninsula has been a border region for centuries with historical multicultural regionalism and recent political unification, at least compared to other European countries. Italy has also a long history of emigration, which began at the end of the nineteenth century and continued until the 1960s.[5] Only during the 1970s did Italy switch from being a country of emigration to being one of immigration: 1973 marks the point at which immigrants outnumbered emigrants.

Since the beginning of the industrial development of the country Italy was characterized mainly by internal flows of immigration, from rural areas of the South to the industrialized regions of the North. Immigration from abroad increased at the end of the 1970s when other European countries such as France and the United Kingdom were closing their borders due to the industrial crisis, thus migratory flows were partly diverted towards Southern Europe. In the industrial areas of the North of the country, immigrant labour became less expensive than Italian labour, even though internal migration never completely stopped. During the 1970s migration was still treated as a national domestic matter and immigration from abroad – even though a modest number of migrants was already present in the country (especially from China, Eritrea, Somalia, Ethiopia and Tunisia) – was completely absent from public debate. Hence, while other European countries had already dealt with the arrival in the public arena of the second generation of immigrants, Italy was far away from the political issue of migration and public debate was still focused on important domestic problems such as political terrorism and the spread of organized crime. This seems related as well to the lack of a serious public debate on the legacy of colonialism. For decades, racism and colonialism have been considered as an incidental, and largely forgotten, component of Italian history (Andall and Dukan 2005).

During the 1980s at least two important aspects of Italian immigration took shape: a substantial increase in the number of migrants, and a large number of illegal immigrants out of government control.[6] Since that time, Italy has considered immigration as an enduring and unmanageable *emergency* for which the country can only give temporary solutions. This has remained until now the widespread representation of immigration flows in the media (Sciortino and Colombo 2004).[7]

These features have been identified as typical of the 'Mediterranean immigration model' – which also include the Spanish, Portuguese and Greek patterns of immigration – (Baldwin-Edwards and Arango 1999; Pugliese 2006; Withol de Wenden 2008). The Mediterranean model of migration is also characterized by the presence of immigrants that shows very complex and fragmented differentiation, according to their national and cultural backgrounds, their economic status, their professional skills and their family situation. Due to such different patterns of immigration, features of the labour market and weak links with the colonial past, the Mediterranean model, which is typically post-industrial, differs from the Fordist model. The immigrant labour force is concentrated mainly in low-skilled professions of the service sector or where low-paid jobs, typically in agriculture or tourism, cannot be delocalized. This kind of model is also marked by a strong difference concerning gender: immigrant men and women frequently present different patterns of inclusion and family formation, heterogeneous national origins, and different expectations. Hence the social context of immigrant flows in Italy is different from what happened in France, in Britain or in other European countries during the industrial post-colonial era of the 1950s or the 1960s.

Nowadays, immigrants in Italy represent around 8 per cent of the population, almost 5 million people. From the outset, immigration was characterized by tremendous diversity, with people coming from over 180 countries and no single group accounting for more than 20 per cent of the total foreign-born population.[8] This diversity concerns not only the great variety of national origins, but also the capillary distribution – especially in the Northern regions – in large cities as well as in small and medium-sized towns, where immigrants work mainly in small factories and domestic services. As far as the settlement distribution is concerned, immigrants are usually included with the Italian population and there is a growing number of foreigners who own a house. This means that in Italy urban concentrations and 'ethnic ghettos' are rare, or limited to minute portions of cities and towns.

Although immigrants in Italy hold educational qualifications not substantially different from Italians (41 per cent of them have a degree or have completed their high school programme, compared with 45 per cent of Italians), and show very differentiated settling patterns, they are mainly perceived as poor people, without appropriate educational qualifications and professional skills (Eurobarometer 2009).

As a matter of fact, immigrants have become a structural component of the Italian economy, occupying the most marginal and least rewarded positions in an economy based on a widespread informal labour market. They are over-represented in low-status jobs (45 per cent of them do unskilled jobs and 21 per cent of them, mostly women, do care work, in particular the full-time home care of elderly people), and their average monthly earnings are about 30 per cent lower than Italians (Caritas 2010). Menial jobs, caring for the elderly and the sick, long hours, heavy or dangerous work in agriculture, the building industry, and road construction and maintenance are mostly carried out by immigrants, although many of them are graduated and did professional jobs before migration.

Hence, most of the immigrants are employed in lower-skilled services, with clear forms of occupational segregation. The *ethnicization* of the job market in particular constitutes one of the most significant components of labour market segmentation for the 'first generation', together with their relevant numbers in the informal economy (Ambrosini 2001; Sciortino 2004). As Italy continues to be host to a large 'irregular' foreign population, this labour force is still managed mostly by means of remedial action, such as mass amnesties. Indeed, a large majority of current foreign residents have acquired legal status through *ex-post* regularization programmes.

In this scenario, political elections have been progressively influenced by matters of immigration and security. The debate around immigration has been mainly dominated by rhetorical emergency issues, and therefore it has focused on reducing and quashing illegal immigration. The attitude towards the first generation of immigrants is generally based on the classical 'wanted but not welcome' for which immigrants are accepted primarily to cover low-skilled jobs with subordinate and silent positions within Italian society.

Only recently have people begun to realize that the migration process is going to become established: the rise of family reunions and of children of immigrants born in Italy and attending the Italian education system is self-evident proof that migrants and their families have become an important and permanent part of the nation.

Being children of immigrants in contemporary Italy

The specificities of the Italian context summarized above have marked the biographies of the first generation of immigrants, placing them mostly in subaltern positions. However the same Italian context seems to affect their children in a contradictory way because they seldom become the focus of public and political debate, notwithstanding sporadic discussions on a new citizenship law more favourable to them. On the one hand, the invisibility of the children of immigrants means that they are seen as migrants, 'birds of passage', doomed to marginal working positions and excluded from Italian society. On the other hand, this invisibility offers some advantages when it contributes to maintaining a fluid and undefined representation of the descendants of immigrants and leaves room for personal agency.

This situation will probably change in the near future and, recently, the more visible presence of immigrants' children has become a rhetoric weapon in the hands of the Northern League[9] and other right-wing parties to contest the projects of a new law of citizenship and more generally to elicit xenophobia as an electoral resource. Nevertheless, the present period of *moratoria* and the absence of strong constructed representations and expectations may be an advantage for this generation, because the children of immigrants are not kept yet in constructed social conflict and they do not have to fight against specific expectations or stereotypes. Their capacity for innovation and criticism can develop in the relatively empty space left by their public invisibility. If on the one hand, such invisibility weakens their claims – first of all concerning a new law on citizenship – on the other hand, it also leaves them a wide space of imagination, and gives them the opportunity to follow different approaches to the contexts in which they live, especially at school and within their peer groups.

Despite their invisibility in the media, the children of immigrants – whether they joined the family or were born in Italy – are a growing presence in Italian public life and their demographic importance is interwoven with the characteristic of being present in the post-industrial and globalized social phase, in a country with an distinctive multicultural history.

According to the latest statistics, minors with immigrant parents represent one million people.[10] Today, around 60 per cent of these minors without Italian nationality were born in Italy and they are 'foreign' only from a juridical point of view, mainly because it takes such a long time to obtain Italian citizenship.

These children were born in immigrant families with very different backgrounds: their origins are from almost all the countries in the world, without the presence of prominent communities at the national level. The economic and cultural capital of these families is also decidedly variable, but usually the first generation of migrants comes from big cities and has a discrete level of education. The history of migration of each member of such families is also an important differentiated variable: in many cases women are the first migrants (especially from Latin America, the Philippines and Eastern Europe).

The children of immigrants who were not born in Italy have probably experienced some kind of traumatic separation during childhood and may have some difficulties integrating into a new school; however, the situation of that growing majority of children of immigrants who were born in Italy or who arrived during early childhood is usually less problematic. Different pieces of research show their valid social inclusion, their will to be active participants in Italian public life, as well as their ability to translate and to adapt their identifications and competences to different social contexts.

As most of the children of immigrants in Italy today are minors and are enrolled in school, education pathways are an inevitable and fundamental observation point. The research on the second generation cannot ignore the status of education of the children of immigrants, and the relationships between that status and the general patterns of inclusion/exclusion. Moreover, education remains the main standpoint of the growing presence of the children of immigrants in Italian public life.[11]

Foreign-born pupils are particularly concentrated at the infant school and primary school levels of education. However, in the last few years, their presence has grown also at the secondary school level where youngsters who were not born in Italy remain more numerous. The higher presence of children of immigrants who came to Italy during their early adolescence, and with more obvious linguistic difficulties, explains their more common choice of a lower level of education and the more problematic passage from compulsory school to upper-secondary school.[12]

The gap between students born or brought up in Italy and students who came during their adolescence is present also in the distribution of learning difficulties and delays. In recent years educational delays of the children of immigrants are becoming a common problem in Italy, with features similar to those of other European countries (Crul and Schneider 2009), while the difference in relation to Italian students grows as the educational level increases.[13] However, students of foreign origin enrolled in *lyceum* (academic upper secondary schools) present a lower level of difficulties and delays and these problems have a frequency similar to that of Italian students.[14] In this case, the children of immigrants are very school-oriented and they invest their emotions and ambitions in the opportunity of higher education, towards university specializations and towards higher professional positions in Italian society, at least compared to the social position of their parents. Therefore, school success is more often the basis of inclusion plans of *lyceum* students.

Such features seem to match traditional evidence in the sociology of education: the selection is conditioned mainly by the social position of the family and by family attitudes towards the future of their children. Parents with a high level of education usually push their children towards *lyceum* and university. The working class with lower levels of education usually make this kind of choice only following the advice of teachers, or if their children have excellent results at school. However, in the case of immigrant families, parents seem more often oriented towards the social mobility of their children.

Overall, despite some marked difficulties, and the high proportion of school delays in the upper secondary school, the number of foreign-born boys and girls who hold a upper secondary school diploma is growing steadily. Moreover, the Italian school system is free and open, without an early selection of pupils. This means that it is possible to enter university education with a diploma from a technical school and not necessarily from a *lyceum*. In the last decades, this has allowed a large number of working-class students – and probably in the near future a growing number of children of immigrants – to reach university education. The results of a recent national survey (Dalla Zuanna et al. 2009) show that the children of immigrants are not only ambitious about their future but that they attach great importance to their professional life. Usually, they are willing to make an effort, they have high hopes and a desire for social mobility.[15]

The Mediterranean perspective: children of immigrants in Southern Europe

The main theoretical perspectives currently used in interpreting the fate of the children of immigrants are based on research carried out in the last three decades, mainly in the US, the UK and continental Europe. Obviously, research literature on the second generation is more consolidated in countries in which immigration flows are a historical phenomenon, rooted in industrial and urban development. In these countries the children of immigrants have been an object of study from which it has been possible to investigate social mobility and identity claims. However, such socio-structural tendencies, cultural claims and public representations are deeply interwoven with the history of migration fluxes of the last century, with the colonial past, and with public debate – in academia and in the media – that have occurred since the industrial era, when national identities were particularly relevant.

Such historical pathways are partially different from those of the Southern European countries, whose colonial past belongs to distant history (in the case of Spain and Portugal) or has been largely forgotten or denied (in the case of Italy), where there have been important emigration flows and where the arrival of foreign immigrants began only in the last three decades, overlapping with the end of the industrial era and the intensification of globalization. Hence, such a generational difference has consequences both for the social construction of the second generation as a sociological category, and for the theoretical framework with which we analyse this generation of immigrants' children.

The rapid overview on data and recent research in the Italian study show us an ambivalent situation in which great potential for inclusion, innovation and imagination exists alongside a danger of marginality, self-exclusion and lack of social mobility. This ambivalence can be considered a constant of the situation of the children of immigrants and it has been remarked upon in several pieces of international research. However, the Italian study presents some historical and contextual specificities which can contribute to assessing to what extent the interpretive patterns developed to analyse a Fordist context of immigration – typical in a country with a long immigration history – can be useful to understand the paths of inclusion of immigrants' children in the 'Mediterranean' Italian immigration context.

This post-industrial model of migration is characterized by a higher degree of differentiation and it is not possible to explain the social paths of immigrant families – and especially of their children – merely on the basis of national origin. At the same time, the socio-economic condition of immigrant families is not always a predictable variable of the social and professional paths of their offspring. On the contrary, the cultural capital of the families seems more important in influencing educational choices and future careers: *lyceum* students tend to come from families with high cultural capital, in spite of their subaltern economic position. Family orientation towards sacrifice, hard work, personal commitment and upward mobility is also a powerful motivator for their children.

Therefore, besides its structural features where adult migrants occupy lower positions, the Mediterranean model has ambivalent consequences for the future of their children. On the one hand, preordained social patterns and destinies have to be challenged, rejecting both passive assimilation and ethnic enclaves, lack of social mobility and emotional overinvestment in upward mobility. On the other hand, in a country such as Italy – where there is not yet a long history of immigration – migrants enter into a fluid hierarchical representation system of ethnic relationships, which assumes different meanings according to contexts, the news reporting in the media and political discourse. Their children can benefit from these variable representations: especially the lack of constructed images of ethnicities and the status of the children of immigrants can be considered an advantage, helping them to build up their own self-representations.

Overall, we may say that – in spite of the difficulties regarding statistics on education – qualitative and quantitative research carried out in the last decade shows that the children of immigrants in Italy are usually well integrated in peer group friendship networks made up of both Italian and other nationalities. They have optimistic plans for the future, a high consideration of their independence, and they consider relying on plural belonging a positive quality. Certainly, research notes different attitudes and projects among the children of immigrants enrolled in high schools to those who have abandoned school or who have chosen lower levels of education. Educational status is, as usual, a point of distinction concerning everyday experiences, lifestyles, family backgrounds, and models of self-identification. The school environment is also different in a *lyceum* to that of a vocational school. However, the generational features that the children of immigrants share and the specific flexibilities of the Italian context make the differences concerning social and economic capital of their families less determinant. Besides possible gaps in socio-economic status and cultural orientations of the families, these young people share some common patterns in their everyday experience – in the models of self-identification and belonging, as well as in the way they perceive and integrate into the Italian context – that can assist their participation and social inclusion.

For that reason, it is important to investigate *when* and *how* – as generational features – the children of immigrants have the opportunity to use their difference as a resource for everyday relationships, in a practical and contextual way, also for claiming recognition and participation in Italian society. This is why it is important to consider not only the structural and macro status of immigrant difference – according to their more general social positions – but also the micro and situated contexts in which such difference becomes a more complex and symbolic stake.

The following chapters will be devoted to presenting the specific ways in which the children of immigrants make sense of their new and often ambivalent social location, and how they claim new forms of inclusion and participation and construct plural and mobile identifications. The following chapters investigate empirically these three aspects, starting with a discussion about the transformation of the idea of locality.

3

A Specific Generational Location

Finding new global locations

Since the end of the last century a number of specific transformations have profoundly altered various aspects of our social experiences. Technological improvements in communications and transport, and a growing 'complex connectivity' (Tomlinson 1999) have modified our concept of local, belonging, and engagement. People are 'more connected' because their lives are increasingly affected by facts, news and commodities that originate in places far away from their context of daily life. Although distant, these places can be perceived as 'routinely accessible, either representationally through communications technology or the mass media, or physically, through the expenditure of a relatively small amount of time (and, of course, of money) on a transatlantic flight' (ibid.: 4).

The idea of locality – that is the 'meaningful space', the place for relationships in which people feel themselves *chez soi*, at home – is profoundly transformed. If, in the past, it was characterized by its 'objectiveness', and imposed itself as a 'given' which was tantamount to community and neighbourhood, nowadays it is mostly perceived as personally constructed, constantly negotiated. More frequently locality can be differentiated from community and neighbourhood.

Community evokes ideas of strong ties and inclusion: it elicits some form of identification with others, who are considered important, significant, with whom we want to have reciprocal relationships, and from whom we expect solidarity and recognition. This space of identification is, in many cases, no longer the mechanical result of being born or living in a particular place. It is instead the result of choices and the capacity to keep up mediated relationships. The community exclusively rooted in a specific territory tends to re-emerge in a reactive and defensive form. It often represents an answer to alleged threats, the attempt to construct spaces for sharing uncertainties and fears, rather than spaces for reciprocal recognition, solidarity, and communal planning. These kinds of communities are often ephemeral: their only bond is the construction of a common looming external threat (Bauman 2001). Especially for many young people, 'their increased mobility and engagement with a global youth culture means that their sense of community may be radically "displaced" as they create multiple affiliations with cultures and spaces beyond their neighbourhoods and cities. For young people, community is not then necessarily forged through a shared, fixed sense of place or continuous networks of trust embedded in these places, but through connections that may also be developed virtually and transnationally' (Harris 2010: 580).

Neighbourhood can be defined by the physical space for everyday life and mundane interactions. It constitutes the environment for actions and it is increasingly characterized by difference and changes rather than by uniformity and routines. It becomes a space of ambivalence. On the one hand, it is a place where it is possible to have direct experience of difference, of the plurality of meanings, codes, languages and behaviours which represent a specific trait of urban experience; a place where different habits and interests confront each other, often as conflicts. Its specific conformation includes forms of power which promote some patterns of behaviours inhibiting others, and which sustain some types of identities contrasting others. On the other hand, it is a space for experiencing new forms of living together, a space where it is easier to resist homologation and to manifest personal individuality. It promotes capacity of choice, mediation and translation.

Locality is defined by its relational rather than by its spatial characteristics, by topology rather than by topography (Lash 1999:282). It is a structure of feelings and values (Appadurai 1996). It has to do with concrete relationships, with conscious, reflexive interactions. As a space for meaningful actions, locality reproduces the complexity and variability of the contemporary global world rather than depending on the reproduction of mechanical routines and conformist behaviours. The growing separation between the 'given' space of neighbourhood and the space of choice constituted by locality strengthens the awareness of the importance of agency: people are taking more of a leading role in the construction of their locality, and can only blame themselves for unwelcome results. Being able to make the right choices and having the resources and the freedom to realize one's own preferences are vital to being the protagonist of one's own destiny. Self-fulfilment and personal independence are connected to the ability to acquire the skills essential for understanding the different contexts and the codes which regulate interactions, for presenting oneself according to context-specific expectations to avoid exclusion or reducing personal opportunities, and for using sameness and difference as instruments for promoting favourable relationships or constructing effective boundaries to exclude potential competitors. Locality is still defined by neighbourhood, but global dimensions are becoming increasingly important, as the significance of what happens locally, the burdens and resources that characterize this space of experience, originates more in global fluxes than in relationships with neighbours.

The familiarity with 'complex connectivity' neither erases distances, nor dooms to homologation and cultural homogenization: we now experience locality and community, equality and difference, and belonging and exclusion in varying, often contrasting, ways. As a result, global connectivity coexists with the permanence of physical distances, while the opportunity to choose which community to be part of coexists with the daily experience of boundaries which hinder personal will. Global connectivity allows new forms of reflexivity to emerge. Giving meaning to everyday experiences in these new localities implies developing specific forms of personal capacity (Melucci 1996b): mixing different languages and managing different codes and rules, being able to use them in the appropriate context; being able to change, switching from one context to another; and developing suitable forms of belonging to allow access without creating ties which are too strong to prevent consistent freedom of motion.

As Ulrich Beck (2002, 2006) put it, from this new form of locality springs a new mix of practices and mundane skills which hold a high degree of interdependency and globalism. People and places become globalized and cosmopolitan from inside. New widespread transnational networks of production, forms of life and consumption are created. While the concept of cosmopolitanism (Lash 1999; Featherstone 2002; Beck and Sznaider 2006; Kendall et al. 2009) highlights the fading of strong forms of belonging, the concept of everyday multiculturalism (Colombo and Semi 2007; Wise and Velayutham 2009) stresses the possibility – and sometimes the necessity – of belonging, simultaneously, to more than one locality, using difference and equality as meaningful elements which need to be emphasized or concealed in relation to different discourses, audiences, situations, the contextual restraints to be faced, or the personal goals to be achieved.

Consideration of locality and everyday relationships in multicultural contexts – the *everyday urban*, as Ash Amin (2002) calls it – as specific situations where new experiences, new symbolic codes, and new forms of action may be brought into being, allows us not only to analyse the daily negotiation of equality and difference, inclusion and exclusion, but also to highlight how these processes may set up the conditions for a new specific generational experience. Being able to manage existence in the everyday urban may represent a new particular set of skills which marks a new generation location (Mannheim 1952).

A significant number of today's youth – at least those among them who are endowed with high social and cultural capital – must be able to cope in an increasingly changing world. They must develop a specific taste for diversity, recognize it and put it into viable schemas for interpretation and evaluation. They must contend with patterns of consumption, information and identification circulating within global flows rather than, as occurred in the past, extract material and relational resources which they find in the local context in which they live. The chance to take disparate elements from these current models in order to put together one's life in a specific way depends on economic and technological opportunities, on the network of accessible relationships and on the individual's own personal abilities to choose. It requires the development of specific skills based mainly on access and management of the symbolic codes used and valued in various contexts, and on the capacity to move from one context to another (Noble 2009; Colombo 2010a). It becomes important to develop the ability to adapt to different relational contexts, characterized by different rules, audiences and interests, coping with the increasing difficulty in transferring what one learns or acquires in one sphere of life to other spheres (Ballard 1994; Melucci 1996b). The ability to count on differentiated cultural references, a certain relativism in one's interpretation of the rules, the ability to adapt and be flexible, and to manage fluently different languages, seem to be fundamental skills that every young person must acquire in order to succeed in an increasingly global world. It is not simply a question of 'accumulative' skills: being able to handle varying contexts implies the ability to 'translate', to 'mediate' what one is or what one has learned in one situation into resources appropriate to others. Thus building a hyphenated identity, for example, is not merely a matter of putting two parts together. Very often what defines the content of the two parts is not automatic but is the result of complex reconstructions that relate to an articulated stratification of local, regional, national and transnational dimensions which are regularly in contradiction of or in conflict with each other (Baldassar and Pesman 2005; Purkayastha 2005).

Being 'included' and respected in one specific milieu does not rule out the possibility of finding oneself in a position of marginality and exclusion in others. In order to be accepted and to play one's cards well, people have to be prepared to present a self-image that is not necessarily consistent and stable, but rather viable in a specific context, multifaceted with varying levels and potentials. The experience of a self which needs to be continuously adapted to different contextual expectations may lead, on the one hand, to forms of resistance which are employed in the reconstruction of a consistency and a stability which are felt to be threatened, and, on the other hand, to the habit of managing a certain degree of variability and individual eclecticism, replacing consistency and continuity as forms of unitary reconstruction of one's own experience with the ability to transform and adapt the self to different contexts. For adolescents growing up in a global, changing and interconnected world, managing this ambivalence may be often more important than being consistent: being able to cope with the context in order not to diminish personal opportunities may be more important than showing an integrity unaffected by the diversity of the situations.

If this ability or need to manage complexity and variability has become a mark of the experience of contemporary youth and is a basic component in creating a 'generation as an actuality' (Mannheim 1952: 303), then it may be possible to view the experience of the children of immigrants as a more general case, able to shed light on social processes which affect contemporary youth as a whole. On the one hand, this perspective acknowledges that the so-called second or third immigrant generations are not radically different from their autochthonous peers who do not have a family history of immigration. In fact, second and third generations have often been described as characterized by some specific form of deficiency or confusion, perennially marginal, unable to be completely like either their parents or their autochthonous peers. Thus, their alleged difference has been privileged against their diffuse similarities. On the other hand, it considers their specificities not only as deficiencies but also as manifestations of peculiar generational characteristics, probably dedicated to becoming generally shared rather than being signs of permanent marginality. The children of immigrants – at least those of them who have access to greater family, cultural and social resources and who invest heavily in higher education and in professional success – can be seen as an 'active minority' engaged in processing new codes and new languages in order to cope with specific historical experience. It is not a question of encouraging an uncritical exaltation of what is produced nor of embracing a conciliatory vision which suppresses the dimensions of the conflict, but of proposing an analytical viewpoint which identifies the social and identification processes activated by these young people as a significant and privileged place where new codes are being produced (not necessarily better, democratic, or exponents of pacific cohabitation and without potential discriminants).

Bearing these premises in mind, it seemed important to try to analyse in more depth how children of immigrants handle the experience of complexity and variability when constructing new meanings for their locality.

Complex connectivity and persistence of family ties

It is quite common among the children of immigrants interviewed to be in contact with relatives living in various parts of the world. They seem to be at ease with the idea of being part of a family network which overcomes any national boundary. They learn to become more engaged in relationships with significant others than with geographical spaces. The family place is not grounded in specific locality but is constituted by actively sharing communication, material goods, information, support and emotions.

> My relatives are scattered all over the world: my grandmother, two aunts and an uncle in Iran, my grandfather in Israel, other relatives in Israel, two of my father's sisters in Romania, and a lot of cousins in the USA and we all get in touch with each other by phone or Internet. I know how they live and if I decide to go to those countries I'll have a place to stay and people who can help me.
>
> (Michael, 17 years old, born in Italy, Romanian parents)

> My grandfather lives in Sarajevo, the other one lives near Belgrade, my uncles live in Barcelona, and then we have friends living in Australia, America, everywhere really, Brazil, everywhere ... and we get in touch by email, we all write in Serbo-Croatian. This being scattered about is a heavy burden, but it's also an opportunity because we are still very united.
>
> (Ana, 16 years old, born in Bosnia, in Italy since the age of 4)

The experience of family diaspora or, simply, of parents' migration, means it is natural to plan their lives globally, without restricting their projects to the local context. The chance of moving to another country where there would be more job or educational opportunities is – although sometimes only in their imagination – a valid prospect. They learn to project their lives from a global perspective. If, on the one hand, this risks fuelling unrealistic expectations of finding better opportunities than real conditions and skills can offer, on the other hand, it means thinking globally, not limiting themselves to what the immediate situation offers. The future can be thought of as detached from geographical restraints and connected to networks which are actively chosen and kept alive. Where people were born or brought up is less important than the relational networks they have created.

Ileana, a 16-year-old girl attending a vocational school, is a good case in point. She was born in Santo Domingo, and was 12 when she came to Italy. She is fond of Manga cartoons and dreams of going to Japan in order to learn to draw them professionally. She is happy to stay in Italy and her best friend is an Italian schoolmate with whom she shares a love of American pop music. She is sure to have a far better education in Italy than in Santo Domingo and is doing her best to achieve good results at school. She strongly identifies with Santo Domingo and loves speaking Spanish with her mother. In order to preserve her Spanish writing skills, she is keeping a diary where she writes only in Spanish, trying to use some new words every day. The last time she went back to Santo Domingo she felt very different from her old friends and realized that, for her, living in that country would be quite difficult because she had already become Italian. If her planned move to Japan fails, she hopes to join some relatives in the United States, and to find a good job over there.

Mirko expresses the same cosmopolitan attitude, stressing the importance of family history as a catalyst for recomposing his personal history in a unique patchwork, conserving everything worthwhile from diverse experiences:

> I'd like to travel all the time ... to live travelling ... for I don't feel I belong to one culture in particular. When I lived in Croatia, having been born in the Vojvodina region, which is part of Serbia ... well, I didn't feel fully Croatian either, so I've never actually lived in the country where I was born ... so I don't feel I belong to one particular culture ... anyway, in this case you feel freer, I mean, belonging to one culture ... well, it's an obstacle, because it holds you back and it limits your abilities. If, on the other hand, you are freer, you don't feel you belong to a specific place, you are more open to new experiences ... For instance, I'm really interested in knowing more about my original culture, I do my best to get in touch with news in my country. I'm most of all interested in our family history ... that really fascinates me very much, and then I try to be informed about all that is happening in Croatia. I read books, I'm really interested ... Well, I'm interested in Italy too ... I mean, I'd like to take with me something of all the places I've been, but without feeling tied to only one of them ... If tomorrow I go to another country, I'd like to take with me something Italian too.
>
> (Mirko, 18 years old, born in Croatia, in Italy since the age of 12)

Family emerges as a constant and solid point of reference. Most of the young people we have interviewed are not concerned with contesting their parents' ideas, expectations or behaviours. They generally set a high value on continuity with family history. Intergenerational conflict is the exception rather than the norm. Accustomed to facing a high degree of uncertainty, the family is often perceived as a stable reference point in a rapidly changing world. Parents are the only people you can always rely on, and in rapidly changing contexts, where nothing is guaranteed, having someone you can trust, someone ready to support you, is considered a highly valued resource.

It may sound rather paradoxical in a country which is often depicted as characterized by the strength of family ties (Banfield 1958) that many of the children of immigrants interviewed accused Italians of not taking enough care of their parents and of not respecting them. Most of these adolescents consider their Italian peers as more individualistic and less interested in taking into account parents' advice than they are themselves. This distinction often becomes the main ethnic marker: what really distinguishes them from their Italian peers is the different value given to family ties.

> In Italy children are inclined to be independent from their parents. In Peru things are very different: family ties are very strong, I mean, it depends on families, but if someone in the family needs some help, everybody feels they must help them, everybody makes an effort, tries to be helpful, no one is left alone when in difficulties. Here things are really different: children never help their parents, they always only ask, they expect their parents to give them money and everything else they want but they never listen to them.
>
> (Nancy, 18 years old, born in Peru, in Italy since the age of 6)

> Look, for us, family is the most important thing ... I mean, Italians are less interested in family, they always think only of themselves, and never of their parents. I think this is the true difference between Filipinos and Italians; Filipinos are much more concerned with their family.
>
> (Catherine, 19 years old, born in the Philippines, in Italy since the age of 12)

Continuity with parents' experience and ethnicity often become synonymous, and the main interest for maintaining the continuity with parents' experience derives from the recognition of the importance of family in assuring a stock of material and symbolic resources to rely on in order to face the variability and instability of their relational contexts. From this point of view, ethnicity becomes not only a sort of insurance against present and future uncertainties: it also constitutes a field for developing a family history and constructing an unbroken link between the past – the family's legacy – and one's own specific experience.

Family values, habits and traditions become stable points of reference for navigating with some confidence the uncertainty of everyday life. They don't need to be practised in order to be effective; in fact, they are often only generically specified. When asked to give some examples of values, habits or traditions which significantly differentiate them from others, the young people interviewed generically quoted family cohesion, respect for parents, capacity to make sacrifices and work hard, differences in cooking and food habits, and some characteristic celebration of public or religious holidays. These particularities often spring from specific family history, but they are considered representative of a more widespread attitude, assuming in this way an ethnic connotation. Family way of life – often rooted in specific family history – becomes a sign of a 'normal but specific' way of life, reinforced and legitimized because it is shared by a wider group of people and transformed into tradition by a language which uses values and customs as its most evocative raw materials. Tightly connected with family history, ethnicity (or nationality, which is commonly considered as its equivalent) turns out to be one of the main factors for ensuring identification and recognition, a marker differentiating 'us' from 'them'.

> I feel more tied to Italy for friends and for the way of life, to go out at night, the places and so on, and I feel more tied to Sarajevo for the people in general, for its culture, which coincides with the history of my family, so I feel Yugoslavian for the values. I'm OK living in Milan: I love the Italian way of life, Milan is a hospitable city although many think otherwise, but my values come from Yugoslavia because I feel that my roots, which are the roots of all my family, come from there.
>
> (Ana, 16 years old, born in Bosnia, in Italy since the age of 4)

The feeling of a close bond with parents' experience is strengthened by a profound debt of gratitude. Many of the children of immigrants we spoke to consider their condition as privileged when compared with both that of their parents and their cousins whose families did not emigrate. They realize that they must thank their parents for the condition in which they currently find themselves; a condition they see as advantageous and fortunate when compared to the opportunities they would have had if their parents had not decided to emigrate. They often express profound gratitude towards their parents who decided to make huge sacrifices in order to ensure their children a better future.

> Both my parents had good jobs in Albania. My father was a cameraman and my mother a journalist. They left these very good jobs and encountered a lot of difficulties in Italy ... they still face a lot of difficulties. It wasn't easy, first of all for my father, he wasn't a boy – he was 47 years old when he came to Italy, well, although he had a good position in Albania he came here, actually starting from zero ... They decided to come to Italy above all for us [himself and his sister], they wanted to make sure we had a better education, and now I owe my parents a huge debt of gratitude, and I must study and graduate, find a good job and give them satisfaction.
>
> (Andi, 17 years old, born in Albania, in Italy since the age of 11)

> I'd go back to Peru only on holiday, not to live there, just for a few months. I mean, if I have to go back, it would not be fair to my parents: they are here to work and made a lot of sacrifices to let me come here and have a good education. All my opportunities would be ruined because now I'm studying to be what I want to be when I become an adult and there I'd have to begin all over again, and the school system is very different from here. I'd have fewer professional opportunities too.
>
> (Milagros, 17 years old, born in Peru, in Italy since the age of 10)

Recognition of the sacrifices made by parents in order to give their children a better future and the children's desire not to disappoint parents' expectations reinforce the idea of the existence of a family history, characterized by both fate and a plan, which now has to be realized and cannot be disowned. A profound sense of continuity with family history leads to a positive evaluation of parental teaching, a sense of pride in family 'culture' and 'traditions'. The bond with parental culture is seen as a 'given' that impacts on character and a deep sense of self. Parental culture associated in a non-problematic way with ethnicity, national belonging and concretely embodied in habits, language and religion is regarded as an 'essential' element of one's own identity, something that is received 'at birth' and that now influences feelings, moral orientation, preferences and behaviour. Family culture is never placed in a void; it is not a totally singular experience detached from broad experiences. It constitutes instead the purest and deepest fabric from which ethnicity sets itself up and takes shape.

So far, ethnicity, as a generalization of family history, has emerged as a point of reference for constructing a personal narrative with some degree of stability amid a flux of experiences characterized by uncertainty, variability and global interconnection. However, discourse about family and ethnicity also emerges as a form of resistance and defence against exclusion. In this case, the specificity of the family, presented under the label of immigrant or under an ethnic definition, is more an external attribution which needs to be opportunely neutralized or managed in order to avoid negative connotations.

Facing exclusion

The importance attributed to family and the efforts to defend it from external misrecognitions,[1] in fact, may also be seen as attempts to counter discrimination and react to the marginal role in which their parents are confined. Manifesting ethnic pride is a way of showing solidarity with the family and opposing the negative representation of immigrants as a social problem.

Children of immigrants – especially the young people we have interviewed, who decided to invest in their education beyond compulsory school and aspire to professional, white collar jobs – try to resist and contest autochthonous negative representations. Most of their parents have a high educational capital but do unskilled work and feel they are treated on a daily basis as marginal, criminal and deviant by the media and in political debates.

In this case, ethnicity is an externally attributed label that children of immigrants seem more engaged in containing and transforming rather than radically deconstructing or repudiating. A first strategy consists in accepting the idea that immigrants are the main cause of social problems, but differentiating between one's own family or one's own ethnic group and other immigrants. The idea that immigrants are the root cause of urban degradation and violence is accepted, but only a small proportion of immigrants – those who are of ethnic groups other than one's own – are blamed for the deviant behaviour.

> I'm not saying that all the people who come to Italy illegally are bad, as my parents were clandestine too and they are good people; it depends on individuals. In my opinion Italy must have more control on immigrants, especially on people arriving from Eastern Europe. I mean, for sure Romanians are unpopular now but most of them are not welcome here. Filipinos are more welcome because they are serious and sincere, if you don't count some exceptional, particular people who are isolated by the rest of the Filipinos. I mean, they are good people, but other people aren't.
>
> (Daniel, 19 years old, born in Italy, Filipino parents)

> I think there are too many foreigners in Italy now, well, if they come here to work ... but if they come here and cause trouble they'd better stay in their country, because it's not fair to mess up a place which is not yours ... for instance, we from El Salvador create some little spaces to celebrate the festival of our country's patron saint, but I think that nobody can be bothered with this, absolutely. First of all we are respecting our traditions ... our culture, even if in another country, because we have it in our blood, but we don't bother anybody. But ... there are people who are really fanatics ... and that is too much ... I don't know, for instance Muslims: there are Muslims who sacrifice animals, things like that. This means they are fanatics, in my view, that's not religion, they are only fanatics. I don't agree, they want to impose their culture. We celebrate our culture in very specific contexts, without being a nuisance; we hold our celebrations with pride, that is the right way.
>
> (Iris, 18 years old, born in Italy, Salvadorian parents)

A second strategy is to blame Italians for being prejudiced against people who work hard and who do their best to guarantee their children a better future. In this case, common stereotypes are more directly contested. Italians who regard immigrants as a problem are biased against them and unable to recognize the quality and importance of their work for the well-being of Italy.

In the beginning, those who came here were really in need: maybe they had a family to take care of, they had to send money home and then they were content with any solution they could find … Really, I'd like anybody who says that we come here to steal jobs from Italians to do the job my father does: he cleans latrines where someone, Italian, has already been … and left everything dirty … So it's really not true that we do nice jobs. My mother takes care of an elderly person, an old grandmother who wets herself, dirties her bed, vomits. It's not pleasant, but we need to do these kinds of jobs … our parents need to do it, but I don't want to do what my parents are doing. They came here to give more opportunity to their children, and here I'm throwing myself heart and soul into studying because I hope to have a better life than my parents have ever had.

(Carla, 19 years old, born in Ecuador, in Italy since the age of 4)

Italian people never pay attention to educational qualifications; they see foreigners and immediately think that all foreigners are good-for-nothings. I mean, Italians think that foreigners come here to work because they haven't got any school qualifications, they know nothing … well, it really bothers me, because they say that we should only be, I mean, submissive, obeying their orders. Well, I say, when talking to my friends, perhaps the first generation in Italy, our parents, work as domestic and manual workers, but we, the second generation, hope to move upwards! Look, I'm not saying I want to take the place of Italians, but at least to have the same opportunities, because we are all equal, I mean, we have different ethnic backgrounds but we all are people.

(Catherine, 19 years old, born in the Philippines,
in Italy since the age of 12)

Why don't they simply oppose discrimination and prejudice claiming equality and sameness, rather than appealing to ethnic and cultural difference? In the current context, distinction is more valued than conformism and difference more than similarity. Being able to show some peculiar attribute is more rewarding than being confused in an amorphous generality. When difference is able to represent autonomy and independence, when it is perceived as something atypical, nonconforming or out of the usual run of things, it often becomes a sign of distinction and creativity. It elicits curiosity and desire rather than fear and repulsion. When ethnicity can be presented as a difference triggering sympathy more than anxiety it seems to become an important way to escape the contradictory colonial injunction to become autochthonous (Fanon 1963, 1966). There is a widespread awareness that equality rhetoric, in contexts characterized by a strong power hierarchy, might work in different ways for different groups. In these situations, to be equal often means the duty of the weaker group to become similar to the stronger one, giving up all the peculiarities which supposedly characterize their difference from the dominant group. Combating prejudice and discrimination with the pure rhetoric of equality risks upholding the request to accept the dominant obligation, to act and think like the dominant group. However, this solution reveals itself to be inconsistent for most of the children of immigrants. In fact, on the one hand, it implies denying any specific positive quality of their parents and family history, as well as accepting that the only viable way not to be out of place or out of date is to be the same as the dominant group. This means admitting the necessity of a radical rupture with the parents' way of life and exposing themselves to accusations of betraying family teachings and solidarity with the group of origin. This also means being ungrateful to their parents and forgetful of all the sacrifices they have made in order to provide their children with a better future. On the other hand, pretending to be seen as totally equal to the dominant group may have paradoxical consequences. In a framework in which the dominant discourse draws a clear boundary between 'us' and 'them', stressing sameness to counter the accusation by the strongest of being too different conflicts with the impossibility of becoming what the members of the minority group – by definition – are not. No matter how much effort they make in order to fit in with the autochthonous group, they would always be considered different. At best, they can aspire to being considered good foreigners trying their best to be similar to the local people.

I have been here for a long time now and I'm really integrated, but, maybe, there is one thing that upsets me; I mean, for instance, when we are talking about politics or the Italian government or things like that, I've heard my friends saying, when they speak about Italy they say 'us' but I have to say 'you', to speak about Italians because I'm Albanian. I mean, I could say 'us' because I've been living here for a long time but I wouldn't, I mean, someone would say 'Sorry? Why do you say "us" when you are Albanian?'
(Andi, 17 years old, born in Albania, in Italy since the age of 11)

Milagros clearly expresses the ambivalence of the recognition of equality by her Italian peers. Beyond any proof of solidarity and friendship, beneath the surface there is always the common idea of a significant cleavage between foreigners and autochthons: a cleavage that indelibly marks a distinction between 'us' and 'them'. She came to Italy when she was 11 years old, joining her parents who had been in Italy for 5 years. She quickly got used to Italian life and tried to integrate. Now, she is attending a good high school, she considers herself more Italian than Peruvian, speaks Spanish only occasionally and with difficulties, and has only Italian friends:

When I came here, my schoolmates were very kind to me; they didn't make me feel a burden [because of] the fact that I'm a foreigner, but it is not easy to be like that because sometimes you listen to the TV and hear 'Eh, foreign people do this and do that', always bad things, and you don't feel part of that group because you behave properly, but ... however, when you say to Italians, when you think of Italians, you don't think of yourself. I mean, I like to stay here and I love the life here but it is always hard for a foreigner, they are always ... they are different, they are very different. I don't know, but you feel ... I mean, also if they don't lay too much stress on my being a foreigner, also if they don't pay attention to this, you feel you are a foreigner, you feel there is something different about you and you think 'My God, what am I doing here?' Sometimes it is very hard, but then I conclude that it's better here, primarily for my future, for my education and everything else. I mean, if I'd got a degree over there it'd be worthless. There I wouldn't be able to find a job; here probably I'll get one, I hope.
(Milagros, 17 years old, born in Peru, in Italy since the age of 10)

When ethnicity becomes an imposed external label and represents a marker legitimizing exclusion or reducing personal possibilities, it is rational to resist it, facing its existence either by turning the meaning attributed to it upside down or by trying to distil the advantageous traits from the disadvantageous ones. When feasible, this second strategy seems to be preferred. Children of immigrants often choose to manage ethnicity by presenting it as a charming difference which may enrich society as a whole rather than a cause for antagonism or a zero-sum conflict. Acceptable ethnicity is constructed by attractive, appealing features which can be appreciated by open-minded interlocutors. People have to be able to preserve their specificity without transforming it into opposition or an excuse for exclusion. Society is thought of as a multicultural ensemble of different groups, each of them conserving different experiences. Having a specific family history – a specific ethnicity – means possessing specific qualities and specific experiences which can be useful – whether enriching, instructive, entertaining or funny – for all the different groups making up the society.

> I feel both Italian and Eritrean. I mean, in the end I love, I mean, I respect the different cultures. I mean, when I have to do something Italian, I do it without making such a fuss, and when I have to do something Eritrean I do it too. I don't know how to explain it better: here there are some rules, which are different from there, and I respect these rules and I respect those ones too. It depends on the context, and knowing different rules is always better. I mean, sometimes I invite some friends round and I've cooked Eritrean food; they were enthusiastic and I love this thing, I mean, I'm different from other people and I love my being different very much.
>
> (Maerge, 16 years old, born in Eritrea, in Italy since the age of 1)

> Coming from another country often gives some advantage; for instance people are often curious when they know I'm from Bosnia, they immediately ask me what's the typical food there. Maybe things would be different if I were black, in that case there might be more discrimination, but in my case people don't immediately think I'm a foreigner and are more curious than frightened.
>
> (Ana, 16 years old, born in Bosnia, in Italy since the age of 4)

Being a foreigner is sometimes interesting because people are interested in you, they ask you: 'Where are you from?', they are curious, they want to know more about you ... and, how can I say this? It is a way to start communicating with others ... they start asking you: 'Where are you from?' ... it's a way to make your acquaintance ... it's nice, I love it.

(Cinthya, 19 years old, born in Peru, in Italy since the age of 7)

In this situation, ethnicity becomes a useful tool, at least at the individual level, to face the contradictory injunction not to be (too) different in contexts where expressing a certain degree of difference is seen as a form of autonomy and takes a high value. It represents an attempt to manage the conflicting needs between being included and being recognized as 'different': two never-ending stressful and demanding tasks. Ethnicity allows a solution to be found to the paradoxical obligation to become similar to the dominant group without having any possibility of becoming one of them (always being remembered as different, that is inferior, subordinate, not accepted, precarious, worthless), as well as respecting and valorizing parental ties but not accepting to share or reproduce their marginal social status. In order to be effective (that is assuring recognition and countering discrimination without fostering exclusion and reducing personal opportunities) ethnicity has to be a sign of distinctiveness rather than segregation. The usefulness of ethnicity as a tool for claiming recognition as well as for resisting negative representations is particularly clear among the young people we have interviewed. They have a good amount of cultural capital (enough to appreciate the potential value of difference in current societies) and, at the same time, they experience social hostility and discrimination, hindering the full realization of their goals. In this position, showing a certain degree of ethnic pride may well be helpful to fulfil different tasks: demonstrating gratitude and continuity with their parents, claiming respect from their autochthonous peers and on this basis participate under the same conditions in the social arena, exhibiting a peculiarity which fascinates and generates curiosity.

Beyond family ties

Although continuity with family history seems to be one of the main concerns among our interviewees, the necessity to gain a satisfactory degree of autonomy is just as important. The need to guarantee a certain amount of balance between maintaining continuity with family experience and parental teaching, and breaking loose from what has been felt as fetters reining in complete self-fulfilment creates explicit tensions. These tensions are managed by modulating the two polarities rather than by making a clear-cut choice of one pole only. Continuity and change are the necessary and ineradicable elements of daily experience and must be managed in accordance with situations and goals rather than by demanding exclusive choices which may be consistent but overly rigid (Butcher 2011).

> The culture of parents should never be forgotten because of its origins, to know where we come from, we can compare it to the study of humanity. Why do we study history? To find out what men did before us, and we have to do the same thing with the history of our parents and our origins [...]. I think, from a certain point of view, that we have to be able to remember our own traditions but we must also know how to adapt to the situations in which we find ourselves, to the environment in which we find ourselves. It's like blending these two things; we have to know how to live with these two aspects. That's what I'm trying to do.
> (Titus, age 19, born in the Philippines, in Italy since the age of 8)

Esteem of family history and cultural traditions is viable only when it does not hinder other important goals, primarily when they are not the cause of exclusion or marginalization in situations in which personal opportunities and realization are at stake. Living in Italy means being able to use as best one can all the openings offered by the Italian context.

> If you came here you have to do your best to live here. I mean, there are a lot of people, also from my country, who came here and always stay together: they don't go to school or any other place where you can meet Italian people, they don't mingle socially, so they cannot integrate ... I see many people from my country who stay together and they always retain the narrow-minded mentality that there is there, they always stay there, in their little, old world, also in the way they dress or behave ... if they don't change these habits ... I mean, you have to adapt

to ... the moment, don't you? the place ... I mean, if here in Italy there is a particular mood now, you have to ... I mean, you don't have to behave like a sheep which goes in the same direction where all other sheep go, but if that is the mood, you should take that into consideration; you cannot go against the stream, because if you do so you have to face other problems.

(Oscar, 21 years old, born in El Salvador, in Italy since the age of 8)

Maintaining a strong bond with family history does not mean a mechanical reproduction of fixed models transmitted by parents. Traditions must be adapted to contemporary needs. Conditions change and with them, culture must also change. Although important, culture cannot always be rigidly defended from transformation nor considered exempt from any criticism. Traditions and culture always need to be reconsidered in the light of the contextual peculiarities. The specific rules valid in a specific context, personal attitudes and the goals one sets for oneself require taking a critical look at culture and tradition and being able to select the useful features while modifying those which may be counter-productive.

Our parents' culture should not be forgotten, but I am not saying, however, that we have to be fixated, glued to how they are, but we must change a little, just that we have to keep the ties with our parents' culture.

(Shanika, 19 years old, born in Sri Lanka, in Italy since the age of 13)

Excessive ethnic closure is considered more of a limit than a support. It is important to maintain a dynamic bond with ethnic and family traditions but it is still more important to be able to be open minded and not to prejudicially close oneself off into an insular community which could be protective but nevertheless reduces personal opportunities. The constraints of a tight-knit community are particularly evident among children from Chinese families. The Chinese community in Milan is one of the oldest and is more residentially segregated than other immigrant groups. Elderly Chinese people, although they have been living in Italy for a long time, often speak Italian with difficulty and seldom have stable and deep relationships with Italians. The Chinese adolescents we interviewed regularly complained about the closure of their community, blaming parents and relatives for anachronistically reproducing an outdated culture which is no longer alive even in China.

> I feel very different from my parents ... we, the young people, we have a new way of thinking ... for the Chinese of my father's generation, earning a lot of money is the most important thing ... it's always the first priority ... in order to earn money they are prepared to give up a lot of things, for instance, to have fun or to go on holiday ... but for me ... and I see this is the same for my friends, work is important, of course, because it allows you to do something ... but it is important to have free time too yourself too ... about money, then, for me it has ... just a symbolic meaning; money never brings you happiness ... even though, unfortunately, to be happy nowadays you have to do well in business.
>
> (Yue, 18 years old, born in China, in Italy since the age of 8)

> I cannot understand a lot of Chinese customs or behaviours, for I'm Italianized, so to speak ... For instance, my father says Chinese girls should not smoke, because in China girls never smoke, while boys do ... well, this is rather foolish, because I'm for sexual equality, so it doesn't matter to me if you are male or female, because, ultimately, you are a person. But my father looks at smoking as ... some form of male power, or something evil for women, and so I don't agree with him at all ... I don't agree with him either about how a girl should behave with other Chinese, in our Chinese community. For instance, she should never appear to be fed up, she always has to be pretty, perfect ... In my opinion the Chinese mentality is far more open in China than among the Chinese in Italy, because Chinese immigrants in Italy have kept the mentality which existed 20 years ago and brought up their children with that mindset, but their children rebel because they have an Italian mentality. Instead, in China there was slow progress and it's been easier for granddad and grandma to change their mind according to changing times.
>
> (Yiyu, 17 years old, born in Italy, Chinese parents)

The tension between maintaining continuity with parents' teach-ings and changing family habits in order to achieve appropriate autonomy is a common problematic point among the young people we have interviewed. A community which is too tight-knit is perceived as a reduction of opportunities. Although respect for parents' teachings is held in great esteem, most of the young people consider being able to adapt themselves to the expectations of the context just as important. To live on a par with their peers it is important to understand that other people can have different habits, that the world is changing quickly and that attempting to preserve unaltered any aspect of tradition ends in unbearable, detrimental isolation.

Finding mediation between continuity and change is considered more useful than a clear-cut choice between them; mediation which is only possible by managing family history in order to identify useful aspects and put the rest aside. In this way, ethnicity is actively selected, keeping what may be used as a valuable characteristic and rejecting what may represent an obstacle or excuse for exclusion. Carrying on traditions doesn't mean conserving them unchanged. On the contrary, it means being able to adapt them to new contexts and in so doing preserving them without missing out on new opportunities.

> I think you should never forget your own culture, because, in the end, it's you, you were born there and that is your culture. There are things that you may not share, but it is your identity ... You should never forget your own roots, but sure, if there are things you cannot agree with in your culture ... this shows that you care, that you want it to improve, you don't want it to look bad to others ... I feel that I have the Egyptian culture, but I also have my own ideas and some of them go against Egyptian culture, but I don't care, because if Egyptian culture includes some things that are wrong, it is not right that if I am an Egyptian, I have to go along with things I do not agree with.
>
> (Christine, 17 years old, born in Egypt, in Italy since the age of 9)

Mediating, keeping a distance, drawing distinctions, and adapting to the situation are all strategies taken into account to better achieve one's personal goals, rather than demonstrating a coherence that risks being interpreted as intransigence, integralism and an excessive attachment to the past. For young people growing up in a globalized, multicultural, changing world, managing the ambivalence deriving from the contradictory desire to preserve continuity with family traditions while participating without exclusion in a common social life is more important than coherence: to fit the context in order to maintain personal opportunities is more relevant than showing an integrity which is not affected by the situation.

Fluctuating between *culture* and *way of life*[2]

In order to help make the selection of what has to be preserved and what needs to change, an important distinction between *culture* and *way of life* is often introduced by our interviewees. Although they rarely use these two terms in a coherent way, they nevertheless feel it useful to introduce some form of distinction which may be helpful in managing the ambivalence between continuity and change, and respect for parents' teachings and accomplishment of personal autonomy. Moreover, the distinction allows them to resolve the apparent contradiction between the desire to be recognized as different – sharing the condition of otherness and foreignness with their parents – and the desire to participate on a par with their peers in the society in which they live and where they are planning their future.

When young people talk about their experience, they make a distinction between two separate ways of thinking of themselves: one, more stable, deeper, which can be described using words such as 'roots', 'values', 'blood' and 'identity', which we summarize with the mundane meaning usually associated with the term *culture*; the other, more fluid, which can be described using words such as 'practices', 'acquired customs', 'habit' and 'choice', which we condense into the expression *way of life*.

I was born in Tirana, the capital of Albania, and I came here when I was a child but I do still feel Albanian. I'm applying for Italian citizenship because Italy is part of the European Union and with the Schengen Treaty the Italian passport is more useful; but I'm Albanian, I mean, I accept with pleasure the Italian culture but I do feel more Albanian, although I speak and write in Italian better than in Albanian [...] I no longer have many contacts with Albania, I have no friends there and also my relatives are becoming very old. Most of them have died now, so I have no more opportunities to go there, and I feel good in Italy,

I'm happy to live here. Because I came here when I was very young, I assimilated the Italian mentality very quickly and in any case I feel a little bit Italian too. I got used to the Italian way of life and I live in that way. That is my way now, but I'll always be Albanian, I mean, even if I lived there for only a few years I feel Albanian, because it is not an external bond: it doesn't matter the way I live, it is an internal mood, it is something personal, deep.

(Juxin, 17 years old, born in Albania, in Italy since the age of 3)

When I got Italian citizenship my friends all said 'Oh, look, you've got Italian citizenship!' and I said 'So what?' I mean, it's not as if a person changes according to his citizenship, a person is what she is! I feel attached to my traditions back home, and anyway my family belongs to that country, but I think that it does not matter where you are born, in the sense that you are linked ... I am obviously linked to Italy because in any case I grew up and live here, and besides, I like Italy. But I think it is a good thing to be attached to traditions because that's where your blood comes from anyway, in the sense that you are attached. Even if you live somewhere else, there's got to be something that links you, because they struggled so long for nationality and for the sense of nationality, so why throw it all away? I mean they worked so hard to get there and then you say 'No, I don't care', no, I don't like that; it would be like a betrayal.

(Romeena, 19 years old, born in Italy, Sri Lankan parents)

I am and I'll always be Ecuadorian, but you have to have experiences of some things, I mean, if you live for a long time somewhere ... you change, you become part of that place, you embody a lot of things from that place ... I've lived here for 15 years now and I live differently from the way my cousins are used to living in Ecuador. I feel Ecuadorian, and I'll always be Ecuadorian, but I also feel Italian, because I do a lot of things nobody does in Ecuador. They are two different things, and you have to have experiences of their difference in order to be able to talk about them.

(Carla, 19 years old, born in Ecuador, in Italy since the age of 4)

The deepest and most embedded habits – which we sum up with the term *culture* (in its mundane meaning) and are usually equated with ethnicity, nationality and family history – are evoked when young people want to refer to an inner core which is presumed to constitute the basis for the more authentic and personal part of selfhood. *Culture* constitutes the raw material from which individuality is then structured. It cannot be ignored because it is where personal substance comes from. Although *culture* does not mechanically determine personal characteristics, a widespread essentialist point of view often transforms it into a substance, a 'given' that impacts on character and the deep sense of self. Parental *culture*, associated in a non-problematic way with national belonging, language and religion, is seen as an 'essential' element of one's own identity, something that is received 'at birth' and that now influences sensitivity, moral orientation, preferences and behaviour. *Culture* is also considered a sort of lowest common denominator that ensures facility of understanding, elective affinities and the most direct communication among those who share it.

In this case, it is evident how 'strategic' (Spivak 1990), 'popular' (Noble et al. 1999) or 'auto-' (Werbner 1997) essentialism can be a viable way for the practical articulation of an irreducible difference, crucial to assuring a space for resistance against external negative representation as well as to act as a catalyst point for the construction of a shared sense of identity in particular circumstances (Gilroy 1987, 1993).

Possession of a specific *culture* is commonly thought of as defined by birth, and deriving from the bonds with one's own family, parental teachings and emotional attachments. The origin of the family established, depending on individual cases, by national or religious belonging counts much more than the place of birth or where one grew up in determining that 'profound' character, given and unchangeable, on which autonomy and the ability to make personal choices are founded.

> I feel very Sinhalese ... because I have the real personality of a Sinhalese person, I've got ... my traditions, I've got ... well, I respect the principles that I was given when I was a little kid, you know. Even if here when you see Italian kids, you feel like changing ... but ... what your parents taught you is stronger ... even religious values, let's say ... here maybe lots of kids aren't ... don't believe in God, that sort of thing, but I ... being Sinhalese, well, it's really a way of understanding things.
> (Shan, age 18, born in Sri Lanka, in Italy since the age of 7)

Losing contact with one's own *culture* means 'betrayal' of one's own essence, changing one's own nature.

> We all have our own cultures and we must respect them, because it's as if it were a betrayal of one's own identity not to respect it and to take on the culture of the place where one lives. No! I mean, my own culture I keep for myself, I admire it because it represents what I am ... we all have our cultures, our languages, our traditions and we should never forget them. I am against the foreigners who ... there are Egyptians who come here, and they really give me a jolt ... they're glad to have forgotten their language, they're glad not to talk to Egyptians any more and to talk only to Italians. The Italians are fine, they're good people, but you are an Egyptian, you betray your people, your traditions, no! This is betrayal.
>
> (Christine, age 17, born in Egypt, in Italy since the age of 9)

Way of life – usually equated with personal taste, style and preferences – is the result of personal learning and individual experience; it is a process of slow but unavoidable embodying of the customs, habits and outlook on life peculiar to the place where the person grew up.

In this case, change, mix and fitting the context prevail over essentialism, and the ability to adapt to circumstances is valued most. Stressing the influence of the situation justifies the experience of feeling themselves as deeply and irrevocably different from their parents and their cousins living in the family's country of origin. To resort to the idea of *way of life* rather than *culture* means assigning the final justification of such a difference to the influence of the situation, rather than a personal betrayal or a voluntary breakdown of communal values and traditions. These are not fixed and unchangeable but require adapting in order to be kept alive, useful, and up to date.

It is worth remarking that *culture* and *way of life*, essentialism and relativism are not the alternative strategies of different people. They represent instead different moments of negotiation that each individual performs in different situations. Moving between *culture* and *way of life* should not be seen as contradictory, but as positional (Baumann 1996; Noble et al. 1999).

The influence of the context on personal characteristics becomes evident when children of immigrants compare their behaviour, mentality and future expectations with those of their cousins living in their parents' country of origin. Growing up in Italy necessarily entails learning specific attitudes and behaviours that make it difficult to accept the living conditions of their cousins. Growing up in Italy means becoming accustomed to the Italian way of life, assuming the mindset of their Italian peers, comparing duties and future expectations to those of their Italian schoolmates rather than to those of their peers living in the parents' country of provenance.

> I've grown fond of my cousins, and all my relatives in Egypt, I mean, I miss them, I miss all of them, but ... I mean, I wouldn't live there ... it's the last thing I'd do [*laughs*]. There, it's another culture, there it's another mentality, it's different from mine ... I couldn't stand living there ... it's the last thing I want to do ... the way of life in Egypt is duller, lifeless. Here I have a lot of fun every day, there I have ... I mean, I have to respect more rules, that is.
>
> (Mimmo, 17 years old, born in Italy, Egyptian parents)

> I've been here since I was six years old and when I go back to El Salvador I feel like a fish out of water ... I am used to living here, I've got friends, habits, behaviours ... my mother wishes to go back there when she retires, it is the same for my father ... but I think differently: I've got used to the life here, I don't like to be considered as a parcel which is sent there, I prefer to live and work here ... I said to my mother 'Mother, you brought me here and now I'm staying here, you have to take responsibility for consequences, it wasn't me who wanted to come. I thank you for bringing me here, I prefer thousands of times living here ... here I've become more open minded, I'm freer and now I cannot live there'.
>
> (Francesco, 17 years old, born in El Salvador, in Italy since the age of 6)

For most of our interviewees, being part of a specific ethnic group – that is, sharing a specific family history – depends on fate, it is a constitutional part of inner substance, and it is not chosen nor can it be betrayed. Becoming Italian, on the contrary, is the result of habit, it originates from everyday routines. It depends on contexts and, since young people live in a different context from their parents, they have to work out new ways of life in order to be in tune with the situation in which they are involved. Being able to understand and master the right codes ruling relationships in a specific context represents the basic skill required to be admitted and not fall short of others' expectations. Fitting the context requires behaving with proper demeanour (Goffman 1956), demonstrating the capacity to be a person worthy of recognition and allowed to have a say. If people want to find their opportunities and establish the best conditions for achieving their goals, they have to act in accordance with the dominant way of life.

> Sri Lanka is my country and I'm proud to be Sinhalese, but I fit in everywhere ... and, in the end, I feel more Western, at this point I feel Milanese, I mean, I've spent all my adolescence here ... for instance, when I talk with my friends in Sri Lanka, I realize how different I am from them. I mean, with them I cannot talk about certain things, while I can do so with my Italian friends, with them I can talk about everything: my parents, my boyfriend, school; my Sinhalese friends would never understand me ... I mean, I recognize myself as part of both of them, but I feel more Sinhalese for my history and more Italian for my thinking, because now I live here and the Sinhalese are too narrow-minded to live here.
>
> (Shanika, 19 years old, born in Sri Lanka, in Italy since the age of 13)

The distinction between *culture* (stressing the importance of family ties and ethnic belonging) and *way of life* (stressing youth experiences and the necessity to be independent from close ties which reduce opportunities rather than increasing them) proves useful for managing ambivalence deriving from the contrasting will to maintain continuity with family history yet to compete equally with their peers for personal self-fulfilment in a global context. Points of reference for future plans are made up of everyday situations, which are inevitably embedded in complex networks of interdependence. In order to effectively be a part of the favourable circumstances offered by these situations and to fit into both family and autochthonous networks, it is necessary to be open-minded, recognizing that codes and rules change according to different contexts, being able to move from one context to another without being excluded, and balancing continuities and changes.

Dual competence

Ambivalence does not mean contradiction or disorientation. On the contrary, it justifies avoiding radical decisions between choices often claimed to be irreconcilable. Rather than expressing a state of confusion or indecision, it highlights the value attributed to continuity with the family bond as well as to the capacity to fit into changing contexts. It shows the ability to use both continuity and change, differentiation and adaptation, and reification and relativism as useful skills which can be employed in different contexts for different goals. It expresses the preference for a 'both/and' logic, rather than for an 'either/or' one. Recognizing the importance of the contexts, and relativizing rules, values and codes, young people may construct a more complex and layered representation of themselves which better fits their everyday experience of living enmeshed in multiple bonds of belonging created by the proliferation of social positions, relational networks and reference groups. Ambivalence has become an important tool for facing the necessity – common for all of us living in globalized contexts – of acting with a certain degree of autonomy in different situations which are regulated by different and often contrasting rules. As Alberto Melucci so effectively remarks, 'we have become migrant animals in the labyrinths of the metropolis, travellers of the planet, nomads of the present. In reality or in the imagination, we participate in an infinity of worlds. Each of these worlds, moreover, has a culture, a language, and a set of roles and rules to which we must adapt whenever we migrate from one of them to another. Thus we are subjected to mounting pressure to change, to transfer, to translate what we were just a moment ago into new codes and new forms of relation' (1996b: 43).

The young people interviewed seem at ease in moving among different representations and discourses; they can regulate without excessive stress what they feel as the deepest part of themselves, tied to parental culture, and what is perceived as a more practical and goal-oriented part, influenced by the place in which they live. When the continuity of family ties and traditions are emphasized, the essential reified trait of culture is used as the central reference: it signals the desire to maintain close personal relationships, it helps describe the feeling of involvement and it brings in the emotional dimension. When emphasis is laid on opportunities in life, on plans for the future, on self and professional fulfilment, the ostensible, essential character of culture inherited from parents becomes relativized: it appears diluted or needs to be adjusted to the different contexts. In this way, children of immigrants paint a very nuanced picture of themselves, always connected but never totally corresponding to the experiences and the expectations of either of their parents, their cousins living in the family country of origin, or their peers with whom they share daily relationships and projects for the future. They position themselves in a peculiar social space where being connected is more important than showing coherence, being mobile is more useful than being inflexibly loyal. They inhabit a new form of locality in which everyday, mundane relationships require the capacity for adjustments, translations and transformations.

At the level of everyday interaction that 'dual competence' (Baumann 1999) emerges which allows the individual to manage both the reified aspect of culture and the relative and instrumental traits of habits and customs.

Managing ambivalence reveals itself to be an important skill in order to generate a new social collocation in which young people can find new space for personal freedom and autonomy, loosening family ties without completely severing them. Young people's locality is constructed by mastering uncertainty and persistent change by means of the capacity to switch codes and languages when they move from one situation to another. Dual competence in using reification and relativization rhetoric allows them to make their specific experience accountable, even if it may appear characterized by apparently incompatible elements. In fact, these young people become more and more familiar with situations in which they measure themselves against vague and unforeseeable circumstances, which may represent vital potentialities (the capacity to think outside the box, globally, without being rigidly tied to conventions and routines) as well as powerful restraints (the impossibility of transferring what has been gained in one context to another, facing the prospect of being excluded and marginalized despite possessing the right formal title to be accepted and included).

Creating stability out of precariousness is viable only when the products of stabilization are strong enough to appear plausible, accountable and defensible, but malleable enough to be adapted to the contextual exigencies. Coherence with the contexts is more important than a more abstract and generic coherence with alleged inner characteristics. Coherence in changing contexts cannot consist in being the same, without transformations, regardless of external circumstances (often the ideal conception of coherence for former generations, living during classical modernity). It means matching continuity and transformation instead, showing a specificity that testifies autonomy and agency as well as the capacity to fit the situation, adopting the right code and showing the proper demeanour.

The capacity to use a dual competence and make a distinction between culture and way of life appears particularly important in constructing a viable representation of self which matches the necessity to stabilize excessive fluidity with the willingness to fit into the situation.

Finding themselves in a new, specific social position – living in a more complexly connected and fast changing world, and being different from their parents, cousins living in their family's country of origin and their Italian peers – children of immigrants are engaged in giving meaning to their new experience, balancing reifications (stability, security and continuity with the past) and relativization (necessity to change and adapt to situations). Separating *culture* from *way of life* – but being able to use them both simultaneously – these young people are able to justify not wanting to loosen the ties to family history while at the same time desiring to participate equally with their peers in Italian social life.

Ethnicity takes on new nuanced meanings too. Being relevant in signalling continuity with family history and traditions – and in so doing assuring the possibility of permanence amid continuous change – or revealing itself a useful tool to counter discrimination, ethnicity is praised and equated with the alleged 'natural' core which constitutes the inner self. In this case, ethnicity is presented as the deepest and most basic characteristic, which was not chosen and cannot be changed at personal will. However, in situations in which ethnicity might become a rigid and negative label causing exclusion, emphasis on difference is weakened and equality emerges as the main register. Ethnicity becomes something which needs to be continuously tailored to new contexts; it cannot only be preserved or reproduced, it has to be adapted and translated. The capacity to shift from one argumentation to another – from difference to equality, from *culture* to *way of life*, and from continuity to change – depending on context, audience and personal goals – emerges as one of the most striking generational skills.

4
Multiple Belonging

The complexity of belonging

The struggle to find a particular social location in which continuity and change can be managed without making a clearly defined choice between the opposing alternatives is also evident when belonging is at stake.

Belonging is a semantically complex notion (Yuval-Davis 2006a, 2011; Anthias 2006), deeply entwined with group identification, ethnicity, nationhood and citizenship. It is related to social location, formal recognition of rights, emotional attachments, social and political participation, as well as recognition of equality and difference. It is closely connected to at least two major dimensions, analytically distinct but closely related: 'belonging as a personal, intimate, feeling of being "at home" in a place (place-belonging) and belonging as a discursive resource which constructs, claims, justifies, or resists forms of socio-spatial inclusion/exclusion (politics of belonging)' (Antonsich 2010: 645).

As presented in the previous chapter, profound transformations in the way in which locality is experienced and endowed with new meanings set the scene for potential innovative generational experiences. The complex connectivity and the increasing reflexivity associated with the necessity to face the changes globalization introduces in everyday life invite a critical re-examination of what is thought of and perceived as 'community', 'one's own home', 'ethnicity', participation and citizenship. Feeling part of a specific community does not derive directly from inescapable destiny; it constitutes instead a never-ending series of accomplishments that demands the ability to mix commitment and choices with one's roots and routes. Belonging not only reflects conditions but enacts identities (Hall 1989) and is, therefore, better conceptualized as a process (*becoming*) rather than a status or a given and stable category (*being*) (Antonsich 2010; Scheibelhofer 2007). It consists of ongoing boundary work that allows differentiation, recognition and the placing of people into specific social locations. Doing the work of continuously positioning themselves, children of immigrants become aware of the complexity of boundaries as well as of the fact that these boundaries are the result of processes of social productions. This awareness potentially enhances reflexivity and the ability to perceive the personal choice of belonging to a specific group as causing political, social and psychological effects. This is not to suggest that belonging is merely free-floating and that people are at liberty to choose their belonging beyond the bounds of common sense, habits, cultural representations, and economic and political power. What we aim to highlight instead is how belonging requires the ability to name and imagine specific location, the ability to construct and cross boundaries between alleged different social positions, rather than simply being the mechanical effect of ascribed characteristics. Claiming specific degrees or forms of belonging in different situations has to do with the capacity to choose, as well as with coming to terms with the force of external powers imposing labels and positions which affect inclusion and exclusion and which cannot be modified by simple personal will.

Belonging emerges as the output, always partial and 'under construction', of the ongoing process of 'manoeuvring' between diverse discourses of the self and different levels of identification (Poynting et al. 2004). It is influenced by the dynamics between structural aspects of the social contexts in which young people act and the ways they deal practically with these contexts, their resources and their constraints. Experiencing multiple belonging, they learn to manage their level of participation in and identification with particular contexts in order to better realize their goals, while at the same time reducing personal losses.

The idea of *differential belonging* introduced by Aimee Carrillo Rowe can be used to draw attention to

the ways in which we are already constituted in and through often overlooked modes of belonging, and also to suggest a resistive command [...] Differential belonging, like differential consciousness, allows us to move among different modes of belonging without feeling trapped or bound by any one in particular. The point is not to be correct, consistent, or comfortable. We need not, or cannot, be the same person everywhere – in different communities, on different occasions, at different times in our lives. We may move among various stages of belonging throughout our lives. Our relational needs may shift over time and across space. And as we move among these sites, the contradictions and crises that arise are most instructive of our becoming.

(Carrillo Rowe 2005: 32–3)

The capacity to maintain differential belonging is not only a useful skill for intellectual elites engaged in deconstructing alleged certainties and expanding personal awareness; it also constitutes a necessity for young people living in constant motion between contexts, adopting specific rules and expectations that cannot be automatically applied or confirmed when moving from one situation to another.

Feeling at home needs continuous construction, selecting from different opportunities, making choices which allow stability without freezing out further possibility of change that could offer something better. Far from being the mere result of ascribed characteristics, belonging emerges as a blurred and mobile location which, in order to be kept fluid and useful, needs the development of specific generational skills. Being able to display the right level of belonging in a specific situation mirrors both the way in which young people understand and interpret their place in the world, as well as the social resources to construct the specific position they have at hand. This shows the interplay between social structures and the agency of young people in claiming space within those structures (Anthias 2002a).

The possibility to manage one's own belonging becomes a strategic feature connecting emotional attachments, identifications, ethical and political values as well as entitlements, status, participation and citizenship. The politics of belonging – that is, discourses and practices of building boundaries, claims for recognition, manifestation or concealment of difference, expression of solidarity or hostility – involves formal recognition of rights, full participation in social life and emotional attachment to specific communities. Citizenship and identities, in addition to 'ethnicities, cultures and traditions' – all signifiers of borders and boundaries – play a central role in discourses of the politics of belonging (Yuval-Davis et al. 2006: 3). In point of fact, claiming different forms of belonging in different contexts opens doors to more nuanced forms of participation that call for a more articulated idea of citizenship and recognition of rights. Thus, the politics of belonging becomes a distinctive social field where identities, hierarchies, alliances and communities are constructed, negotiated and resisted, in the endless attempt not only to fix and naturalize the difference between belongingness and otherness, but also to escape the danger of being entrapped in boundaries or labels that prevent the expression of personal will and ability.

As Skrbiš et al. (2007: 262) observe, the politics of belonging usually presupposes 'a range of human actions that are imbued in politics, charged with emotions and symbolically codified. Not surprisingly, the exploration of various ways in which belonging is lived and experienced often resembles a journey into semiotics of images, gestures and practices'.

Analysing the ways in which children of immigrants are actively engaged in the politics of belonging – going to great lengths to play a role in the definition of what is involved in belonging, in being a member of a community, claiming the right of participation, on an equal basis, in social life, or resisting negative locations which are the cause of exclusion and discrimination – allows us to better understand how transformations introduced by the globalization processes and the intensification of complex connectivity are affecting the relationships between social position, membership, participation, entitlement, identification and self-fulfilment.

Analytically, it may be useful to distinguish between different facets of emotional attachments, which correspond to distinct politics of belonging, using different rhetorical accounts in order to achieve different forms of recognition, claiming different rights and producing different self-representation. In fact, the young people interviewed show themselves to be capable of coping, in relation to contexts and objectives, with a plurality of forms of belonging, which are connected with nuanced emotional attachment and which range from the claim of universalistic forms of identification, in which equality and similarity resulting from being part of a unique community of human beings are given priority, to the call for recognition of specific memberships in which particularism and difference are emphasized.

What is more relevant is that they are able to use both universalistic and particularistic accounts in order to express, depending on the situation, differentiated belonging, and are able to switch from one rhetorical register to the other every time they feel it useful or necessary. A complex, mobile and layered idea of belonging emerges. Three main constellations of emotional attachment, tightly connected with different facets of citizenship and claiming the recognition of particular aspects of personal characteristics, may be analytically introduced to account for how belonging is dynamically expressed by the young people interviewed: *admittance, allegiance* and *involvement* (Colombo et al. 2011). These represent different – but intertwined and all usable by the same person in diverse situations – politics of belonging, showing different ways of being or becoming a member of the community and the complex articulations between rights and obligations, entitlement and engagement, participation and identification, and equality and difference characterizing citizenship in the contemporary, globalized world (Delanty 2000; Isin and Turner 2002; Joppke 2007a).

Admittance refers to formal aspects of recognition. It stresses the universalistic claim to be equal, to not be excluded on the basis of prejudice or systematic, institutional discrimination. It implies the emotional attachment to a common, universalistic community and the recognition of equal respect and dignity for all human beings, regardless of physical, social, historical or cultural differences.

Allegiance involves stronger feelings of belonging to a specific community. It stresses the importance and the 'unavoidability' of difference; it is often based on the idea of the existence of particularistic and essential characteristics that can be neither hidden nor betrayed without losing autonomy and identity.

Involvement entails more specific recognition of personal characteristics. It has to do with participating as an equal in society, having a say in matters regarding public life, being allowed to express preferences or dissent. It mainly refers to the chance or the desire to be part of a 'community of opportunities' in which anyone has the same options to participate on behalf of specific interests and to have a stake in the life and future of the community. Recognition of equal rights is as important as recognition of personal difference because mere admittance is not enough if people are admitted into the community but are prevented from expressing their particular preferences. On the other hand, a difference that isolates into a strong but separate community reduces opportunities and rules out potential rewarding relationships.

These three aspects of belonging are also connected to three facets of citizenship, which itself is characterized by multidimensionality.[1] The formal dimension – to have an official status and a passport – can be distinguished from the participative dimension – to be considered part of society, allowed to have a say, and to express and defend specific opinions or interests – and from allegiance – to feel part of a specific community of destiny.

This distinction enables us to analyse how these different constitutive dimensions are connected or disjointed in concrete, mundane situations in order to express an articulated and mobile idea of inclusion and exclusion, equality and difference, rights and duties.

Documents that matter

Most of the young people interviewed expressed great interest in obtaining formal recognition of Italian citizenship. It is mainly considered as a legal status, an 'official document' attesting the legitimacy to stay in the place where one lives and as protection from discrimination or prejudice. An instrumental conception of citizenship seems to prevail, while its emotive or symbolic dimensions remain in the background. In this case, it is conceived as a legal device that might avoid the complications of and frustration with Italian bureaucracy.

It is difficult to grasp the widespread interest in obtaining Italian citizenship without considering the current Italian regulations and the obstacles foreigners face when they deal with the Italian administrative system.

Also due to the massive emigration fluxes of the Italian population towards Northern Europe, North and South America and Australia which, from the second half of the nineteenth century until the seventies of the last century, had characterized its history (Pugliese 2006), Italian citizenship law appears as an 'ethnic law', privileging bonds with offspring of long-departed Italian migrants rather than promoting integration of foreigners living in Italy. In fact, the most straight forward ways of acquiring Italian citizenship are by *ius sanguinis* – having Italian ancestors – or by *ius connubii* – marrying an Italian citizen. Children of foreign parents who are born in Italy are not automatically recognized as Italian, let alone entitled to stay in the country. On the contrary, they need to fulfil a series of complicated requirements in order to apply for Italian citizenship.[2] Therefore it is not surprising that, in spite of a constant increase in migrant settlement in the country, the number of people acquiring Italian citizenship is extremely low.[3]

The rules are even stricter for children born abroad to foreign parents and coming to Italy during childhood. In this case, they must wait three years after their eighteenth birthday before applying for Italian citizenship. During this interim period they, as well as the children of immigrants coming of age and failing to obtain citizenship, have to apply for a regular residence permit. This often means long, exhausting queues, as well as facing intransigent and, occasionally, humiliating interaction with police or other bureaucrats as the following extracts show:

> Even if I don't have citizenship yet, I already feel Italian, I mean, I don't know, to be honest, for me to be an Italian is to be as I am, as I am now, Italian, because I am what I am because I grew up in this place, with a specific point of view, with these kind of people; I live here, I obey the law, I have rights and duties like all the people who live here have ... I feel 100 per cent Italian, so I don't understand why I cannot have Italian citizenship right now ... after all it is always the same story, yes, I am Italian, but I haven't got the citizenship ... so you feel different because you only have an alien's residence permit to stay here in the country where you were born while everyone else can stay here without permits ... you must have a permit, you don't have the freedom to live in the country where you were born, you have to apply for a permit, and if you are lucky, it's OK, otherwise you have to go back to a country where you have never lived and you barely know ... it really makes you feel different, it makes you feel incomplete ... I know that citizenship is only a piece of paper, nothing will change with it, maybe only greater freedom to travel, but for me it is important, it has always been important ... I always feel the lack of it as an unequal and pointless discrimination ... I never understand why I cannot have it.
>
> (Adian, 18 years old, born in Italy, Eritrean parents)

Citizenship would be convenient because it would allow me to save a lot of time, in my opinion, all the time you need to have your residence permit renewed, because for this you really have to hand in a lot of paperwork, and with the citizenship I wouldn't have to desperately always look for a regular job in order to be granted the permit, I mean, after a while all this really stresses you.

(Alexis, 20 years old, born in Peru, in Italy since the age of 3)

Considering the bureaucratic complexity and the arbitrariness involved in obtaining a regular permit to stay in Italy for anybody not considered part of the Italian blood community, it is not surprising that most of the children of immigrants interviewed considered Italian citizenship so important.

Being accepted as people

The necessity of facing the daily struggle to be recognized as eligible to stay in the place where one was born, lives and is planning one's own future brings to light an initial potential constellation of belonging. In this case, the emotional feelings attached to belonging have to do with the desire and the necessity to be considered 'human', and not to be excluded from places or situations concerning daily, mundane interaction. The politics of belonging are, thus, mainly led by universalism and equality. Being admitted, on an equal basis, in the different contexts making up the common framework of everyday relationships, constitutes a prerequisite for taking one's own chances on the same terms as others in fair competition transcending prejudice and discrimination. Admittance has to do with being accepted on equal terms in daily situations: being excluded, or not recognized as equal in these situations is felt as a profound, unjustifiable injustice.

Admittance is close to the idea of 'assimilationist belonging' introduced by Aimee Carrillo Rowe (2005: 33): 'In assimilationist belonging we want those in power to recognize us as equals. Even though we recognize ourselves as different, and are recognized that way by others, we don't emphasize those differences when we are assimilating. We want those in power to value our universal humanity over our departures from what's valued by dominant culture'.

Not being excluded, being considered as 'human', and having the opportunity to belong wherever one chooses or desires, no matter one's origin, language, religion or other kind of physical or cultural differences, are the core requests. Claiming equality beyond difference may have an effective rhetorical strength when asking for concrete inclusion while resisting exclusion and prejudices. Insisting on equality may help to weaken boundaries erected by a hegemonic culture separating those who are considered legitimate members of the community from those seen as alien.

For the young people interviewed, being regarded as 'equal' to their peers with Italian parents is considered 'natural' and 'obvious': sharing the same conditions of youth and the same daily experiences makes any distinction that creates discrimination unjustifiable and indefensible. Taking part in the same 'way of life' should be enough to be recognized as part of the same community and to be entitled to participate on the same terms in social life. Those who share the ordinary point of view, common patterns of consumption, rules, skills and future expectations must have equal opportunity for personal and professional fulfilment, regardless of any personal difference. In this case, culture, traditions and ancestors must not be considered as relevant: everyone must be treated as equal. Distinction, when necessary, must be based on personal worth, not on alleged ascribed characteristics.

Claiming admittance widely employs rhetoric of equality and tends to leave difference in the background.

> Language, culture and all these things shouldn't matter at all, they shouldn't make any difference between people; people are different in their behaviours, in the way they accept other people, for these things. Language, religion and culture must only be personal matters.
>
> (Ahmed, 17 years old, born in Italy, Egyptian parents)

> Everybody should be treated the same way, and their nationality should not have anything to do with it, with the fact that we are foreigners or not ... personal abilities count for more, not nationality ... we are all equal and what distinguishes us from others are our personal abilities and not the group to which we belong ... I feel just like other young people and I want others to

see me that way, for what I can do, not as a Filipino or an Italian or any other.

(Titus, 19 years old, born in the Philippines,
in Italy since the age of 8)

Being excluded on the basis of origin or cultural difference is perceived as unfair discrimination. The everyday experience of living the same situations, and sharing the same future expectations and the same dreams as their autochthonous schoolmates entitles the children of immigrants to expect equal rights and opportunities, and to be recognized as part of the Italian demos.

I don't think it is fair that a foreign guy cannot become a cop or a *carabiniere* [member of the Italian military police], for me it's not right. Maybe you were born here or have lived here most of your life but you cannot do it ... I know I cannot do it, and I'd like to become a cop ... and it is unfair that I cannot do it just because I'm a foreigner ... it is unfair because I live here, I go to school here, and maybe sometimes I study much more than some schoolmates of mine but, just because I'm a foreigner, it is unfair I cannot do that when other people can [...] Because, even though someone has different nationality, we are all the same, in the end we all are human beings and, in any case, our goal is to get on in life. I don't think this is just my goal, I think it's yours as well ... I mean, everyone wants to get on in life, so I believe we are all the same.

(Shanika, 19 years old, born in Sri Lanka,
in Italy since the age of 13)

The wish to be considered as legitimately belonging to the social context in which they live and to be part of Italian society does not equate to the desire for total assimilation. It highlights the aspiration to be recognized as equal, to have equal dignity and to participate on a par with everyone else in the social arena, to show their skills and to play their cards right (Riccio and Russo 2011). The legal status of being a citizen constitutes a prerequisite for participating on equal terms in social life rather than the final recognition of full homologation. According to the young people in this study, it means equal opportunities rather than sharing the same identity.

Citizenship doesn't mean feeling Italian: instead it shows people that we are the same as they are, we respect the law and pay taxes, it shows them that we are not poor people. OK, we came here to find a job, but we came here and we do our best to find a job, to pay taxes and all these things.

(Veja, 17 years old, born in Italy, Ghanaian parents)

Being refused admittance to situations that are considered a mundane part of everyday experience generates strong feelings of discrimination. Interviewees feel dispossessed of the due recognition of human beings deserving respect; this reduces their chances of participation under the same conditions as everyone else in the common ongoing effort to get on in life and fulfil personal goals. Belonging, in this case, means being recognized as human beings having the right to *exist*, to *stay*, and to *live* legally in the place where one goes about one's daily life. Stressing equality over difference represents an effective rhetorical tool to avoid exclusion, counter discrimination, and which offers the opportunity to participate in social life without significant handicaps.

Obtaining formal recognition of Italian citizenship is not only considered important in order to be granted equal opportunities, but also because it is connected to obtaining an Italian passport.

The passport assumes a particular symbolic meaning. It is regarded as a conditional right of access to the 'cosmopolis' of global communications (Balibar 1988). Travelling without being delayed or stopped at national borders is seen as a status that allows admittance to wherever people think they have the best chances of achieving personal objectives and realizing their purposes in life. Admittance to or exclusion from 'Western societies' appears as a crucial dichotomous device distinguishing those who are entitled to fully participate in the global flux of commodities, ideas, opportunities and aspirations from those who are entrapped in situations of institutional misrecognitions that confine them to their restricted neighbourhood.

Many of the young people interviewed describe personal experiences in which the lack of an Italian passport prevents them from behaving as their 'Italian' peers do. One of the most common stories has to do with the frustration of being unable to join their peers on a school trip abroad. The lack of an Italian passport and a residence permit nearing expiry cause either the denial of an international visa or huge difficulties in returning to Italy after the trip. Being forced to relinquish these collective moments causes resentment. These renunciations are experienced as evidence of unjustified and unjustifiable discrimination. Not having access to the social space that entitles their peers to all the required rights for full participation in the modern 'cosmopolis' constitutes one of the main institutional devices that produce new forms of exclusion. Not being admitted into the social space of formal citizenship means exclusion from those economic and cultural opportunities that require skill and willingness to move, flexibility and constant connection to global fluxes, in order to become real and effective.

> Citizenship makes everything easier. For instance, over the last five years I've attended this school and every time I had to go abroad with my class it was a big problem. Every time I had to go to the police to ask for a permit, stuff like that. It's such a pain! So I want citizenship to avoid the hassle, even when the police check you ... what is more it is a certainty for the future. Because if you live here in Italy, in my opinion, you have many more opportunities for your future, whereas if they send you back to your country, there, you have fewer possibilities. I'd like to stay here, in Italy, but I'd like to have some experience abroad, I mean, it would be a dream to go to ... maybe find a job, I don't know, maybe in France. It would be great to have such an experience. I have two uncles there, in Paris. And then, maybe, it's really a big dream ... go to the States, at least for a trip, then if I find a job, if I have that chance, yes ... everything American fascinates me ... starting from what you can see in the movies. It may seem childish but I love it, I love their way of life ... It's a dream but I'd love to have the chance to try ... and with an Italian passport maybe things would be easier.
>
> (Mohcine, 19 years old, born in Morocco, in Italy since the age of 5)

From this point of view, citizenship means first of all admittance, the formal right to enter any place that can increase personal opportunities, not being stopped at the door, not being excluded on the basis of prejudice or ascribed categories. Right of admittance has to do with the recognition of equal opportunity; it involves behavioural and attitudinal aspects rather than innate characteristics. It relates to the 'way of life', that is to say, to actions of free will and personal choices, while far less importance is attributed to blood, ancestors, religion and ethnic or racial characteristics.

Admittance on an equal basis is also a prerequisite for consideration as a human being deserving respect and proper personal recognition. Possession of a formal document attesting the legitimacy to exist, to stay and to be respected is vital for resisting everyday situations in which a foreign background equates to inferiority, deviancy or being out of place. Showing the right document sometimes constitutes the minimum requirement for recognition as a person, while, in other situations, it can be an effective tool for countering racism.

> Having citizenship also means being treated in a different way. I would like to have Italian citizenship. It would be great, if I had Italian citizenship then maybe at customs they would see the Italian passport and let us go. Usually they stop us and check us; with Italian citizenship we would be like one of them ... and then they look at you from a different viewpoint, they look at you as a person.
>
> (Albena, 18 years old, born in Bulgaria, in Italy since the age of 9)

> I always introduce myself as Egyptian, because I'm not truly Italian ... I mean, yes I am, because I was born here and I've lived here, but my true origins are Egyptian ... I always introduce myself as Egyptian, then if someone speaks or behaves like a racist I say: 'look, I'm Italian as well, you shouldn't behave that way' ... but I like to give people a chance; when I say I'm Egyptian I'd like to see if they behave with me differently from how they usually do with other Italians ... and if I see they behave differently, if they have prejudices, then it is important to be able to show them the passport and say: 'Look, I'm an Italian citizen'.
>
> (Moussa, 18 years old, born in Italy, Egyptian parents)

When recognition as a person entitled to participate on an equal basis in social life is at stake, stressing equality over difference may be a useful rhetorical tool to avoid exclusion. In this case, belonging stresses the opportunity to 'feel at home' in the place where people live their own everyday experiences, while the politics of belonging is engaged in weakening the boundaries which create insurmountable differences between those entitled to be part of the community, taking advantage of all the privileges deriving from this belonging, and those regarded as alien and excluded. The formal recognition of belonging to the community in which one lives, attested by the concession of formal citizenship, still matters as official acknowledgement of the right to stay and to be considered as a person. It is a prerequisite for not being excluded, for unrestricted, equal and effective participation, and for showing one's own abilities and individuality.

Stressing equality in order to obtain admittance is not without cost. Assimilation strategies always have to pay the price of participation in the definition of and the provision of legitimacy to some form of 'normality' that imposes itself as a standard for the evaluation of who and what is admissible and who and what has to be excluded. The children of immigrants interviewed share with their Italian peers the idea that only those who behave properly and are of use, only those who contribute to the well-being of society, in that they are employed, obey the law, pay taxes and are economically self-reliant should be considered as part of the society.

The universalism supporting the claim of equal admittance dismisses relevance of any difference related to ascribed characteristics, leaving uncontested and legitimizing the dominant pattern of normality. By invoking equality as protection against exclusion, it risks undermining the capacity to credibly criticize the dominant idea of normality as well as the conformation to the space in which one asks to be admitted. From the uncriticized point of view of the dominant group, boundaries defining inclusion and exclusion, and belonging and foreignness equate with boundaries separating good from evil, and normal from deviant.

> Citizenship should be given to everybody ... you want to live in Italy? Fine! Get your documents in order, work, support a family ... don't bother other people, then everything is OK and you have citizenship, but if I see a foreigner who rapes someone, jail doesn't solve anything, he should go back to his own country directly and nothing else ... because at that point, you don't want to be a citizen and so I would send him back to his own country.
>
> (Adel, 21 years old, born in Egypt, in Italy since the age of 4)

There are people now who come here only to create a disturbance, I don't like them. If it depended on me, I think like the Northern League thinks: send all of them back to the country where they or their family come from ... I'm not Italian, but I think that way: there are people who come to generate disorder, well, they don't have to come. In my opinion, they are people nobody wants, I mean, there are people who come here to find a good job, they want to get on in life, and these people deserve some help, they must have a regular residence permit; but those who come here only to cause trouble, immediately out. There must be a distinction between those who come here to get on and make a contribution and those who steal or do things like that.

(Abder, 21 years old, born in Morocco,
in Italy since the age of 15)

The general idea that admittance should be a guarantee on an equal basis is not at odds with the idea that it must be reserved only for those who behave properly. The apparently universalistic claim that nobody should be excluded from a community due to 'blood' or other immutable characteristics is no longer valid when moral traits are taken into account. According to several young people in this study, belonging entails sharing moral values and must be earned. The idea that belonging constitutes a 'reward for proper behaviour' can potentially legitimize exclusion. It distinguishes between people of class A (the 'right ones', the 'good citizens') and people of class B (the 'marginal', the 'bad' or the 'non-citizens') (Dean and Melrose 1999; Lister et al. 2003). The former must be guaranteed and protected while the latter must be left to their fate and, in any case, excluded from the rights guaranteed by citizenship. The universalistic and inclusive principle that Marshall (1964) considers to be the basis for the modern idea of citizenship which tends to broaden participation in public life as much as possible and to reduce economic, cultural and social divisions is replaced with a particularistic and exclusive principle transforming citizenship into a set of obligations, commitments and responsibilities towards the community and converting rights into rewards that must be earned through active and compliant behaviour (Ong 1999). The 'natural' division based on blood and origins is transformed into a 'moral' distinction that is just as obvious and incontestable.

Belonging as allegiance

The relevance given to being accepted on an equal basis and the demand for an assessment of personal values founded on individual skills and abilities rather than on ascribed factors does not mean complete dismissal of difference or the wish for full assimilation. There are situations in which the emotions attached to belonging require the recognition of specific differences and the feeling of being part of a specific community. When identity issues are at stake, the classical rhetoric of roots may be useful for drawing boundaries which clearly distinguish between a space for 'us', where it is easier to feel accepted, safe and immediately recognized, and an external space, where one is continuously exposed to the uncertainty of the relationship with the 'other'.

Belonging equates with allegiance, and the politics of belonging implies the construction of effective boundaries that distinguish and protect. Making a difference capable of defining an identity and creating a space of safety and resistance against potential external threats constitutes the main conditions for 'feeling at home' as well as for claiming and justifying the necessity of some form of distinction between insiders and outsiders.

When belonging equates with allegiance, being different is more important than being merely admitted. Self- and external recognition of difference are perceived as the crucial condition for creating a space of protection and solidarity that permits personal fulfilment, autonomy, dignity and respect. Carrillo Rowe calls this mode of belonging 'separatist': 'In separatist modes of belonging, we not only recognize our differences, but we value them and seek to nurture them solely among people "like us". This mode of belonging can be vital when the work of engaging the wider world becomes draining. Separatism offers an important site to dream, to create visions and try them on with others who begin with similar assumptions, politics, and experiences' (2005: 34).

Belonging as allegiance can be sustained by the will and the effective ability to use specific differences as boundary markers creating an effective distinction between 'us' and 'them', as well as by the necessity to react to and resist forms of external aggression or discrimination. In the first case, the reification of culture and traditions is emphasized. In the second case, stressing a separatist belonging is mainly a reactive answer toward racism and exclusion.

Sharing a reified notion of culture and difference makes it difficult, for the young people interviewed, to feel 'totally' equal to their autochthonous peers. As we have shown in the previous chapter, *culture* – unlike *way of life*, which is conceived as determined by the context in which one lives – is thought of as connected to parental teachings and community ties, and comes from sharing specific history, habits and language. For these young people, *culture* is seen as acquired by birth and people belong to a community by fate. It constitutes a distinctive marker that cannot be ignored or easily given up without betraying one's own most essential and deepest 'nature'. So, being born into a foreign family marks a crucial difference that cannot but be accepted and sustained.

> I prefer to knock around with Latin American people ... I don't know, it's easier, we are more united, we are all the same ... for instance, if you are walking in the street and you see someone strolling along, after a while we start looking at each other and we start speaking, so we get to know each other, become friends and then we start going out together. Things are easier with people who come from my country: we immediately feel on the same wavelength, we are all like-minded people.
>
> (Maria Eugenia, 18 years old, born in Peru,
> in Italy since the age of 14)

The essentialistic rhetoric entwines culture with identity and reinforces the idea that cultural differences exist as 'facts' and mark effective and meaningful diversities. The 'true sense of self' derives from an original and natural difference linked to a collective destiny that must be taken as a given, to hereditary values which must be preserved and reproduced.

> Citizenship has to do with the future you are going to construct, both for yourself and your children. If you want to have your future in Italy, you have to be a citizen, you cannot say 'I live here' without thinking of citizenship. Holding citizenship means that you are part of that community, that you are engaged with and committed to that community. Citizenship means that you have

all the rights and all the duties to be a member of that community. After that, if you want to keep your ties with the place where you were born, that is another question, in this case there is always a tie ... In my opinion, citizenship and identity are not strongly tied to each other, because if I take Italian citizenship I still remain what I am, I still hold all the ties with the country where I was born. I don't change as a person. To be a person is not connected with a document where it is written who I am. Citizenship is just bureaucratic stuff, which can help you both at the economic level and for a better integration with other people, but what you are is bound up with your family, the place where you were born, where you come from.

(Amed, 20 years old, born in Egypt,
in Italy since the age of 8)

In belonging as allegiance, people reify difference and use it as raw material for the construction of visible boundaries that allow internal solidarity and guarantee the expression of individual peculiarities. In this case, belonging means sharing the experience of living with 'familiar' people, who have the same language, history and desires. The desire to belong, which is an expression of personal allegiance to a specific group, cannot be satisfied by generic admittance on the basis of universalistic equality. It involves the recognition of a deeply rooted difference, which can neither be given up nor betrayed. It implies the sensation of being part of a group of people sharing the same fundamental and constitutive substance and, on this basis, they are able to fully understand each other. They can communicate and be supportive because they are made of the same material. The reified character attributed to culture and its capacity to work as an effective boundary marker principally emerges when young people consider their personal life and their likely future partners.

When I think of my future husband first of all I want him to be of my own culture, my own religion. Because I don't believe I can get on well with someone who has a different religion, different culture. I know people who have married an Italian guy, or vice versa, and when they have had babies they didn't know on which side they are ... are they Catholic or Muslim? Hindus or Muslim? I mean, this is confusing, and I have to look at the future of my children. So, I don't think I can marry someone of different religion, I prefer someone who has my own culture and my own religion.

(Rufaida, 18 years old, born in India,
in Italy since the age of 11)

I'm really in love with my girlfriend. She is Peruvian like me, I wouldn't have it any other way, she is the ideal girl for me also because we have the same traditions, the same culture, we think the same about all the important issues ... we have a lot of things in common ... Things would be very different with Italian girls, they are ... not all of them, I don't like generalizations, but usually they are less sincere, less reliable; rather than a real relationship they only want a fling.

(Jefferson, 20 years old, born in Peru,
in Italy since the age of 8)

I cannot imagine an Italian boyfriend, because ... I'm not at ease with them ... also if I like him, I couldn't ... first of all the language, if he cannot speak Arabic I feel something is missing ... but maybe this is not the main point ... nor is the religion ... I don't know why, it's something coming by itself ... because I feel at ease only when I speak with Egyptians, because also with Moroccans or Algerians it doesn't work ... I'm at ease only with Egyptians ... because my culture is Egyptian, I cannot but share it with the love of my life ... so I prefer an Egyptian, even if I've never lived in Egypt, I was born here and I prefer to stay here.

(Aiat, 18 years old, born in Italy, Egyptian parents)

Belonging as allegiance is also a useful tool for opposing prejudice. When young people face discrimination or negative labelling, they may valorize their difference in order to claim recognition and respect. They use ethnic difference as a boundary to increase internal solidarity and as protection against external threats. In this case, ethnic belonging constitutes a reactive move against exclusion and misrecognition (Kibria 2002; Purkayastha 2005; Skrobanek 2009). The widespread experience of being considered by their autochthonous peers and, in general, by Italian society, as invaders, unwelcome, potential deviants or alien to the 'normal' way of thinking and behaving, leads to defensive reactions which strengthen distinctions. A viable form of defence, in fact, consists in valorizing the very same difference that is externally imposed as a negative attribute. In this case, a reified conception of culture may constitute a suitable strategic resource to face episodes of racism and discrimination. The idea that culture is a proper basis for individual character supports the claim for respect of difference, since recognition of human differences is the sole 'universal' form of recognition which grants equal dignity to all human beings without forcing them into hegemonic and constraining categories. Calling for the recognition of one's own difference, presented as a personal characteristic not willingly given up, represents a form of resistance against a misrecognition that humiliates and devalues each individual or the group with which people identify.

> I've got a lot of friends, I mean, many of them are Italian ... well, they are mostly schoolmates, but my best friends are all Arabic, they are Moroccans like me, because in the end Moroccans understand me better, they share more things with me. I mean, it's always been difficult to get to know Italians, we know each other but ... they always keep their guard up, they always make you feel you don't fit in, you are different ... When I was a child I had fewer problems with Italians, I simply didn't pay attention to what they said or thought. The troubles started later, when I grew up I understood they are different, that, indeed, we think differently, and cultures are different, as well as behaviours, values and a lot of other things.
>
> (Kenza, 18 years old, born in Morocco, in Italy since the age of 2)

Reactive belonging, which stresses the unavoidable allegiance with a specific group due to alleged ancestral and 'natural' ties, transforms the difference – attributed by the dominant group as a negative label – into a positive mark. Ethnic difference becomes the foundation for a diverse humanity, which defines values and power differently and holds on to the deepest human principles against the greed, decadence, false conscience and egoistic interests of the current dominant group. Ethnic belonging assumes importance in adolescence, after experiencing discrimination and racism, rather than deriving mechanically from a 'natural' habit acquired by birth (Aparicio 2007). It requires awareness, personal commitment, a sense of solidarity and a mutual project for the future.

The difficulties in obtaining formal citizenship contribute to the development of reactive, separatist belonging. In a general context in which children of immigrants are increasingly obliged to take civic and language courses, sign 'integration contracts' or follow 'citizenship paths' (Joppke 2007b; Bauböck and Guiraudon 2009) in order to obtain a document attesting their right to live as their autochthonous peers are allowed to live uncontested, the children of immigrants may consider these requirements as forms of unjustified discrimination that can be countered only by reinforcing separation and stressing difference. Asking young people born in Italy and living their everyday existence alongside their autochthonous peers – sharing the same experiences, practices and dreams – to prove they truly deserve to be considered legitimate to stay, may contribute to transforming citizenship into a device for discrimination rather than fostering participation (Ong 1999).

> I still haven't got Italian citizenship, I still haven't got it because under Italian law I'm a Senegalese citizen ... but I was born here and I've been living in this place all my life ... I cannot see why I cannot have it ... I've got a lot of friends, we all do the same things, playing basketball, meeting at the bar ... but I cannot vote, I mean, I want to speak up for myself! I want to have my say. Why are there other people who are regarded as Italian but they are not interested in politics or they don't obey the law and they can vote, while I cannot? And they expect me to swear on the Constitution, to swear loyalty in order to obtain citizenship! Why shouldn't other people do that, while only I must do it? Why must I alone request permission to vote? ... It seems to me a very unfair thing ... I mean, I have to swear loyalty in ... here, in the country where I was born. If I was born here I must have Italian citizenship!
>
> (Loum, 19 years old, born in Italy, Senegalese parents)

If belonging to the broader society is forbidden or problematic, looking for a more hospitable shelter in an encapsulated community (Werbner 2005) may be the most viable option. Feeling at home may mean, in this case, staying only with those who can understand us because they are like us, identical to us.

When belonging equates with allegiance, it exaggerates the alleged mutual difference and expresses the idea of deep sharing based on common roots. The common essence constitutes both the external cause and the personal reason for staunch solidarity. Belonging, in this case, means feeling to be among the like-minded, protected and distinguished from external aliens. Ethnicity, nationhood and pan-ethnic identification become locations of viable and effective belonging because they draw boundaries that distinguish between external hostility and internal solidarity. The allegedly common substance constituting the deeper character of everyone belonging to the same community assures camaraderie and mutual support, it guarantees the necessary recognition for adequate personal self-fulfilment.

However, the essentiality of identification supplies a kind of raw material that can be useful only in specific situations and for specific purposes. Difference has to be adapted to contexts rather than mechanically reproduced. Real situations always require the ability to manage the tension between reification of identity and the need to cope with changeable and differentiated experiential contexts. Equality and difference, and universalism and particularism are not mutually exclusive and are, rather, in continuous flux to ensure recognition of self, inclusion, participation, autonomy and the opportunity to develop one's own personal abilities.

Being recognized as people deserving a hearing

Admittance and allegiance do not exhaust the range of possible emotional attachments or potential politics related to belonging. There are circumstances in which 'feeling at home' depends on being recognized as individuals with specific personal characteristics that deserve respect rather than being simply accepted. In these situations, belonging relies more on having the opportunity to actively participate in communal life than feeling safe but separate, while the politics of belonging consists in claiming recognition of personal uniqueness and being considered as autonomous. The politics of belonging stresses the right to express personal preferences rather than claiming admission on an equal basis or having the right to preserve, in isolation, one's own diversity. Belonging, here, does not mean being equal: it signifies having the same opportunities and being recognized for one's own uniqueness.

Involvement concerns this more articulated level of belonging. It has to do with the feeling of being engaged in public social life and having the right to intervene directly in it in order to manifest a personal point of view, defend private interests, and express individual preferences. The possibility of conflict and the manifestation of one's own difference as discernible from other potential differences remain central aspects. Involvement entails a sophisticated and nuanced idea of equality and difference, which may be used in diverse ways to claim diverse degrees of inclusion and participation.

In this case, fully belonging cannot be reduced to assimilation, a form of participation in which the opportunity 'to be here' has to be weighed up against relinquishing any recognition of personal peculiarities. These have to be regarded as the legitimate basis for the expression of individual preferences.

Neither can belonging be limited to recognition of difference, which implies separation and isolation. Acknowledgement of personal and collective specificities may be important not only because it assures protection and preservation of traditions but also because it allows the individual to have a say, to give a personal opinion about decisions concerning communal life, in order to have some power to influence it. Taking part in social life is as important as being recognized as different.

Belonging, in this case, means having the complete right to participate as well as being allowed to fully express personal interests. It implies being free to criticize other points of view, and to expect people to take these expressions or criticism seriously, deserving to be heard and taken into account.

> Look, if I decide to live here, it's because I like it here, I feel that this place has now become a part of my life ... I am the one who decides ... then if I decide to live here it is right that I have my say, that I am accepted and can contribute to making things go well here ... if I have some good ideas that can help, they must not tell me: 'You can't talk because you are a foreigner!' I want to have my opinions heard and I don't even want them to say: 'First become an Italian and then you can talk'; no, I want to live

here and therefore I want to say what I think, but I also remain a Kosovar.

(Marcus, 21 years old, born in Kosovo,
in Italy since age 13)

When belonging means involvement, great importance is given to autonomy, agency, and the opportunity to intervene directly to shape one's future. As for the 'supremacist' belonging presented by Carrillo Rowe (2005: 34), when we claim this particular form of belonging 'we recognize our differences and want them to be recognized and valued. We believe that these differences make us better, that they provide us with a particular vantage point on social relations that create new visions for social change. We want to share those visions with the wider world to transform the sites of belonging we inhabit'.

Involvement has more to do with sharing the same way of life than sharing a common culture, traditions or values. Sharing the same way of life means being able to express personal autonomy and individual preferences; it implies manifesting particularity rather than conformity. Personal difference has to be adequately recognized but it cannot be a cause for exclusion. Belonging as involvement entails the recognition of the right to stay and to move, to be accepted on an equal basis and to fully express one's own difference.

Thus, involvement ends up by indicating the possibility to participate in social life without being forced to assimilate or give up personal characteristics. Due to the daily experience of being compelled to switch constantly from one context to another, in which rules, communication codes, opportunities and expectations are different, involvement implies forms of belonging which are always partial, plural and changeable. Belonging, without assimilation and without being entrapped by boundaries that turn into cages, necessitates the opportunity to move across these boundaries and to be adequately recognized in different contexts. The ability to be flexible, changeable and adaptable depending on the situation becomes a new generational skill, that was much rarer among previous generations, often used to learning a narrow set of uniform, if not monolithic, roles to play out faultlessly at every moment of the day, if not during their whole lives.

Involvement means recognizing that people are more complex than that which can be synthesized in one unique belonging (local, ethnic, national, religious, etc.); it is more complex than a single choice, it involves ambivalence and multiple loyalties.

> I'm Russian, but I don't know any more ... I've lost a lot of the Russian culture I had before ... If I go to Russia now everyone will think I'm a foreigner ... because I don't dress like them any more, they don't recognize me as Russian ... You surely lose something, obviously I have breathed so much Italian air that I recognize myself in a lot of Italian things. I have Italian citizenship, I'm Italian ... but that doesn't mean I'm less Russian ... it's more complex than a single choice.
>
> (Kristina, 18 years old, born in Russia,
> in Italy since the age of 5)

Belonging as involvement entails the skill of adapting oneself to the specific expectations of the different situations in which one is involved, as well as the external recognition of being fully entitled to participate, have a say and defend one's own interests. Playing a part wherever it is possible to gain some advantage, some opportunity to improve one's own social position, or, simply, have some fun, is a necessary skill towards developing self-fulfilment and self-confidence. Involvement means feeling fully accepted as an individual, a prerequisite for being the protagonist of one's own life, having the chance to participate on a par in everyday life, and having the right to plan a future where one lives.

> Look, I feel both Italian and Eritrean ... because I was born here but my roots are over there, and I think this is an advantage ... I think that traditions are very important; I'm very proud of my traditions, but you have to adapt to the situation ... I mean, on the one hand you have to adjust, but, on the other hand, you don't have to conform to the customs of the majority, I mean, you have to be yourself ... I feel at ease with my friends because they accept me for what I am. There are things we agree on and others we don't ... but everyone is free to have a voice ... we are all different, we all came from all over the world: there are Italians, Eritreans, Egyptians, English and from everywhere else, and we have good times together, because everyone is accepted as a person ... we know that we are different but this makes things

more interesting because nobody is interested in convincing others to give up their traditions.

(Fortuna, 18 years old, born in Italy, Eritrean parents)

Young people participate in a diversity of worlds, in which different languages, roles and expectations have to be used in order to fit the situation and to communicate effectively. Failing to assume the right code in the right situation is cause for exclusion and marginalization.

Moving freely from one context to another, being allowed to show personal ability and to fully express personal difference are all facets of what Alberto Melucci (1996: 52) called personal capacity. Being part of different communities, fully participating in each of them, without being forced to give up personal differences or to show an exclusive loyalty which prevents taking up the opportunities provided by other forms of belonging, represents necessary facets of that individual set of resources a person uses in order to act autonomously and to be recognized as a person by others.

From this point of view, Italian citizenship makes sense only as an additional recognition, when it acknowledges the Italian side without consequently requiring the denial of other identifications and other loyalties. Citizenship cannot be considered as an abandonment of any previous identification in order to embrace a new one. On the contrary, it is seen as the necessary deployment of the irreducibility of one's own identity into a unique dimension. Dual citizenship constitutes the recognition of the deeper character of identity, inevitably hybrid and plural. Equality and difference are not opposed, rather they constitute two different aspects of the same personal experience, each of them giving sense to a specific part of the self. Without contradiction, children of immigrants are engaged in claiming recognition as being legitimately Italian and, at the same time, the right to be differently Italians (Zinn 2011).

You see, I really feel like this: Italian and Moroccan ... because after all ... I am what I am ... I mean, even if I say 'I'm of this or that extraction' ... in the end everyone can see that I'm this way, Italian and Moroccan ... Yes, and after all I like it ... I love my culture, I love the fact that I'm Arabic, I'm proud of this, I don't want to keep it secret. So, yes I'm Italian and Moroccan ... I feel strongly Italian too, otherwise I wouldn't have all this hope of obtaining Italian citizenship.

(Kenza, 18 years old, born in Morocco,
in Italy since the age of 2)

Citizenship is never fully equivalent to identification; the young people interviewed make a sharp distinction between, on the one hand, the recognition of formal rights and the bureaucratic dimensions that legitimize the presence in a specific community and, on the other hand, the feeling of belonging and national identification. Citizenship has mainly to do with *inclusion* – that is, the opportunity to participate, to have the right to a voice and to take part without discrimination in social life.

Fluid and differentiated belonging

Involvement requires the capacity to select, mediate, translate, and move from one situation to another, understanding the differences and the peculiarities existing in each context. It entails the opportunity and the ability to belong to different groups, showing knowledge of the rules governing the relationships in each situation in order to be accepted and to participate on an equal basis, but without the promise to be fully and exclusively loyal to only one community.

The children of immigrants we interviewed often live on the move, forced to keep changing when they cross the countless boundaries marking the contexts of their everyday experience. As Alberto Melucci remarks, in a globalized society: 'We find ourselves enmeshed in multiple bounds of belonging created by the proliferation of social positions, associative networks, and reference groups. In simply conducting our lives, we enter and leave such systems far more frequently and in a far more rapid sequence than we did in the past' (1996b: 43). This fluid existence changes the way in which belonging is experienced: feeling and effectively being part of a specific community is not something deriving from innate, ascribed characteristics. It rather depends on the capacity to adjust personal behaviour and expectations to those valid in the specific context in which one is acting. Being able to adapt is more relevant than showing a coherence that may be interpreted as incapacity or lack of will to recognize the complexity of different situations. To understand and use differences, to know how to behave in different contexts using different codes is a daily, mundane necessity if one wants to feel adequate in different situations and to gain the greatest advantage from them. An excessive attachment to one sole group, to one sole language or to one sole code is considered excessively rigid and does not allow one to manage effectively in the flux of contemporary life.

Young people become accustomed to dealing with ambivalence (see also Butcher 2004); even though differences are considered an obvious and natural 'given', they are not regarded as valid in the absolute. Instead, they are 'comprehensible' and 'plausible' only in relation to time, place and to personal goals. Knowing how to recognize and use different codes that set up valid rules in different contexts is considered a positive skill. What is important is not to claim a specific difference but to recognize its partiality; to be aware that its validity and consistency inevitably depend on contexts. A skilful user of difference knows when to apply the right codes at the right time, in the right place and with the right audience.

> I feel both Italian and Eritrean, and that's basically because I like it, I mean, I follow both cultures. When I have to do something Italian, I do it without making a big fuss about it, and when I have to do something Eritrean, I do it ... for example on Sundays I always go to church in Italy, but when I go to Eritrea, I have to go every day and I go. But I don't know, it's like here there are laws that are different from there and I obey these laws and I also obey those. My mother wants me to be half and half, and follow Eritrean and Italian traditions. When it comes down to it, I don't make a distinction, I mean ... I like both of them and when I need to, I use one or the other.
>
> (Sara, 20 years old, born in Italy, Eritrean parents)

Fitting the context is more important than a strong, exclusive belonging. Differences are perceived as 'local rules', which cannot be compared or exported with success from one situation to another. They make sense only if they satisfy the expectations of the context.

> Living here I feel I have something more; I mean, knowing new things is always better, it makes you richer, it makes you more

interesting and important ... So coming here to Italy has been an improvement, and living here I feel more like my Italian friends, but it depends on the situation you are in. I mean, when I go to Romania I feel like them too ... it depends on the place, on what you have to do ... knowing both here and there I have no problem, I can manage in a way that is more Italian as well as in the Romanian way ... it depends on the situation ... I'm both Italian and Romanian because I know how to behave when I'm with Italian people and I know that things may be different when I'm with Romanians ... the most important thing is being able to understand the situation.

(Stefan, 18 years old, born in Romania,
in Italy since the age of 11)

In this way, belonging is always partial, temporary and conditional, but it doesn't lose its relevance. The necessity to show different attachments in order to have the possibility to move from one context to another, to cross boundaries without being stopped or delayed, and without reducing the chances to play one's own cards well, promotes a differential belonging that relativizes memberships. As Carrillo Rowe (2005: 34) put it:

In differential belonging, we recognize the lessons that come from moving among these various modes of belonging. While each mode provides a vital component to our growth and the formation of our politics, becoming stuck in any mode or seeing modes as mutually exclusive can be counterproductive. It is precisely the movement across these modes that allows us to be politically productive. Our separatist belongings can nurture the work we do when we are assimilating; our supremacist belongings can provide insights into our revolutionary belongings. We may engage in more than one mode of belonging at the same time, and the emphases on different modes of belonging will shift throughout our lives.

The young people we have interviewed demand much more than the recognition of the specificity of their ethnic culture (as many of their ethnic leaders do); they are fully embedded in their hybrid condition and claim recognition *and* participation. They contribute to constructing multiple and mobile youth 'ethnicities' (Amin 2002).

The capacity to deal with ambivalence requires a dual cultural competence (Baumann 1997, 1999): the ability to manage the dominant discourse which considers difference, culture, community and ethnicity as 'given', reifications that people receive as 'natural' fate at birth which cannot be eluded or changed, as well as the ability to handle demotic discourses, attentive to the exigencies of the context and available for mediations, which consider those same things – difference, culture, community and ethnicity – as relative and malleable, something one makes rather than has, something which has to be translated into the specific jargon in use in any specific situation.

Dual cultural competence becomes a necessary skill because being autonomous and self-fulfilled in a global society may mean not only claiming mobility rights, multiple belonging, and hybrid and changeable identities, but also fighting for the recognition of common cultural roots, shared history, and the preservation of specific languages or habits from the tyranny of the dominant group, making use of alleged essentialist and reified identities (Yeğenoğlu 2005).

In this ongoing shifting between reification, resistance, mediation and challenge, the concept of integration changes: it no longer only refers to being accepted, on an equal basis, by a local or national community; it also means being allowed to participate, without exclusion, in the global flux, claiming the right, if necessary, to freely manifest one's own differences and expect public recognition. Equality and difference become tools for claiming participation and avoiding exclusion. What is really at stake is not the recognition of strong and stable identities or differences, but inclusion in, or exclusion from social contexts that may offer relevant material, symbolic, affective or ludic opportunities.

Children of immigrants attending high school seem to be in a favourable position to develop dual cultural competences. They may often rely on families with high cultural capital, who attach vast importance to education as an effective channel for their children's social and professional success. Strong family ties and high school attendance ensure the achievement of a thorough knowledge of their parents' cultural world as well as of that of the society in which they are planning their future.

Such high cultural capital paves the way for the development of an elevated level of reflexivity. This allows immigrants to transmit to their children a valid knowledge of the culture of their country of origin, so that their children can be proud of their family history and can value their roots. Moreover, it promotes a deeper awareness of the cause of their parents' migration, stressing the social, economic and cultural deficiencies which allegedly characterize their countries of origin. Reflexivity is also used to judge the society of settlement, which is neither completely and acritically accepted nor radically rejected. In this way, children of immigrants are encouraged to maintain selective ties with the world and tradition of their parents as well as with Italian society. Thus, they learn to valorize their capacity to manage diverse situations and to apply, in a fitting and differentiated manner, the correct rules for different audiences and contexts.

The daily relationships with their autochthonous peers constitute a pull towards conformity: to learn the local language, to adapt to and share with the majority the dominant way of life and patterns of consumption. To become accustomed to – although in a selective and partial way – the majority's patterns of thinking and behaviour makes it difficult to realize personal projects when one is rigidly confined into one sole ethnic group. An excessive ethnic closure risks reducing opportunities, leaving no space for wider recognition and inclusion. In order not to limit personal opportunity it may be useful to accept the shared language and codes set up by the majority, without giving up some traits of difference that may be useful markers of personal value. Living only within the boundaries of the ethnic community is too restrictive and constraining for young people who aspire to participation on a par with their autochthonous peers in the current cosmopolis of global interconnections.

Having said that, awareness of personal location, pride in one's own origin, and responsibility towards what is conceived as 'one's own community' make complete identification with the autochthonous community impossible. The idea of the existence of a significant difference from 'natives' is also generated by the pervasive and constant experience of being discriminated against. Daily confrontation with the life and fate of their autochthonous peers highlights noticeable episodes of racism and discrimination. Although children of immigrants may have greater skills and expertise, they often perceive the presence of a glass ceiling that prevents them from reaching the social position acquired by their autochthonous peers. This contributes to the development of a critical attitude towards the effective degree of tolerance and openness of the society in which they live, and prevents them from fully belonging to it. The ongoing entwining of the experience of being forced to adapt to different contexts with the permanence of an essentialistic lexicon for identity and culture contributes to the formation of varieties of particularistic cosmopolitanism in which defence of allegedly personal peculiarities pragmatically mixes with being accustomed to living with the 'other''s difference. All this promotes development of a practical, post-national citizenship (Soysal 1994; Tambini 2001b), which uses universalistic arguments when claiming particularistic recognition, and uses difference when claiming inclusion, participation and respect. A practical split of belonging into the different dimensions of admittance, allegiance and involvement means that belonging is turned into a battleground where protection of equality – a requisite for autonomous participation and appropriate self-fulfilment – and difference – as recognition of personal freedom of choice, autonomy and criticism – may be simultaneously claimed and granted.

For the young people we interviewed, multiple belonging does not stand for indecision or confusion. It means being able to adequately fit the different contexts – with a satisfactory competence in their different languages and rules – in which people are engaged daily. Moving from one context to another without reducing personal opportunity or being excluded is more important than showing unique, strong belonging.

5
Complex Identifications

Hyphenated identification

The necessity to show multiple and differentiated belonging in order to improve personal opportunity and better fit the different contexts in which young people are involved has implications also in group self-identification.

The importance given to ethnic identification by children of immigrants has always been a focus for attention. In the framework of melting pot ideology and Fordist organization of society (in which integration is viewed as a straight-line trend that culminates in the eventual disappearance of ethnic groups into a single host society), allegiance to a specific group has been mainly interpreted as the expression of a static identity, indicating the degree of assimilation achieved by the immigrant's offspring. Identification with the country where one lives or with the parental ethnic group – in this schema, natives have nationality, while foreigners have ethnicity, and the former is destined to take the place of the latter while the civilization process succeeds – has only three possible outcomes: assimilation, exclusion or crisis (Child 1943).

Assimilation corresponds to a successful path of total adaptation to the majority group; a process of adaptation that requires children of immigrants to rid themselves of habits, languages, behaviours and associations that mark them as 'immigrant' and to become 'natives' as completely as possible. The failure of this desirable path leads to ethnic closure and isolation. In this case, a strong retention of ethnic ties is cause for a more conflictual relationship with natives and is associated with social exclusion and marginality. The full identification with either the 'natives' or with the ethnic group has often been seen as a clear choice between two conflicting worlds. Both choices have their social and psychological costs but both lead to an adequate resolution of psychological tension. Clear and strong identification with a single group confers a satisfactory level of inclusion and emotional attachment, which are necessary to develop autonomy and self-esteem. Life becomes more complex when people are unable to make a clear choice between the two allegedly incompatible groups. In this case, the incapacity to choose a precise identity leads to a precarious position and produces *apathetic reaction* (Child 1943) or *crisis* (Park 1928). Being at the meeting point of two cultures, to the extent that these cultures collide, the conflict itself is experienced as a personal problem. People suspended 'between two cultures' develop 'a new type of personality, namely, a cultural hybrid, a man living and sharing intimately in the cultural life and traditions of two distinct peoples; never quite willing to break, even if he were permitted to do so, with his past and his traditions, and not quite accepted, because of racial prejudice, in the new society in which he now sought to find a place. He was a man on the margin of two cultures and two societies, which never completely interpenetrated and fused' (ibid. 892).

The incapacity to choose between two different cultures, to assume a defined identity, produces a profound disillusionment, 'spiritual instability, intensified self-consciousness, restlessness and malaise', but also represents a stimulus for changes and fusion of culture, for fostering 'the process of civilization and of progress' (ibid. 393).

From this perspective, assuming a hyphenated identity implies an internally divided and never completed identity, oscillating between two cultures and feeling a tension or a conflict arising between them. It is a fragmented and incomplete identity because neither one of its two constitutive parts can be stable, authentic or sure. Hyphenated identity is not an easy position. While leaving room for more freedom and innovation, it is characterized by a perennial state of crisis. People unable to choose a single, defined identity are insecure, they face communication problems (bilingualism is seen as cause for confusion and the inability to fully master a language), and cannot be trusted (allegiance towards the country cannot be shared with allegiances towards other groups). Hyphenated identification is always suspect. As Theodore Roosevelt said in a 1915 speech to the Catholic group the Knights of Columbus: 'The men who do not become Americans and nothing else are hyphenated Americans; and there ought to be no room for them in this country. The man who calls himself an American citizen and who yet shows by his actions that he is primarily the citizen of a foreign land plays a thoroughly mischievous part in the life of our body politic. He has no place here; and the sooner he returns to the land to which he feels his real heart-allegiance, the better it will be for every good American. There is no such thing as a hyphenated American who is a good American. The only man who is a good American is the man who is an American and nothing else' (Roosevelt quoted in Kennedy and Bailey 2010: 268).

Although the classic assimilationist perspective tends to look at hyphenated identification mainly as a sign of integration failure, current research on the so-called new second generation shows that among the adolescent children of immigrants, this form of ethnic self-identification is widely becoming a common way of presenting and describing themselves, pointing to a different way of interpreting their presence and participation in the society in which they reside.[1] The children of immigrants are likely to identify themselves through multifaceted definitions which encompass just as much the attraction of the culture, the social network and the traditions of their parents as the total and unconditional identification with the society in which they live and wherein they are planning their own future (Aparicio 2007; Baldassar and Pesman 2005; Kasinitz et al. 2008). The young people we interviewed confirm this trend. They recognize themselves as part of Italian society while maintaining strong affective ties to their parents' original group.

Different ways of interpreting hyphenated identification

Symbolic and instrumental

Current interpretations of the ever more widespread tendency among adolescent children of immigrants towards multiple hyphenated identification are still diversified and not always convergent.

Some scholars read this growing willingness to see themselves in an articulated way as an indicator of the spread of a symbolic ethnicity (Gans 1979, 1997). The persistence of identification with the parental ethnic group is mainly cultural. It is not founded on the permanence of the actual ethnic networks and organizations to which they belong on a concrete and continuous basis. It is more a question of forms of expression which claim recognition of a specific and particular identity, an instrument of valorization in itself and of social inclusion rather than the manifestation of crisis, isolation or dissociation from the majority. Ethnic cultures and organizations become less and less important for children of immigrants, and ethnicity becomes a way of feeling and expressing personal identity (Gans 1992). Ethnicity inevitably diminishes its capacity to constitute a network of strong and binding ties, and is reduced to a voluntary affiliation which can be expressed with broad personal freedom.

As Gans explains (1979: 9): 'as the functions of ethnic cultures and groups diminish and identity becomes the primary way of being ethnic, ethnicity takes on an expressive rather than instrumental function in people's lives, becoming more of a leisure-time activity and losing its relevance, say, to earning a living or regulating family life [...] Ethnic symbols are frequently individual cultural practices which are taken from the older ethnic culture; they are "abstracted" from that culture and pulled out of its original moorings, so to speak, to become stand-ins for it'.

In an increasingly multicultural society, to call oneself 'Egyptian *and* Italian' or 'Peruvian *and* Italian' would be a way of celebrating one's own difference without feeling excluded, marginalized or segregated. If anything, the expression of a specific ethnic difference would be, in many cases, a sign of cultural assimilation, since symbolic ethnicity, rather than being a mechanical reproduction of the cultural aspects of the family's group of origin, tends to be an endorsement of attachment to the cultural traditions of the majority. People claiming hyphenated identity merely decorate their identification with the majority with the frills and superficial modifications referring to a different (appealing, exotic) symbolic language. Rather than an indicator of difference, it is used to indicate a specificity that valorizes inclusion. In this perspective, hyphenated identification refers to a weak and voluntary ethnicity, intermittent and strongly subjective. This ethnicity demands little or no involvement and is not a discriminating factor in relationships with others. It is an easy and discontinuous way of expressing a facet of personal identity, that does not conflict with either other facets of the same identity or other ways of life.

From the standpoint of segmented assimilation (Portes 1996; Portes and Rumbaut 2001) or acculturation processes (Berry et al. 2006), the spread of hyphenated identification indicates the advantage of maintaining solid ties with the parental ethnic network. In an hourglass economy and in a segmented job market where there is a clear distinction made between jobs requiring high professional skills and those requiring only physical strength, the children of immigrants must enter the job market with top professional and cultural skills already acquired. They therefore need more help and support because they find themselves obliged to acquire in only one generation those social positions that the children of immigrants of the Fordist context took several generations to attain, passing from unskilled workers to specialized workers and then to the middle class (Portes et al. 2009). Conserving strong ties with their parents' community, which can represent a solid and real support for overcoming difficulties and discrimination, while acquiring the necessary skills for competing on a par with their 'native' peers in a competitive job market, offers more opportunities than either a rigid closure into the ethnic group or a mimicry strategy that risks leaving people without adequate and necessary help. A hyphenated identification indicates both the desire to integrate successfully into the society of residence, and the recognition of the importance of family ties in achieving high professional and economic status. United families with a high level of cultural and social capital successfully transmit to their children great pride in the family history which stimulates interest in maintaining a bond with their 'ethnic' traditions and culture; pride that also acts as protection against discrimination and nourishes self-esteem and the awareness of their own qualities. The tie with the ethnic network acts as a 'moral force' which, by binding the individuals to the expectations of the group, protects against deviance. The maintenance of a strong identification with parental culture and tradition is then an expression of economic rationality – maintaining bonds that allow them to have greater resources at their command to cope with a segmented and increasingly demanding labour market – and a form of protection against any form of discrimination and racism. Hyphenated identification mirrors a selective acculturation in which the learning of the language and way of life of the majority take place simultaneously with the preservation of key elements of the parental culture. Children who are involved in the new society while retaining their ethnic heritage, who are proficient in the national language and use it more than the ethnic language, but who also maintain their ethnic language, and have friends from both their own group and other ethno-cultural groups, including the national society, show the most positive psychological and sociocultural adaptation. They show a higher level of life satisfaction and self-esteem, perform better at school and have fewer behavioural problems than peers who adopt ethnic or national identifications (Berry et al. 2006). Hyphenated identity, when it expresses a real selective acculturation, is 'associated with positive outcomes because youths learn to appreciate and respect the culture of their parents and because command of another language gives them a superior cognitive vantage point, as well as a valuable economic tool' (Portes et al. 2009: 1082).

Transnational and reactive responses

The prospect of transnationalism (Levitt and Glick Schiller 2004; Levitt 2009) tends to see the spread of hyphenated identification as evidence of the spread of transnational practices and social fields. Hyphenated identification would describe the current condition of immigrants who are bound by multiple loyalties extending beyond a specific place and a specific community: immigrants who experience the 'bifocality' (Vertovec 2004) of lives lived 'here and there' based on information, interests, practices and sentimental ties that transcend the dimension of the nation-state or the physical locality. The growth of hyphenated identification would be a sign of the decline of the nation-state and would force sociological analysis to overcome a 'methodological nationalism' (Levitt and Glick Schiller 2004) which regards the territorial dimension of the state as adequate and necessary to comprehend social life.

From this point of view, hyphenated identification is more than just symbolic. It is 'real' because the experience of maintaining communication across national borders becomes part of daily life (Somerville 2008) and identification needs to mirror this 'plurality of locations'. Hyphenated identification is a new way of thinking of self, better able to account for the continuous experience of being immersed in a network that extends and crosses the borders of various nation-states. It manifests the awareness of being included in relationships and practices that cannot be described as one sole belonging. It is a sign of a form of identification based on lifestyles and consumer patterns taken from the transnational social space, on abilities and opportunities to maintain long-distance relationships rather than those founded on proximity and the sharing of physical space. It indicates that the individual's experience of real, concrete and daily relationships mirrors a self-image that is always 'fuller' than that which a national identification can portray. Current immigrants and their offspring live in a new particular space that promotes new forms of identification. Children of immigrants inhabit innovative social transnational spaces where the two different patterns of identification transmitted by parents and native peers are not enacted in two separate contexts but in one original, interconnected social field (Levitt 2009: 1230). In this way, hyphenated identification constitutes a new identity, mixing the pre-existing identities in an inventive way, so as to better face the new experience of living 'across borders', 'beyond nation-states'.

A different interpretation emphasizes how the tendency towards self-definition in accordance with articulated forms of belonging indicates the emergence of a 'reactive' or 'racialized' identity imposed more by external prejudices than by personal choices of expression (Kibria 2002; Purkayastha 2005; Skrobanek 2009). External negative labelling based on racialized characteristics prohibits minorities, marked as non-white and thereby devalued, from having a symbolic or optional race/ethnicity (Vasquez 2010); they have, instead, to face an imposition of ethnic difference which excludes or reduces personal opportunities. Young people, especially those of the middle class with a high level of cultural capital who want to be 'integrated' and considered on a par with their peers thus run up against prejudices and racism and find themselves obliged to give a new meaning to the label of ethnic difference imposed upon them from the outside. A consistent, often implicit, common rhetoric uses phenotypic traits as markers to distinguish between 'white' (that is an authorized member of the community) and outsiders. Many children of immigrants aspire to integrate but, due to their phenotypic traits, family name or religion which are considered marks of non-whiteness, are labelled as foreign and discriminated against. They have to face processes of racialization that push them to re-elaborate their idea of ethnic belonging, giving a positive value to what is seen by the dominant group as a marker of inferiority. Hyphenated identification, in this case, is widespread among young people who are categorized as 'non-white' as a form of reactive racialized ethnicity. Claiming a hyphenated identity (e.g. Egyptian-Italian) allows them to claim legitimate inclusion in the majority (they claim to be Italian), while taking pride in their racialized difference that the majority considers cause for exclusion. Hyphenated identification is not a personal choice; young people, despite their interest in integration, are constantly reminded that 'natives' regard them as insurmountably different. The double identification marks the recognition of the impossibility of being totally, definitely and solely 'native'. The valorization of ethnic belonging does not derive from a habitus, from a family socialization within cultures and community networks referring to the parents' country of origin; on the contrary, it is the result of subsequent awareness that fully manifests itself only in adolescence when the children of immigrants experience discrimination and stereotyping, when they become conscious that other children consider them 'different'. Positive and proud enhancement of what is imposed as a brand of inferiority is an attempt to overcome the marginalization in which they find themselves. Hyphenated identification would therefore demonstrate a reaction to the existence of a 'glass ceiling', an obstacle that many children of immigrants experience in their efforts to become full and active participants in the society in which they live.

A different point of view

Although helpful, the interpretations put forward to account for the growing tendency towards identification in an articulated and plural way seem to overemphasize the 'content' of hyphenated identification rather than the processes by which this form of identification is expressed, made accountable and legitimized. In so doing, they risk depicting hyphenated identification as a new 'type' of identity, transforming it into a reified entity, something that people 'are' or 'have'.[2] If we look instead at hyphenated identification from a constructivistic, processual point of view, it is not a 'new' category, set beside the classical identification either with the ethnic group of the parents or with the majority group. It constitutes instead an important part of that generational skill that allows people to manage ambivalence, to move across boundaries, and feel at ease in different contexts where different rules apply. A hyphenated, fluid and adaptable identification allows the avoidance of radical choices between supposedly irreconcilable features. Rather than expressing a state of confusion or indecision, it highlights the value attributed to both the continuity with the family bond and the capacity to fit into changing contexts. It is not a new, fixed form of identification, placed alongside a rigid identification with the past and the family's tradition and an amorphous, passive form of assimilation. Instead it represents the capacity to use both continuity and change, differentiation and adaptation, and reification and relativism as useful skills that can be employed in different contexts for different goals.

Hyphenated identification – at least as it is currently used by the young people we interviewed – represents a transformation of the idea of identification: it is not absolute, stable and clear but always changing, adaptable to the situation and ambivalent. So it undermines classical identifications rather than simply adding a new type to them. More than a new category, it is a process, something that needs to be performed in specific ways in specific contexts. Children of immigrants enacting hyphenated identification are not something new; they *do* something new instead: they manage multiplicity and mobility better. They are not only *in-between*, a new mix, suspended between two incompatible worlds, as they are *both*: they claim the possibility to be more than a unique category, to move from one to another while remaining fully part of both.

The central point, then, is not to calculate how much 'ethnic' or 'national' there is in the hyphenated identification – trying to fix a new category – but to highlight the capacity to use both of them for different goals and for different audiences. Hyphenated identification does not exclude a full identification with either the ethnic group or the majority – so it is not in direct opposition to either of the classic forms of identification: assimilation or ethnic closure (Hammack 2010). It represents the ability to use difference in order to express different facets of personal identity, how to fit best into different contexts, and have more opportunities to achieve personal goals. It expresses a new use of identification: it is more oriented to showing the capacity to fit into different specific and changing contexts than to showing a strong and coherent identity which is indifferent to the situations.

Hyphenated identification cannot be conceived as a new fixed category because it is mainly a rhetoric resource to use when claiming a specific boundaries collocation. Even those who are regarded – in some specific situation and from a static, classificatory point of view – as having been assimilated or characterized by ethnic closure, may use differentiated identifications to express their ethnic collocation. To be ethnic in a globalized context has less to do with fixed categories and more to do with the ability to use the right code in the right situation. Probably, it is less useful to think of people as having ethnic, national or hyphenated identities and more useful to think of people as active agents able to use different forms of identification and to modulate their relative intensity in relation to different contexts.

Resisting categorization

Although hyphenated identification has always constituted a viable and widespread method for the children of immigrants to represent themselves, 'being more than one thing' may have a profoundly different meaning nowadays than it did in the past.

First of all, it seems to be a way of avoiding reduction and negative external labelling. Complete assimilation and rigid closure within the precincts of one's own group are generally considered unacceptable and negative solutions. Two of the main forms of integration contemplated in the hypothesis of segmented assimilation – full assimilation in the dominating middle class and strong recognition in an oppositive but marginal culture – are both considered undesirable options.

> I feel 100 per cent Italian ... in fact the way I live is different from my cousins [who live in the Philippines]. My cousins would never dream of going out alone with their boyfriends, because the thinking there is a little backward, even going around holding hands is different ... but I don't find it hard being a Filipino, actually I am proud to be one ... I even asked my parents to speak more Filipino at home so that I can learn it better ... I don't want to lose this part of me.
>
> (Julie, 17 years old, born in Italy, Filipino parents)

> My parents are pretty closed, they don't open up much. They were born in Morocco, they live here but it's as if they were in Morocco. Not me. I'm different. I was born in Morocco too and this ties

me to Morocco but it's different ... I would never live in Morocco
because there they have a different mentality from here. By now
I am more used to the ... Western mentality because I've been
in Italy for so many years ... and I'll stay here in the future ... so
then it's no use being so attached to Morocco.

(Mohcine, 19 years old, born in Morocco,
in Italy since the age of 5)

They feel compelled to associate with both cultures, however they do
not want to neglect one or the other. The hyphen is a symbol of the
struggle of the second generation immigrants to blend in with the
norms of the culture of the majority while maintaining the traditions
of their family. Although they can accentuate one side of the hyphen
over the other, the identification they express is far more fluid and
complex than the dichotomy suggests.

For a long time it has been very difficult for me to answer questions like: 'Are you more Italian or more Eritrean?' because the
answers are intricate. I can decide: 'OK, now I'm Italian and
I send my Eritrean side to sleep completely', otherwise I can say:
'I have my origins, I have my roots, I trust in them, I stand by
them and rely on them'. But for me, my turning point arrived
when I became aware and I accepted being a mix of different
things, not only of my two cultures, but of a lot of other things
I've lived and incorporated ... I'm ... I'm a real mix of different
things ... a lot of things, a puzzle. But not really like a puzzle,
because a puzzle is made up of separate pieces, which are side by
side. Even if they fit together and make a nice picture, they are
still only next to each other, so I prefer to speak of fusion, because
it is difficult to understand where one thing begins and the other
ends. I'm really that fusion, the real point of that fusion is me ...
and that point is already full of people, there are a lot of us in that
situation, and this is something new: it is a new way of thinking
about yourself, no longer compelled to be only one thing.

(Aline, 21 years old, born in Italy, Eritrean parents)

By claiming a hyphenated identification, young people highlight the
ongoing process of identity negotiation that embodies instances of
both conflict and integration (Hammack 2010: 378): a process that

implies constant fluctuation between a desire for particularity and a
desire for universality. Due to their specific social collocation they
aspire to both inclusion and recognition: they do not want to be seen
as different – always being asked: 'Where are you from?' – while at
the same time they do not want to have their difference ignored –
nobody asking them about origins. As Ghassan Hage (2010: 117)
points out, vacillation 'between the desire for the universal and the
particular is very much the norm among most racialized people.
Indeed, it could be argued that it is this vacillation, more than the
aspiration for the universal, that is inherent to the human condition.
When people aspire to integrate in a new cultural group, or choose
to continue to be part of a group they were born into, they do not
just fear being particularized and having their universality denied,
and do not just fear being universalized and having their particularity denied. They fear both, and being "fixed" in both. That is, they
fear not being able to have a space where they can vacillate at will
between the universal and the particular'.

Hyphenated identification offers such a space for vacillation; it
does not provide a new category but the escape from any 'fixing'
category.

> Often other people ask me 'but do you feel more Italian or
> Ecuadorian?', and this kind of question makes us feel really awk-
> ward, because you don't know how to answer such a question ...
> my uncle is used to asking me such a tricky question, and I say
> 'Well, but I don't know what to say'. He asks me 'Tell me, on a
> scale of one to one hundred, how much do you feel Italian? How
> much do you feel Ecuadorian?' 'But I feel myself half and half!'
> Because, anyway, I grew up there, I had my school there, and
> I lived there half of my life, but I have lived here the other half,
> do you understand? I want to tell you something, I want to have
> Italian citizenship and I'll get it, if possible. I'm going to apply for
> it, but by getting Italian citizenship I don't mean to hide mine
> ... I'll get it because I feel Italian, while many other people get it
> in order to be accepted, do you understand? You know, there are
> many children who were born here, with their parents coming
> from my country, and who, when someone asks them 'Where
> are you from?', they answer they are Italian, because they want
> to be seen as Italian and pretend to have nothing to do with

Ecuadorians. Other children grow up with another mentality and say 'I was born here but I'm nonetheless only Ecuadorian!' ... I feel myself halfway; I have nothing to share with Italy, but I still feel Italian! I feel Italian because ... I grew up here ... even if at first it was tough ... at first, when I took the metro, or buses, in my mind I thought 'I'm not from this place, I'm not from this place, I feel odd', but now, when I'm on buses I feel that here is my home. I feel I'm part of this country, even if I'm not totally accepted I don't mind, because I feel I'm part of this country, because when I'm sitting on a bus I think and I say to myself 'Well, I'm going home'.

(Pamela, 19 years old, born in Ecuador,
in Italy since the age of 12)

When I think about being Italian or Filipino, well, I feel I am a bit of both ... I feel Filipino, well, because of my looks, while when it comes to my approach to things, I feel partly Italian ... I mean, I feel both ... I don't think I make a choice ... between being Filipino or Italian ... I don't want to make one because anyway I have strong ties with both of them ... I don't even pay attention to this 'being Italian or Filipino' thing, I mean, I'd rather have these two different cultures than choose.

(Jeremie, 19 years old, born in the Philippines,
in Italy since the age of 9)

Hyphenated identification implies a critical stance towards reductive categorization. To be considered in one sole way restricts opportunities, hems in and trivializes personal skills, because people are necessarily always more than what one single category can claim. Stating the impossibility of being reduced to one sole category emphasizes the effort to escape simplification and definitive choices, as well as the critique of the existing categories, none of which is able to fully encompass real experience. Hyphenated identification reveals that there is no defined, shared form of identification young people want to be integrated into. Assimilation theories also fail because there is no single pattern into which people are willing to be assimilated, nor a single group, culture, way of life or language that can embrace the multiple facets of individual complexity and the necessity to be able to change and adapt oneself when contexts, audience and personal goals change.

A hyphenated, multifaceted and mobile identification is certainly the most commonly used because it best reflects the complexity of one's own personal experience. Not having to choose one sole option but keeping open several corresponds best not only to daily personal experience where equality and difference are open questions to be defined case by case rather than by given elements requiring simple, unproblematic recognition, but it also corresponds to the skills required to pass from one context to another.

Assuming a hyphenated identity means not having to give up multiplicity as well as knowing how to move from one situation to another without the risk of being excluded. To successfully claim a specific difference equates with the ability to understand how to act in a specific situation without breaking the rules, without falling short of others' expectations.

In some ways I feel Italian, maybe because of some habits I have. In other ways I feel definitely Bulgarian; that is, I am in the middle ... exactly the way I feel right this moment, I feel both Bulgarian and Italian. It depends on things ... It's just because of the fact that my origins and the way I am make me still feel Bulgarian, that is, in my soul inside I'm Bulgarian, but in the way I live every day, and maybe even more generally in the way I think, I feel more Italian ... But I think that society is now changing very fast and that you have to adapt to changes in ways of thinking, in the ways of being of various cultures, of various people, I mean, I think you have to know how to change.

(Iva, 19 years old, born in Bulgaria,
in Italy since the age of 11)

The central point in claiming a hyphenated identification is not giving importance to either of the two identifications; it is instead the hyphen itself: the process that allows people to claim a different hierarchy of identification in different contexts, shifting from one another when necessary or useful.

Difference and equality seem to be linked to contextual definitions: they can be taken and used in substantial reified form as well as in procedural relative form. In practical everyday life, difference and equality reveal their ambivalent dimension: they appear to be, at the same time, potential constraints and potential resources for action:

> I think that the fact of having a different culture from that of so many of my acquaintances is an advantage because somehow or other I can identify with the situation of others, depending on the person I am with. Therefore I can understand his difficulties and I can understand his suffering or something of the sort, so you see, this is an advantage ... it's as if I had more tools to understand what is going on ... an extra view so I can see better ... Therefore, from some points of view, it works in my favour, but from other points of view, it doesn't. For example, it works in my favour if someone wants to talk to me, get to know me, find out something about Ghana ... and anyway, something about me. But it works against me when, for example, I go down the corridor and I see people talking about me anyway or something like that, since up to this year I was the only black boy in a school of about 500 boys. So it's a bit tough ... when I feel as if I am being watched ... treated differently, then it gets tough.
>
> (Isaac, 18 years old, born in Ghana,
> in Italy since the age of 12)

It is context that determines when and to what extent equality and difference can be a constraint or a resource. It is the single individual who must know how and when to display or conceal the cultural difference or the similarities of ways of life in the specific situation.

The capacity to both show *and* hide difference (ethnicity) is the characteristic feature of a generational skill that can be reduced neither to a desire for radical, incommensurable differentiation (showing ethnicity or any other form of difference as a mark for rigid retention of particularistic ties or a will for separation and auto-segregation) nor to a desire for full assimilation (concealing any difference). The key point is the capacity to manage the two different competences, which may seem contradictory only when abstracted from specific situations. When situated in everyday contexts of interaction, reification or relativity, retention or transformation, and expressing or concealing difference, the two competences clearly represent different, but not incongruous, possibilities. Choosing between them requires the reflexive capacity to evaluate audience expectations, rules governing the situation, and personal goals, rather than taking a stand, in abstract and rigid ways, for or against only one of them.

Difference as a resource

Being recognized as individuals eligible to have access to different contexts, individuals who deserve a hearing and who could legitimately have a voice requires the capacity to use difference according to the situation, translating personal characteristics into tools to be used to achieve personal objectives. Difference, in fact, in many situations may be seen as a valuable instrument for fascinating, drawing attention, and generating interest. Especially in contexts where relationships have to be established quickly, without the support of previous and deeper reciprocal knowledge, and with no guarantee they will last and be successful, useful or, at least, not dangerous, showing some peculiar characteristic that can be seen as interesting, enriching, or just funny, may facilitate acceptance and may ensure the opportunity of having a say.

The children of immigrants we interviewed use both strategies of differentiation and belonging within a framework that attaches a high price to cultural diversity (Faist 2009), at least the type of cultural diversity that can be seen as enriching the possibility of choice and can be enjoyed as a constitutive part of the metropolitan way of life.

Some facets of ethnic difference, thus, are considered as a valuable extra that increases opportunities: showing some form of cultural difference prevents homologation and the prospect of becoming indistinguishable, voiceless, absorbed by the mass; an extra that needs to be preserved because it may constitute an effective source of knowledge and skills which people may use to construct their original biography, enriching their experience and making themselves more popular and interesting.

Actually, I feel Italian, but I don't want to give up my Egyptian side ... I know I cannot go back and get used to the Egyptian way of life, I know that my future is in Italy ... or maybe in England ... but I don't want to lose this side of me, I don't want to forget where I come from ... On the contrary, I must say that as time passes my interest in Egypt and the Arab world is increasing. I'm very interested in everything taking place there, I'd like my parents to tell me more about what they saw and did ... I was not born in Egypt, I was born here ... I went back to Egypt only sometimes in summer to see my grandparents, and I speak very little Arabic too ... but I'd like to speak it better, to know more things. I love this side of me, I don't want to lose it ... but I also feel totally Italian, indeed I get really angry when someone regards me as a foreigner... what! Me a foreigner? I was born here and I've spent all my life here, why would I be a foreigner? I do what Italians do, I think like Italians think ... I know about Italian life better than many of my mates ... at this point, this is my country ... but I'd like other people to recognize my Arab side too ... why do I have to forget it?

(Amithai, 17 years old, born in Italy, Egyptian parents)

Actually, I can say I'm both Italian and Egyptian, so when I'm here I feel at home and a little bit foreign because I'm half Egyptian, and when I'm in Egypt I feel at home and a little bit foreign because I'm half Italian; but I think I take advantage of this situation, because I know two cultures, and that is good, I mean, it allows me to know two different points of view, and there are the positive sides of both, and I can have them both, and this makes me richer.

(Nadia, 18 years old, born in Italy, Egyptian parents)

Ethnic difference is seen as a 'relational resource' which stimulates and opens the door to relationships (Kibria, 2002), something that may fascinate and generate interest. To summon up some form of (exotic) ethnic difference may represent the opening move towards getting involved in a new context and making new acquaintances, it may improve popularity among peers.

I'm happy in Italy, I feel this is my place ... however, there are things about Egyptian culture that are better than in Italy like, for example, devotion to family and parents and friendship, there's a greater sense of friendship ... on the other hand, there are things in Italy that I like better, like all the comforts, greater study and employment opportunities, freedom ... I try to keep both and make the best use of them. I'm now hoping to take Italian citizenship ... this is important, because if you have an Italian passport you can travel anywhere ... however, I don't want to give up being Egyptian totally ... that has its advantages too ... it's a great civilization ... also, I like going to Egypt and feeling at home; we have a house by the sea, at Sharm-el-Sheikh. Last year, I invited two classmates ... they were very envious ... then, when I took them there, showed them around, showed them what life in Egypt was like, I knew my way around and I knew where to go ... I showed them everything and now they're always asking me 'When will you invite us to Egypt again?' After that holiday, they think more highly of me.

(Hassan, 17 years old, born in Egypt,
in Italy since the age of 12)

You can see from my face too that I am not Italian, so I cannot say that I am Italian, that is, only half, because I have lived here but I do not belong to this land. Yes I was born here, I have lived here, I have relationships with many, many more people than in Egypt ... I think like a lot of Italians, maybe I don't think like a real Egyptian any more. I mean, I have an Italian mind, but if it really comes down to it, I am an Egyptian underneath, I am not Italian and I am not ashamed of this. Actually I am proud of it. Actually lots of people are very pleased to learn that I am Egyptian ... 'Hey, that's great, you're Egyptian!' and so it is a good thing. It is also this diversity which connects me with people; even with friends you stand out, I mean, I don't know, you are more visible, people are more curious to know you ... So diversity often ends up bringing you together, so in this way it can also help you in relationships.

(Moussa, 18 years old, born in Italy, Egyptian parents)

Ethnic difference, far from being a factor that guides and shapes behaviour, is identified as a resource that can help achieve personal goals and can be used or put aside according to the relational contexts involved. Ethnic difference, when used in the right way, respectful of the expectations of the contexts, may represent a useful tool for relationships: showing a specific difference may constitute a way of becoming more interesting and more easily accepted, it may facilitate participation and belonging. The advantage drawn from hyphenated identification, bilingualism, or the capacity to manage different cultural codes 'is not just a marker of hybridity as some new configuration, but part of a strategy that also reproduces belonging, to an ethnicity, a national identity, or a peer group, depending on social context at any given time' (Butcher 2008: 385). Ethnic difference may become a resource that young people use in order to make their position more attractive and further their own opportunities. It may become an instrumental tool, which has to fit the different contexts.

> I do my best to feel good and so I either choose to act Italian or to act Ecuadorian, I see which is the most convenient one, I don't know how to say ... I can act Italian and I can act Ecuadorian and at that moment I say 'Hey, I like acting Italian better, so I'll behave like Italians do, or like the Ecuadorians!' but this doesn't create problems for me at all, because I know that whatever I do, there are different consequences ... Knowing both the Italian and the Ecuadorian ways of thinking, I have more chances of choosing things, I think more about what I've got to do because I can do things the Italian way and the Ecuadorian way.
>
> (Melanie, 19 years old, born in Ecuador, in Italy since the age of 16)

The young people interviewed seem engaged in managing the continuous fluctuation between identification and differentiation. A fully autonomous identity must find a way of coping with the opposing needs of feeling part of the significant contexts in which one lives and, at the same time, being different, emerging in one's individuality, assuming a specificity that allows recognition. Being accepted without getting lost in the crowd, being recognized as distinctive without being defined as deviant – these are the required skills.

Ethnic difference shows all its ambivalence: on the one hand, it proves to be a resource when it assists in the activation of relationships, arouses curiosity and allows distinction; on the other hand it may end up being a restraint when it is rigidly imposed from without and is a vehicle for discrimination or an excuse for segregation. Hyphenated identification, then, mirrors as young people learn to manage dual skills in the use of difference, hiding when it may be a source of discrimination, and emphasizing when it can be used to claim the right to participate or to signal specific individual qualities (Semi et al. 2009). The dual skill further enables young people to consider and present their difference as 'essence', as a characterizing given that must be accepted and recognized as constituent and unchangeable, as well as the result of contingent choices that can always be modified, the result of intention and ability to make individual choices (Baumann 1996).

Differences should not be lost nor should they be imposed. A proper use of difference puts respect for the rules of the situation in first place and is guided by a pragmatic need: never be out of place, stay in tune with the situation to avoid being excluded.

> Culture is important. It defines who you are, how you are ... you cannot break away from family ties, from the things you have learned ... in some way those things are you, it is your way of being ... but you should never be too attached to your own culture. I mean, you have to know how to adapt – like me – adapt a little to the culture that is in Italy instead of importing your own culture and setting it down right here ... I mean, if someone has a tradition, he doesn't necessarily have to lose it, but if someone imposes his culture, then I don't think that's right ... that's a mistake, because he doesn't understand that he has to live with others ... he will always find himself out of place.
>
> (David, 20 years old, born in Peru, in Italy since the age of 3)

The skill of adapting ethnic difference to the varying contexts appears particularly important when young people reflect on belonging and identification. In this case the chance to make cultural difference count as an element of distinction comes into play alongside the interest in the possibility to participate without exclusions or handicaps on a par with their peers in Italian life. The desire for inclusion and participation cannot therefore turn into assimilation. It must manage equality and difference in such a way as to ensure a certain degree of recognition and inclusion without implying total homologation.

When skin colour and gender matter

Children of immigrants can be better perceived as skilled cultural navigators, with a sophisticated capacity to manoeuvre their way through a wide variety of social arenas, which are often organized around different and sometimes radically contradictory moral and cultural conventions. 'Their capacity to cope with "two different cultures" (although rhetorically useful because instant sympathy can certainly be expected if they ascribe their personal difficulties to their condition of "culture conflict") doesn't mean being psychologically confused' (Ballard 1994: 30). On the contrary, their specific social location allows them to develop and fine-tune their code switching skills, expressing themselves with equal ability in two or more codes. While Roger Ballard presents code switching mainly as the capacity to fit two different contexts where two contrasting codes are applied, concealing the other part, the 'betrayal' implied by assuming the code of the 'enemy', it might be more usefully understood as the awareness of the importance of being 'more than one thing', of being able to master different languages at the same time and to move from one to another when necessary. It is an important skill for resisting reductionist categorizations and claiming participation while countering assimilation.

However, the ability to move backwards and forwards, to switch codes, may be a problem when stereotypes impose negative labels or structural inequalities constitute exclusionary boundaries. Ethnic difference always swings between at least two meanings. On the one hand, it may be a sign of particularity and specificity, a sign of diversity that allows recognition and individuation, self-fulfilment and autonomy, a characteristic that sustains dialogue and communication. On the other hand, it may be a sign of diversity that justifies separation, a trait that excludes and isolates, that makes communication and dialogue difficult (Waters 1990).

In many cases, gender, skin colour or eye shape, as well as family name or clothing style, may make code switching impossible or ineffective: only people who fit racial standards can credibly show hyphenated identification and present themselves, with some chance of plausibility, as both ethnic *and* national. While many children of immigrants can call on their 'plurality of selves' to fit a number of different social situations, the voluntary nature of personality or cultural shifts should not be overstated because, depending on the situation, their flexibility can be limited by racialization or other forms of negative labelling (Vasquez 2010: 60).

In situations where ethnic difference is looked upon favourably, continuity with parents comes to the fore and it is highly prized as an extra that confers a special status as an interesting or unique person and paves the way for new relational opportunities. In situations where ethnic difference is seen as a stigma, the national facet of the hyphenated identification is emphasized. In this case, presenting a hyphenated identification may constitute a valuable way of facing exclusion. Claiming they are truly Italian, when other people contest this identification, is a way of resisting discrimination and denouncing the double bind into which the majority has cast them: 'promising equal access to its material and immaterial resources to anybody who obeys its rules but constantly denying these rewards to those it does not define as its legitimate members. No matter how much they comply with the rules' (Räthzel 2010: 547).

> Sometimes I'm really proud to be Algerian, other times I'm really proud to be Italian, it depends, but facing racists I feel deeply Italian … to racist people I say: 'I'm Italian and you must shut up, you must respect me' … with people who tell me: 'Shut up, foreigner! You have no rights to be here, you'd better go back to your country', I feel frustrated, and I shout out my being Italian because I want them to respect me and not be racist towards me … I was born here and I've spent all my life here; I study hard, I'm involved in Italian politics, I'm more Italian than you and you tell me I'm a foreigner and I cannot speak! I can't stand that! You must shut up.
>
> (Asma, 17 years old, born in Italy, Algerian parents)

Exclusion and racism may also trigger a reactive stance. When people feel they are excluded because of their being considered alien, because of some rigid categorization that judges them as inferior, they may valorize precisely those aspects that are seen as a stigma. In this case, claiming an ethnic identification means resisting the dominant definition of the situation and reversing the stereotype: what other people consider negatively is valued most.

> With people with prejudices I tend to feel attached to my parents' culture … I feel like an Italian, because I was born here, I grew up here, I speak the language … but when someone is a racist, I tend to favour my Egyptian side … because I am proud to be an Egyptian and I don't like hearing people speak badly about

it ... I want them to recognize me as an Egyptian. Even if I feel more Italian than Egyptian, with racists, I want them to recognize that being Egyptian is not a minor thing ... with them I bring out all my Egyptian difference and I become a real nationalist.

(Amre, 18 years old, born in Italy, Egyptian parents)

Many young people interviewed see racism and ethnic discrimination as evidence of the impossibility of being really accepted as equal. Paradoxically, the existence of racism makes the reified and essentialist idea of cultural difference more relevant and concrete, because it strengthens the importance of the ascriptive character given to race, religion and ethnic origin. In this way, racism may end up by supporting a reactive form of valorization of difference, which justifies the upholding of distinctions and boundaries based on collective belonging. Ethnicity becomes a constraint that can never be totally overcome, and, ultimately, determines individual behaviour and character.

Even with citizenship some things cannot change ... even with citizenship people don't look at me as an Italian citizen because ... if a person doesn't know me, if he sees me for the first time, he doesn't think I'm an Italian citizen and he has to treat me as an equal, as an Italian citizen ... because my skin colour is different. If I were white and got Italian citizenship I would be satisfied, I'd become Italian inside and outside, completely ... I can became Italian inside me, but not outside.

(Supun, 19 years old, born in Sri Lanka, in Italy since the age of 10)

Only in the last 30 years has Italy become a country of immigration. In spite of its internal cultural diversity, it has represented itself as a 'racially homogenous' country, and the process of racialization is still an ongoing, open process. There are no fixed and settled racial or ethnic categories, instead they change quickly when the news and political discourse point out some specific ethnic/national group as the cause for rising criminality or urban decay. Italianness has seldom been defined by phenotypic markers; it has been constructed mainly against other white Europeans, so whiteness has not represented – up to now – a viable raw material for marking ethnic or racial boundaries. It has instead been taken for granted. Kinship and religion have counted for more than skin colour in defining who belongs to the community and who does not.

> When I say I'm Egyptian I don't get any problems; people say: 'Great! Egypt is a fantastic place and Egyptians are wonderful!', but when people find out I'm Muslim, everything changes, and I feel they are hostile: you really do feel it on your skin … Some time ago I wore the headscarf and people stared at me as if I was an alien, or worse, a terrorist … I even quarrelled with my best friend because she said Islam was a barbaric religion … I almost cried … I cried because I didn't expect such a thing from my best friend … but she was Italian and she didn't understand me.
>
> (Romisaa, 21 years old, born in Egypt, in Italy since the age of 1)

Dominant everyday discourse creates an insurmountable cleavage between 'natives' and 'immigrants', rather than between 'white' and 'coloured'. It is at this level that children of immigrants find a new form of solidarity to face racism and discrimination. Recognizing themselves as 'immigrants' allows them to create a more solid basis for resistance and collective action than ethnic or pan-ethnic identification (Espiritu 1992).

It is not by chance that two of the most widespread and active organizations of children of immigrants in Italy have religion (Giovani Musulmani d'Italia (GMI), Young Italian Muslims) or the simple fact of being sons or daughters of immigrants (ReteG2 SecondeGenerazioni, NetworkG2 Second Generation) as their basis for association (Frisina 2010; Riccio and Russo 2011; Zinn 2011). Both of them recognize the multiple identifications of the young people and go beyond the ethnic line, addressing the issue of citizenship, taking sides in the struggle against discrimination and racism, as well as supporting the acknowledgment of children of immigrants as legitimately Italian. Both of them affirm the full Italianness of children of immigrants, while asking for respect and recognition of their diversity in religious faith and cultural choices. Rather than claiming a radical and insurmountable diversity or total assimilation into the majority, they stress the plurality of being Italian, contesting the argument that a single pattern can summarize the multiplicity of individual experience. They claim the right to be Italian *and* different, they assert that being Italian *and* children of immigrants are not mutually exclusive options.

The general contraposition between 'natives' and 'immigrants' contributes to lessening the relevance of ethnic identification in claiming respect and protection against discrimination. Wide-ranging identification and universalistic arguments appear to be more legitimate than particularistic claims. Asserting their being Italian, their contribution to the well-being of the country, and their respect for the rules of the majority are ways of emphasizing their being part of the main society and thus deserving more rights (Wessendorf 2007, 2010).

Kristina, a young woman born in Russia and who arrived in Italy at the age of five, gives a good illustration of the capacity to use both the universalistic and the relativistic rhetoric. The former is used when participation, inclusion and more rights are at stake, the latter when specificity and difference can be presented as a relational resource:

> I feel Italian, I've spent most of my life here and I think and behave as Italians do, but other people always see me as an alien ... This is a big problem in Italy, there is a lot of prejudice against immigrants: Italians always think that we are all criminals or prostitutes, even if we were born here and we've spent most of our lives here, we are seen as aliens ... We help this country, without our work things would be worse. My parents have a regular residence permit, they have regular jobs, pay their taxes and behave properly, but they are always foreigners ... I think that is not good, I mean, people who want to live here and behave like everyone else, who pay their taxes and are useful for the country should have more rights: they should be treated equally, there should be no difference between natives and immigrants, the country where one was born shouldn't be important.

> [...]

> I feel indeterminate, a perfect pastry dough, a perfect pie, well done, I mean I stored ingredients from both sides. I took the best parts of both cultures and I mixed them in order to create my unique personality, so I have some facets which are more Russian and others which are more Italian, and I think that each part

helps me to be more complete, more interesting. I'm very proud of my Russian side, even if I'm no longer really Russian, I mean, I've mixed everything together in order to give more flavour to my personality. However, people cannot be linearly defined by a single culture; each person is unique and people who change contexts, who don't always live in the same place have more ingredients, so to speak, to create their original pie.

(Kristina, 18 years old, born in Russia, in Italy since the age of 5)

Within this framework, ethnicity assumes a specific meaning: it is useful when emphasizing particularity and individual richness rather than racial difference. It is more of a personal attribute than a viable basis for collective action.

It is not only racialization that influences the way in which ethnicity is expressed, highlighting or concealing one or the other side of the hyphen: gender plays an important role too. In general, it is possible to say that racialization is harsher for men than for women, who are allowed a greater degree of movement between the different facets of hyphenated identification (Warikoo 2005; Vasquez 2010).

Immigrant men usually have a more negative representation: they are depicted as violent and criminal, as a problem for public order. Consequently, male children of immigrants are more often reminded of their foreignness, which is a mark of their impossibility of belonging to the national community. Thus, they can claim to be Italian only in specific situations, where they can use difference as a fascinating resource. It is more difficult for them to evoke their Italian side to claim more rights. In this case, they are often labelled as illegitimate, pretending to be Italian when the evidence of their racial condition indicates otherwise. On the other hand, due to the prejudices which characterize the perception of immigration in Italy, any claim for more rights or recognition which uses the rhetoric of ethnic difference coming from young men tends to be seen as an aggressive move, an attempt to impose alien rules on indigenous customs (Colombo 2010b).

Women may have more room for manoeuvre. In many situations they are more easily accepted as Italians and when they express some form of ethnic difference, it is often framed in a specific form of racialization that tends to view foreign women as exotic, erotic and sexual (Vasquez 2010: 56). In this case, ethnic difference is likely to be seen as an extra that makes them more interesting and more fascinating. It is a completely different matter when religion is at stake. Due to widespread Islamophobia, women wearing a headscarf are usually regarded with suspicion, if not as a threat to the identity of the majority. They are considered behind the times, excessively bound to tradition, incompatible with the respect of freedom and autonomy that characterizes the Western way of life.

As Sirma Bilge (2010: 10) observes, 'paradoxically portrayed both as a *victim* (passive) of her oppressive patriarchal culture/religion and male kin, and as *threat* (active) to Western modernity and culture of freedoms, the veiled Muslim woman has been turned into an allegory for undesirable cultural difference'.

Wearing the headscarf is generally seen immediately as a sign of foreignness, of not being Italian, making hyphenated identification more problematic.

> I've always had problems at school. My classmates are almost all right-wing, racists. I had a lot of problems because of my headscarf ... they didn't accept me and ... I mean ... they saw me as a foreigner and said 'Go back to your country!', I mean, I was born here and I don't like people saying those things to me ... I think of myself as more Italian than many others ... but people think that being both Muslim and Italian is impossible.
>
> (Asma, 17 years old, born in Italy, Algerian parents)

It is important to highlight that race, gender, class and other social differences interact and frame the opportunity to switch codes and use hyphenated identification in a dynamic way. Intersectionality[3] represents an important analytical tool to understand how the differentiated and mobile identifications emerge and the structural limits they have to face. The ways in which these social differences interact are complex and cannot be understood by the simple addition of their diverse effects. To be a middle-class, young, black woman makes some aspects of identification rhetoric more plausible, effective and justifiable than others in ways that are specific to this social position. When the intersection of these social differences changes, the space for switching codes and the dynamic use of hyphenated identification also change.

In general, it is possible to say that not being considered the bearer of discriminatory racial markers, nor showing behaviours or cultural attitudes which are interpreted as a threat to the way of life of the majority, create the favourable conditions for the emergence of a fluid and dynamic hyphenated identification. This is more difficult when cultural and material resources are limited and when discrimination and racism impact heavily on people's lives.

Tactical ethnicity

The tendency to introduce oneself using hyphenated identifications reflects generational experience: it manifests the need to manage multiple identifications that elude the possibility to be over-synthesized.

It does not seem feasible to reduce the spread of hyphenated identification to one sole cause. The development of intermittent, light and personal forms of symbolic ethnic identification which exalt individual difference, the ability to use ethnic networks instrumentally in order to improve social, economic and professional success, the new experience of living in transnational contexts which require the ability to mix different codes to avoid exclusion, and the capacity to express ethnic pride in the face of discrimination and racism, claiming respect and recognition of ethnic difference as a means for inclusion and participation, are all important aspects explaining the importance that hyphenated identification assumes for contemporary children of immigrants. However, in addition to these factors, which certainly play a central role, the hypothesis that new and specific generational experience is leading modern-day young people to develop the need and the ability to manage difference, to move from one context to another and to adapt what they learned from their parents to diverse situations, may deserve closer consideration.

For the children of immigrants, hyphenated identification is a useful tool to signal the desire to be included, to participate actively without, nevertheless, having to become fully homologous with the majority. It signals a desire for integration that cannot be reduced to assimilation. A certain degree of difference coming from the recognition of a solid bond with tradition and family experience is deemed inalienable. However, this *cultural* difference is seen as an extra qualifying identification that encourages rather than limits full integration.

To be *both* Italian *and* foreign does not mean becoming isolated, using difference as a sign of incommensurable diversity, but it does mean sharing a large part of the dominant way of life without having to give up personal specificity. It is a relational resource rather than a stigma or a source of psychological confusion. Fluctuating between one identifying pole and another increases reflexivity and makes it possible to criticize extreme and excessive stances considered unreasonably inflexible and demanding a loyalty that reduces opportunities.

The ability to move backwards and forwards seems to mark the emergence of a *tactical ethnicity* that takes contexts into account as well as being able to use different references in different situations. Management of ambivalence rather than consistency seems to give direction to the manifestation of tactical ethnicity: being able to cope with situations in such a way as not to be excluded and not to miss out on those precious opportunities for self-fulfilment is more important than the ability to demonstrate integrity and consistency that do not let themselves be influenced by context.

The idea of tactical ethnicity is close to Okamura's concept of situational ethnicity (1981). Both stress the importance of context and avoid the reification of ethnicity. Both place primary emphasis on the situation of social action and focus 'on the way in which individuals appraise the behavioural choices open to themselves given the constraints imposed upon them by the wider setting' (ibid.: 453). However, while the concept of situational ethnicity insists on the role of situation – and the actor's perception of that situation – the idea of tactical ethnicity attracts attention to the capacity to manage multiplicity and ambivalence as a necessary skill for continuously constructing or deconstructing boundaries and personal social locations. It aims to highlight not only the fact that the structure and the expectation of the contexts – and the interpretation that individuals give to them – are affecting the individual's invocation of one ethnicity or another, emphasizing or concealing difference, but, mainly, that ethnic difference may be used to advocate a specific interpretation of the situation, collocating social boundaries in specific ways and making them more or less porous. In this case, ethnicity is not only the 'outcome' of specific situations, but it is precisely what is at stake in specific situations because the way in which (ethnic) difference is defined constitutes one of the most important raw materials for the construction of meanings, social relationships, power hierarchies, inclusion and exclusion, opening up opportunities or legitimizing exploitation.

Given the importance of difference, the capacity to use hyphenated identification cannot be simply dismissed as purely symbolic. As proposers of symbolic ethnicity suggest (Gans 1979; Waters 1990), ethnicity for children of immigrants may become a way of expressing personal identity rather than a real commitment to conserving ethnic traditions and organizations. It has less to do with 'real' and 'concrete' patterns of behaviour, thought and social organization, and more to do with the personal capacity of choice. It may become an easy, superficial and intermittent means of expressing their particularity in ways that can be appreciated and which do not conflict with other lifestyles, something that makes them both special and simultaneously part of a community. However, the idea of tactical ethnicity aims to draw attention to the fact that the expressive character does not totally erase the important function that ethnic identification may play in determining inclusion or exclusion. The fact that hyphenated identification promotes a form of ethnicity that is not interested in 'conserving', without changing, customs and ethnic organizations, is proof of the lessening of ethnic importance only if we consider ethnicity as a 'thing', a 'given' that has been built in the past and now there is no alternative but to preserve it. Otherwise, if we consider ethnicity an ongoing process, the symbolic aspect is not merely 'superficial' and without real social cost; it constitutes instead an important tool for a specific definition of the situation that can open up opportunities or close them off. Differences in the ability to manage this tool appropriately, especially for people who have to face different contexts where different rules define the condition for social relationships, may give important advantages or may be cause for exclusion (Song 2010; Khanna 2011).

This is not to say that ethnicity expressed by hyphenated identification may be completely understood as instrumental (Portes and Rumbaut 2001; Jiménez 2010), or strategic (Stanczak 2006), nor that children of immigrants are totally free to express or conceal any form of ethnic attachment at will. Claims of belonging and assertions of identity may be effective only if they are 'accountable', only if their intended audience accepts those claims and assertions as plausible, legitimate and justifiable.

On the other hand, ethnicity expressed by hyphenated identification cannot be completely understood as a reaction against external negative labelling and racial discrimination (Kribia 2002), a matter of pride, survival and resistance (Song 2003: 141). It is not an 'automatic' response to external constraints. The process of boundary construction is not only reactive, an answer to pressures from the external environment, it is also creative, a product of internally generated dynamics (Espiritu 1992: 176).

Tactical ethnicity aims to call attention to this ambivalence. It is as much instrumental as it is reactive. Adapting to contexts is characteristic of 'tactics', finding expedients in order to obtain something, exploiting situations and slipping in the moment the opportunity presents itself (de Certeau 1990). It is neither a completely self-determined achievement nor an injunction that was totally imposed. It arises, instead, from the need and the ability to construct a moving multiple identity that is continuously being defined and that can and must be differentiated depending on the contexts, the audience and the goals. The main purpose is to avoid being excluded from environments that can be advantageous and necessary for full self-fulfilment. This goal is best achieved tactically rather than with strategic, well prepared, but rigid planning. Tactics exploit and depend on opportunities, and what they achieve is always precarious; it cannot be maintained forever. Tactical opportunities reside in blind spots, areas of ambiguity and ambivalence, cracks that open up in the control and surveillance of power, in the contradictions and the silences of dominant discourse. Often, tactics are unable to radically challenge this power; nevertheless they can slip in and carve out a space for independence, they can open up valuable opportunities. As for the concept of tactical cosmopolitanism introduced by Landau and Freemantle (2010: 380) – although we mainly stress the importance of belonging and the relevance of a tactical use of both equality and difference, and not only the capacity to overcome exclusion emphasizing cosmopolitan rights and rhetoric – tactical ethnicity draws on various, often competing, meanings attributed to equality and difference in order to allow people to insinuate themselves, however superficially, into the network and spaces needed to achieve specific practical goals.

Finally, the capacity to adequately express hyphenated identification cannot be totally understood by conceptualizing ethnicity in cognitive terms (Brubaker et al. 2004). While taking into account the micro-mechanisms that enable and prompt situational shifts in identification, and recognizing that many of the processes involved in expressing identification and belonging are unselfconscious and quasi-automatic rather than deliberate and controlled may help us to give a less restrictive account of human agency, the idea of tactical ethnicity intends to stress the fact that hyphenated identification may become a political resource used as a basis for the assertion of collective claims. Expressing, resisting or concealing a particular difference may be of key importance for the actor involved in a specific relationship, as it can function as a resource in setting boundaries, in fostering processes of inclusion and exclusion, permitting and denying acknowledgement, contesting or supporting the definition of the situation and the existing distribution of power.

To summarize, we can suggest that the idea of tactical ethnicity may be useful to refer to the development of a mobile and globalized ethnicity consisting of elements taken from various contexts and ready to change and adapt even further, of an 'effective' ethnicity that opens up to opportunities rather than closing them off. Furthermore, it refers to a 'distilled' ethnicity that selects some traits and blocks out others, that develops in a critical and reflexive way and that focuses on what from time to time proves to be useful, reasonable and legitimate. Tactical ethnicity presents itself as a useful tool characterized by and extra set of components: the usefulness of this tool does not reside in the quality of any one single component, it lies instead in the personal skill in using them appropriately within the context. This capacity cannot be merely considered as a personal competence; it depends instead on the structure of the context and the relationships of power within it, as well as on the personal capabilities to recognize the rules valid in a specific context and in mastering them in accordance with personal goals and external expectations.

In the case of the children of immigrants we interviewed, the management of tactical ethnicity does not give up full recognition either in Italian society or of a specificity linked to family history. Instead these children represent the birth of a new generation of hyphenated Italians who question the current idea of Italianness and develop the specific ability to deftly and successfully navigate different contexts and be considered 'insiders' in more than one group (Vasquez 2010: 47). The deployment of tactical ethnicity, fluid boundaries, multiple belonging and hybridism constitutes a repertoire of socially useful subject positions appropriate for different contexts (Noble et al. 1999: 40). From the point of view of a tactical use of ethnic difference, hyphenated identification brings to the fore the importance and the ambivalence of the ongoing processes of inclusion and differentiation, which embody instances of both conflict and integration, and resistance and participation. Moreover, it shows how the capacity to manage ambivalence, more than displaying a rigid coherence, is becoming a prized generational skill for young people interested in obtaining the best they can from the different contexts available to them in which they can take their chances.

6
Children of Immigrants in Search of Justness

Living on the move

In the previous chapters we have offered an insight into the children of immigrants in plural and differentiated contexts and locations, in the process of coping with belonging and identifications, claiming inclusion and participation, dealing with constraints and opportunities. We have pointed out the relevance of their generational experience, their common belonging to a 'generation location', together with their native peers, and their specific relevance as a 'generational unit', characterized by specific capacities and challenges, skilful in the use of continuity and change, of differentiation and adaptation, of reification and relativism.

Overall, we have painted a distinct portrait of the children of immigrants, particularly the ones who can be considered an avant-garde or an active minority, given their educational and relational resources. Belonging to a family with a high level of education and cultural capital, and having steady relationships with 'autochthonous' friends can help to develop reflexivity, critical capacity, and competence to negotiate different identifications. It is precisely this capacity to manage situations and to fit into the context that define a pathway towards inclusion, relatively independent from economic or professional status. In contemporary globalized societies, upward inclusion is not just an issue of economic power and professional success; it is something more connected to the capacity to know and manage contingent rules and identifications.

In a globalized world – where identities and references are no longer merely geographical locations, but are increasingly relational – contingency and *situatedness* (Appadurai 1996) become the theoretical and practical framework from which the children of immigrants' agency can be better analysed. It is mainly in contingency that difference – far from being a factor that determines and shapes behaviour – can be identified as a resource to help achieve personal goals, to be used or put aside according to the relational contexts involved.

The emphasis on contingency certainly does not mean the end of discrimination and reified identities; it should not lead us to overestimate individual freedom or to underestimate structural constraints. The children of immigrants cannot always use difference at will, and each context can reveal threats of domination. Constraints and power relationships shape the degree of freedom they have in defining themselves, and ethnic difference can become, at any moment, an external label, a burden to be resisted and transformed. This can dramatically reduce the space for autonomy and prevent them from participating equally with others in the social arena, from showing their skills and from playing their cards right.

Despite such difficulties, the capacity to use difference in relation to context becomes a personal and collective resource when discourses and practices regarding ethnic belonging and identification are at stake. On this point, we have introduced the idea of 'tactical ethnicity' in order to account for a contextual use of difference, whose ambivalence has to be managed, rather than resolved by a radical – but restraining – choice of only one option from the many available. As de Certeau suggested, the tactic is not a strategy, but rather the ability to use different references in different situations, privileging adaptability over coherence and integrity, coping with the constraints of the situation. Moreover, the typical use of hyphenated identifications – here and there, *culture* and *way of life*, continuity and change, parents' culture and personal autonomy – reflects a need to manage ambivalence and pluralism, avoiding reification or obligation of synthesis. The challenge is to overcome the apparent contradiction between the claim of difference and the desire to participate on an equal basis, with the same personal autonomy as their peers.

This exists more for historical reasons than for subjective qualities. Although some individuals are more skilled than others, the personal capacities we have described are not to be considered just as a personal gift, but as a generational experience. They are related to a historical context of complex and plural connectivity, where cultural references and products, communities and groups no longer necessarily refer to specific places, nation-states or social strata. For the present generation of young people this means having at least the potential opportunity to collect information, objects, tastes, cultural references, rules and habits from disparate places, putting them together in a personal way. Tactical ethnicity and hyphenation are a wider generational characteristic of these young people, related to a generational experience of pluralism. The ability to adjust oneself to the situation, to translate experience learned in different contexts, and to manage difference and multiple belonging plays a central role in a globalized and pluralistic society, and becomes a necessity. Being able to deal with difference, without considering it an incommensurable reference, becomes a fundamental resource. This is particularly evident for those people – such as the children of immigrants – who claim simultaneously both recognition of particularities and equal treatment, and who aspire to full social inclusion while avoiding assimilation or homologation.

Tactical ethnicity, hyphenation or the capacity to adjust must not be considered either instrumental or, on the other hand, a sign of subordination and weakness. Certainly, such attitudes can be present, especially when the constraints of the situation oblige people to move towards more opportunistic choices or conflicting positions. However, tactics and the capability to adjust are principally the means by which the children of immigrants endeavour to make their identifications and choices of belonging accountable, legitimate and plausible. Therefore, they always try to cope and deal with their environment; their choices of identification are not a simple reaction to the constraints before them but rather the attempt to interpret and transform the context, to adjust and 'repair' it, valorizing opportunities and minimizing the risks of exclusion and control. Since in most cases context determines when and to what extent difference can be a constraint or a resource, the children of immigrants must learn how to manage difference or similarities in contingent and changing situations.

The focus on contextualized experiences and on the capacities of adaptation, improvization, mediation, accountability and claiming can be summarized by the concept of *justness*. In this chapter we explain how the reference to justness can condense both the generational experience of immigrants' children and their ability to manage constraints, contingent rules and identifications. We argue that this analytical tool is useful to synthesize the intersection between historic changes and situated, single experiences.

From coherence to justness

In a situation in which the capacity for mediation and the contextualized use of difference become indispensable skills for full social participation, the principles of coherence and integrity have ceased to be the real objective. As opposed to previous generations, roles and strong identities are no longer preferable to temporary back-up and references. Unified – and reified – identities, coherent belonging to an ethnic group, or incontestable loyalty have become instead the sign of an inability to coexist in a situation of inevitable pluralism. Equal participation in social life is more important than demonstrating coherent consistency that would rule out dealing with the context. In this case, there is a preference for coherence and harmony with the context – rather than with a reified idea of culture and identity – indicating a certain ability to change according to circumstances, and to match continuity with transformation.

Again, this is not to be confused with trivial opportunism, which is always possible, but such attention to the context has to be considered as necessary. As a matter of fact, in a globalized and individualized society, where single actors are taking more responsibility for their actions, the role of individual agency in coping with difference and pluralism cannot be celebrated as the pure triumph of personal will and taste. On the contrary, this ability to cope with the context and its constraints shows us how the children of immigrants use both essentialism and relativism of difference as rhetorical devices for the production of meaningful accounts and practices. Being skilful in such a way as not to be excluded and not missing out on opportunities is still the objective.

The concept of justness can help us to better explain the meaning of such a transition from unconditional coherence to context coherence. If, on the one hand, the concept of generation is useful to understand the *diachronic* historical changes for which the children of immigrants can be considered as a generation unit, with specificities that distinguish them from previous generations of immigrants' descendants, on the other hand, the concept of justness can be helpful as a *synchronic* theoretical tool, to point out the ways in which the children of immigrants manage their identifications, justify them and claim them as appropriate according to the situation.

What is justness?

When analysing the agency of the children of immigrants, we have pointed out the relevance of context to their opportunities, constraints and contingencies. On this point, the position of the descendants of immigrants is no different from that of other social actors; hence we have insisted on historical and generational relevance in order to understand contingent situations.

More generally, the globalization processes and the disconnection of space and time (Giddens 1990; Tomlinson 1999) have certainly fostered the importance given to contingency and immanence as analytical dimensions, and to the coordination of action in the here and now. However, this importance is also related to processes of differentiation and pluralization, for which people must learn how to choose and coordinate different options and values in different situations, and to mitigate the conflicts or uncertainties related to such undefined choices.

When describing this framework, we find it useful to rely on the concept of *justness*, which we can define as a 'mediating concept' – borrowing Bourdieu's notion – as it includes, simultaneously, an idea of situated fitness to and harmony with the context, a process of justification of practices, and a reference to a claim of justice as fairness and validity.[1]

Up to now, the concept of justness has been applied mainly in philosophical debates; and it is not one of the objectives of this book to analyse the results of the attempt to use the concept of justness as mediator in the historical, philosophical ambivalence between validity and contingency. However, if we are interested in understanding the way in which the children of immigrants cope with different cultural codes in their daily life and, by means of their identifications, the relationship between their values and their practices, their references to what is right and their concrete behaviour must be taken into consideration.

Although justness has rarely been applied in sociology, certain scholars have already worked on the heuristic value of this concept. We can briefly recall here two theoretical views which have extensively applied this analytical tool in their research: those of Jürgen Habermas and of Luc Boltanski, together with Laurent Thévenot.

In his complex reasoning, Habermas (1999) uses the concept of justness with a specific meaning: if, on the one hand, transcendent cultural truths aspire to universalism and incommensurability, on the other hand, their justness is always subjective, temporary and contextualized. Justness as harmony is relative and *personal*, even though it can be, and has to be, shared with others. The ability to find a form of justness is a personal resource, as well as an opportunity, to be encouraged or held back by the context. Consequently, as a 'personal effort' set up in pluralistic contexts and among relative values, justness cannot be merely a personal form of self-persuasion; it needs to be communicated and perceived as a 'good reason' – that is to be justified – and it has to aspire to a broader validity.

In short, according to Habermas, even though justness is contextual, constructed, fallible and immanent for its subjective performativity, it cannot be merely an agreement around a temporary 'convention' of social rules. Justness is not only a justification, it is also a claim of validity. Habermas (1999: 225) considers it as an *epistemic concept* even though its validity is not assimilated into an incommensurable truth.

In Habermas' definition justness is linked to justifications, trials and practices but requires the recognition of a community to become a claim of validity: on the other hand, claims of truth always transcend justifications and local values. In a pluralist society, transformed by globalization and migration fluxes, justness becomes a central concept. Since claims of validity, and even the idea of justice no longer overlap with universal truths, justness becomes a stake in the negotiation between plural values and references.

The definition of justness given by Boltanski and Thévenot (2006) is partially different and more involved in the classical sociological topics of normative consensus and legitimate social order. The two French sociologists have tried to understand how social order is still possible in a significant phase of growing pluralism and individualization. Their answer is based on the concept of justification, but also includes that of justness.

According to Boltanski and Thévenot actors coordinate with each other by using their acquired competences, and by justifying their choices towards plural moral conceptions. Drawing upon American pragmatism, ethnomethodology and Goffman, they argue – contesting openly Bourdieu – that people have the capacity for self-determination. Such a capacity is more visible in moments of disruption of social order, in situations marked by dispute, when rules of social integration necessitate justifications, arguments and valid reasons. Justification has a subjective foundation but it starts from normative backgrounds of shared convictions, conceptions of justice, practical commonality and material artefacts. Such backgrounds are plural and people argue over the appropriateness of the justification models that they employ.

Boltanski and Thévenot explicitly use the concept of justness 'when a technical mode of justification is in question' (2006: 34). Justness is rooted in a specific context and related to a situated *convention* that actors endeavour to establish. However, according to these authors, justness is also close to the concept of fitness, but not only in the sense of being adjusted to a context or a constellation of references. This production of fitness is not merely an adaptation; it is an effort 'to adapt the context to oneself'. As a matter of fact, justifications and attempts at justness produce new conventions and convictions, unfinished adjustments and temporary agreements. Disputes and contradictions produce justifications, but not necessarily rules or norms.

Drawing from the observations of Habermas and Boltanski/Thévenot, we can observe that the concept of justness has been applied in sociology to account for the justification of values as well as of practical actions based on the search for personal equilibrium, in harmony with the context in which one is involved. Hence, justness – which represents both a claim of validity and a practical status – becomes an interesting analytical tool to observe how the children of immigrants claim recognition of difference and, at the same time, equal social treatment.

Justness does not correspond either to a habitus – to embodied cultural dispositions organizing the ways in which individuals see the world – nor to a simple adaptation to expectations, due to socialization or strategic calculations of costs and benefits. On the contrary, the idea of justness recognizes the personal and unique individual adjustment to a temporary and situated context, in a way that is claimed to be recognized as right and legitimate, in accordance with more general principles of justice. Hence, signing up to justness means denouncing inequity, partiality and favouritism.

This idea of justness gives an account for the relationship that children of immigrants have with their difference and how they use it. For them, fitting into the context means coping with the situation, but also deciphering and adapting it to themselves, tactically evaluating constraints and opportunities. Such fitness is possible if difference and similarities can be justified as plausible and accountable. And finally such contextualized adjustments are always based on the claims of fairness and equality. This is why the *search for justness* on the part of children of immigrants is not a simple and passive 'adaptation' but rather an active interpretation of the context, starting from more general principles of impartiality, denunciation of power relationships, discrimination and abuse, and recognition of one's difference and uniqueness.

To summarize, the idea of justness includes three analytical levels which highlight the positions we found in our research:

1. Justness as *fitness and appropriateness*: as the ability 'to adjust' oneself to the situation, to find a harmonious collocation in the context, avoiding humiliation or embarrassment. The children of immigrants must learn how to manage different situations, when they are at home with their parents or when they are at school with their peers; how to deal with what they feel as their 'family roots' and with the daily experience of exploration of personal independence. This means recognizing that codes and rules change according to context and relationship frameworks, and that it is necessary to develop forms of appropriateness each time. This also means that in daily life the children of immigrants are able to position themselves in line with the situation, privileging flexibility and avoiding conflict; even though this does not mean forgetting or repudiating family roots or cultural pride. They learn instead to manage both the parental culture and the habits of their peers.

Here justness is that sort of contingent appropriateness to the situation, that allows the children of immigrants to feel, at least temporarily, in harmony with the context, without passing through an overwhelming and irreversible process of amalgamation and assimilation, without opposing it as a radical cultural otherness. Justness as fitness refers to the right procedures of behaviour and relational rules, which means neither passive acceptance by means of mimetic attitude, nor aggressive opposition based on resentment.

Justness as fitness is evidently related to tactical ethnicity, to the capability to use different references in different situations, to improve self-fulfilment and personal independence by acquiring the skills essential to understanding the different contexts and codes which regulate interaction. In this case, justness means presenting oneself according to the expectations and rules of the context, in order to promote favourable relationships, to valorize opportunities or to avoid exclusion;

2. Justness as *justification*: as the ability to argue the procedures and the valid reasons to justify one's decision, belonging and identification patterns, which can be negotiated and translated to appear plausible and accountable.

In the previous chapters, we have seen how the children of immigrants are called on to justify their choices and identifications, to have them recognized and justified in return; and we have pointed out how, with these processes, they contribute to changing their environment. Thus, justness is also a transformative and a reflexive process, because the production of justification can change the definition of the situation in which the actors are involved, producing a new equilibrium and new interpretations.

Justness is a form of justification because it is not simply related to the contingency of the situation in which one has to fit. Justness also refers to the capacity to manage pluralism and ambivalence as a necessary skill for the never-ending process of justification, construction and reconstruction of boundaries, meanings, identifications, social locations and relationships. Justifying one's choices of identification or form of ethnicity is not only a reaction to the expectations of the context, but a way of redefining and transforming it as well. Ethnic difference can be used to advocate a specific interpretation of the situation. If we consider ethnicity as ongoing, and not an established product, it is possible to verify how people justify its applications to valorize themselves, to avoid exclusion or to question discrimination. Hence, the search for justness is a way of matching a temporary exigency of adaptation to the context, to the continuing endeavour of adapting the context to oneself and one's difference;

3. Justness as *justice*: contextual fitness, appropriateness, accountability and justification are possible because they are related to some sort of claim of validity. Thus, the idea of justness also includes a reference to a wider claim of justice. The references to justice, equality and fairness have been prominent in our interviews. Discrimination and inequality can be contested only on the basis of a reference to justice.

The idea of justice is relative, as Rawls, Walzer or Habermas have declared in their different theoretical positions. Consequently, if the idea of justice is based neither on an absolute and universal truth nor on a type of inconsistent moral relativism, how we establish what is *right* becomes fundamental.[2] When justice cannot be defined in a unique and definitive way, it can be conceived as a temporary justness in which an equilibrium among countered exigencies can be found. Thus, the idea of justness does not only concern the process of justification or the practices of fitness, it concerns the right to contribute to the criteria with which justice is defined as well.

The topic of 'justness as justice' is particularly relevant when the children of immigrants request explicitly the right to discuss the criteria of justice which apply to them. What is claimed as a right – for example Italian citizenship following an extensive period of residence, entailing studies and 'honest behaviour' in Italy – or what is denounced as unfair – such as being excluded or discriminated against – is based on an idea of justice and impartiality. The principle of equality, and a just society, is often quoted by our young interviewees and considered as important as that of difference, especially when excessive attention to their ethnic difference becomes a justification for discrimination.

Justness as a claim of justice is particularly evident when the children of immigrants face discrimination. We have seen how ethnic identifications can be used in order to claim respect and recognition of difference, expressing ethnic pride when resisting and contesting racial attitudes. In this case, justness is neither a simple adjustment, nor a way of justifying oneself with others;

the search for justness becomes instead a claim of justice related to the specificity of actors and situations. Racism and discrimination are an unmistakable form of inequality and injustice; but here the claim of fair treatment becomes the attempt to avoid reification of ethnicity too. When episodes of racism and discrimination elicit rage and resentment, the search for justness becomes a way of claiming justice and equality, avoiding the reference to a reactive and reified form of difference, refusing to live ethnicity as a constraint or a stigma.

For that reason, the children of immigrants seem particularly interested in a definition of justice capable of holding together the idea of equality and difference: equal opportunities and the recognition of difference, as cultural and individual. Their request for Italian citizenship in particular, is related to a 'politics of belonging' (Yuval-Davis et al. 2006; Skrbiš et al. 2007) for which formal recognition of rights, equal opportunity of participation and sentimental attachment to one's roots can be articulated. Again, such a situated interpretation of justice and fairness, of recognition and equality, is elicited by the processes of globalization and the intensification of complex connectivity, changing the relationships between social position, belonging, participation and identifications.

Difference, merit, autonomy

In the analysis of the search for justness, we can point out specific contradictions, which emerged during the interviews, and which are related to more general conflict between the topics of difference and merit as forms of equality. We have already pointed out how the children of immigrants fluctuate between the claim of uniqueness and difference, and the claim of equality and fairness. Such claims are usually valorized differently according to the situation, but they may also be reciprocally contradictory. Equal recognition of personal merit, or the quest for autonomy in particular may be in contrast with the claim of cultural difference.

1. *When the idea of difference is valorized* as personal uniqueness, in addition to belonging to a specific cultural tradition, pure equality is not possible. Thus, some inequalities are necessary and they

can be accepted on the basis of some specific difference. Here, the problem becomes that of finding the 'right' or acceptable inequalities associated with the recognition of these differences (Benhabib 2002). On this topic, the children of immigrants we interviewed affirm that it is possible to be at the same time both 'equal and different' and that equality does not mean sameness. Thus, they claim justice as justness, which does not need an amorphous sameness, but can accept forms of difference. However, this is possible only in a specific and contingent situation, not as a definitive status. A combination of equality and difference cannot be the result of a search for coherence but rather a temporary moment of justness and agreement.

Such *situatedness* is highlighted by the contingency of identification. The children of immigrants try to overcome the conflict between difference and equality with tactical ethnicity and with the use of hyphenated identification. The reference to hyphenated identification specifically is a way of avoiding a radical choice between supposedly irreconcilable alternatives and values. However, difference and equality remain in conflict, because it is problematic to overlap difference with an idea of universal justice in a pluralistic world. To be ethnic in a globalized context elicits the search for the most suitable rules in every situation.

2. *When personal merit is valorized*, justice becomes the recognition of personal capacity. In that situation the children of immigrants claim the recognition of their abilities and responsibilities in facing everyday trials. Italian society should recognize their merits as people fully participating in the Italian context: at school, at work, in the public space, in daily relationships. The claim of citizenship and of a new law on citizenship is fundamentally based on this conception of meritocratic justice. Again, there is not a claim of coherence of cultural values and identities – such as national identities – there is, however, a valorization of personal abilities in specific social contexts.

Such an emphasis on personal merit is also a way of claiming justice from a subjective point of view. Personal talents must not be obscured by gender, skin colour, body shape, name, clothing styles or religious symbols. Involvement and full participation require recognition of personal skills and characteristics, where personal merit has to be considered more relevant than visible differences. Thus, the focus on merit points out the need to participate in the same opportunities and options as their peers, freely expressing capacity in an open – but also equally competitive – environment.

3. *When autonomy is valorized*, justice is identified with personal freedom and subjective choice: however, personal freedom can be in contrast with equality and merit, as well as with loyalty to groups and values. Freedom and equality are traditionally in conflict. Autonomy is in conflict with merit, because a merito-cratic culture can be an occult form of domination, as well as a justification for social inequalities. Moreover, autonomy may be in contrast with difference, as each person must learn to adjust himself or herself to the context, to avoid being trapped into a reified identity.

As stated by Rawls (1971) autonomy, merit and equality are reconcilable only in a situation of equal opportunity: trials of merit must start from the same position of fundamental equality. This is precisely what the children of immigrants ask: although they are aware of the importance of personal autonomy, the recognition of their merit and effort needs a better situation of equal opportunities, overcoming discrimination and prejudice. Cultural difference can be a valuable asset only if it increases opportunity, is seen as appealing, and opens up the range of per-sonal choices.

Again, it is evident that in most cases the discrepancies between the claims of difference, merit and autonomy could find a balance only in temporary moments of justness: when equal opportunities are feasible; when individuals overcome naive attitudes towards coherent and monolithic ideas of difference, merit or autonomy; when they can minimize the constraints and valorize the opportunities of the context.

Ambivalences of justness

In a pluralist and globalized world, the search for justness becomes the individual attempt to find an equilibrium, a temporary point of stability, an alternative to the search for a definitive and reas-suring coherence in terms of identities and practices. Moreover, it is an attempt to counter the objective constraints of the situation with subjective adjustments, by optimizing personal resources and capitals.

However, this idea of justness must not be considered absolute and definitive: as Habermas noticed, justness is always unstable, relative and subjective. It is related to the contingency of the situation, to the pluralism of values, and to the subjective position of the individual who perceives it. Consequently, the claim of justness can also be instrumental and auto-referential, intrinsically unfair compared to the needs and positions of others. As the search for justness originates from the single actor, it is not necessarily related to inter-subjective or community ties; it is instead primarily a consequence of focusing on the individual. Hence, the claim of justness can have an ambivalent outcome, and even when it takes on the form of a claim of justice it can be opportunistic and instrumental, despite the reference to some sort of fundamental rights.

To understand such ambivalence, we have to consider that the search for personal justness is related to all the major changes of late modernity, such as individualization, globalization and economic liberalism. On the one hand, individualization has elicited the strategic relevance of personal capacity, self-initiative, innovation, flexibility, and personal creativity (Beck 2006; Boltanski and Chiapello 2005; Sennett 2008). This has enhanced new forms of self-governance, characterized by the expanding role of voluntary engagements, the ability to take advantage of the opportunities offered by globalization and transnationalism, and the need to satisfy a personal sense of justice and responsibility (Rebughini 2010). On the other hand, in a world marked by neo-liberal reforms and post-Fordist economic flexibility, individuals are more often in isolated and weak positions. They refuse exclusive belonging and traditional duties, but they also lack reassuring, inclusive identities and communities. In globalized and individualized societies, individuals are obliged to choose, to constantly take decisions alone (Melucci 1996b). Thus, the quest for justness becomes a *model of agency*, more than a value or a moral position.

Justness is intrinsically ambivalent because our globalized and individualized societies oblige the actors – and particularly those who are carriers of pluralism such as the descendants of immigrants – to face contradictory choices. The contexts into which one has to fit are diversified and changing, requiring different tactics of adjustment. The need to shift from one argumentation to another, playing with the register of accountability, requires specific competences of justification, based on a different register of values. The claims of justice can be based on collective and communitarian references, as well as on more universalistic needs for autonomy.

Such reference to justness, to its different forms and to its ambivalence, offers a grid of intelligibility with reference to the behaviours and identifications of the children of immigrants. From the point of view of justness it is possible to draw attention to both the distance from behaviours coherent with reified identities and values, as well as the ambivalence that the children of immigrants manage in their daily lives.

This is evident in what we have called tactical ethnicity: in some situations it could be relevant to point out family history and traditions, in order to counter discrimination and exclusion with the idea of ethnicity based on deep, unforgettable and undeniable roots. In other situations ethnicity might become a negative label resulting in exclusion or stigmatization; in which case, emphasis on difference is weakened and universalistic equality becomes the main register. In addition, feelings of belonging are under constant construction, where ambivalence and contradiction are more frequent than coherence. To feel in harmony or to feel at home needs constant choices that are not related to ascribed characteristics and values, but to different references and mobile locations.

As a product of our time, the search for justness is intrinsically ambivalent, an alternative to coherence. In a globalized and individualized world, being totally coherent, with reference to a culture or to a set of values, means missing out on opportunities and autonomy. A coherent and self-sufficient reference to a unique community or a unique identification is the only alternative for those who are unable to negotiate, select and navigate through a plurality of references. Certainly, the transition from the need for coherence – of roles, identities, belonging, norms – to a justness anchored in contingencies – even though part of more general transformations of late modernity – cannot be considered an irreversible or a unidirectional process. There are evident counter-tendencies towards hyper-coherent, mutually exclusive and diametrically opposed identifications still running against it.

However, the search for justness seems to be a growing need. At least, it is more related to those sections of the population – particularly to those of the younger generations – who can rely on personal skills of adjustment, translation and mediation, whose agency is able to claim and find space in the present social structure. Hence, the search for personal justness is becoming the distinctive mark of a generation – particularly of the avant-gardes of that generation – born into a specific historic context, where the fluidity of references and the rapidity of change impose new, or additional standards of social selection, based on the capacity to find adequate, context-related and never-ending forms of equilibrium and synthesis.

Overall, the search for personal justness becomes the generational response to a context of pluralism and fragmentation in terms of cultural references and lifestyles, as well as in terms of economic opportunities and risks. Thus, justness is a relevant framework of interpretation if we want to study the situation of the children of immigrants not only from the alternative perspective of their socio-economic integration, or their solipsistic capacity to play with differences.

What is at stake is not just the inclusion in a nation and in an economic system, or the opportunity to move up the social hierarchy; neither is it only the chance to freely access multiple, flexible and ephemeral identifications. What is at stake however, is the opportunity to find a personal route to equilibrium and justness in a changing and unpredictable context, where the ability to adapt, and take chances, becomes the main alternative to communitarian enclaves.

In our individualized society, every single actor is pushed to measure himself or herself with specific and singularized trials, with situations of social and economic uncertainty, with the growing importance of the personal capacity to deal with rapid change. In such an individualized environment, the reference to coherent communitarian interpretations and solutions is now insufficient and unsatisfactory. The ability to manage identifications and belonging, the claims of equality and difference, and the capacity to select and translate references in situations of ambivalence become the elements of a permanent search for personal justness. This might lead to opportunistic and selfish attitudes, but it could also enhance the claim of an inter-subjective harmony referring to a wider and pluralistic frame of justice.

Conclusions

In this book we have focused our attention on a specific field of analysis: the children of immigrants living in our globalized, neo-liberal and post-industrial society. We have conducted our empirical research in one context – the Italian context – in which such characteristics are related to the more specific historical and generational features of immigration flows.

The aim was not to present and describe a national case study, but to investigate how new empirical and theoretical specificities are emerging in countries where immigration flows are more recent. We noticed that well-established theoretical frames, useful in understanding immigrant inclusion in Western countries with a long immigration history, can only be partially applied to the specificity of immigration processes in countries where immigration occurred in a post-industrial phase of full globalization. We have tried to develop some new insights into the historic specificities of the current generation of children of immigrants, growing up today in new countries of immigration, where the main characteristics of a globalized environment overlap with a generation location.

The children of immigrants interviewed in Milan do not seem to face the three alternative pathways suggested by the segmented assimilation framework, nor do they face a radical choice between assimilation or exclusion, mimetic or separatist attitudes. Most children of immigrants are proud of their origins and do not want to lose contact with the cultural values and products of their countries; but they are proud as well of their personal freedom and autonomy of choice. Moreover, a certain degree of difference is as important as social equality because it constitutes a specific mark which can improve personal resources and capabilities. Overall, we observed complex and multiform frameworks of inclusion, rather than segmented assimilation. Indeed, inclusion is not only segmented from a socio-economic point of view, but it also depends on symbolic issues, such as stereotypes and claims of recognition, according to the contingencies of the situation. Thus, the construction of inclusion takes on different forms in different contexts, depending on opportunities and threats. This is why it is important to consider not only the structural and macro status of immigrant difference – according to their more general social positions – but also the micro and situated contexts in which such difference becomes a more complex and symbolic stake.

Neither does transnationalism seem to be an adequate alternative in order to interpret the situation of immigrants' children in Milan. Instead of a vocation of creative border crossings or a subjective ability to create original and fashionable hybridities, we have found the capacity to be accustomed, to find a suitable synthesis in each separate context, which cannot be changed simply by individual will and which always presents forms of constraint. This is why we have proposed the analytical grid of justness to report these skills of mediation.

The children of immigrants on whom we have focused our attention share a generation location with their native peers, the historic experience of globalization and disarticulation of space and time. However, the children of immigrants we interviewed are also a generation unit and an active minority, engaged in processing new codes and new languages in order to cope with the specific historic experience of globalization. On this point, we have insisted that the subjects of our analysis are not representative of a general category of immigrant children: they are an avant-garde of immigrant children, a specific segment in which the characteristics we were interested in are more visible.

These young people have neither a single, constructed future in front of them, nor do they face structured habitus to be reproduced; they can easily imagine, however, their open-ended future in places other than where they were born or where they live now, and they can at least aim to join professions other than those of their parents. This not a simple programme of upgrading but rather a work of the imagination made up of memories, desires and creativity. This is not pure fantasy or Utopia; it is linked to irony, resistance to passive acculturation and discrimination, selectivity and the capacity to choose.

The present generation of children of immigrants is familiar with change and instability. Despite material difficulties, prejudices and uncertainties, they have the opportunity – even though not automatically the capacity – to become cultural navigators, explorers of difference, avoiding confusion or fanaticism. In this respect, we have to consider that – compared to the past – the present generation of children of immigrants seems more accustomed to thinking of their professional and biographical future from an individualized, flexible and 'cosmopolitan' point of view. Thus, the most widely perceived threat does not seem to come simply from a subaltern social position – which could be overcome by international and individualized job mobility – but from the reification of difference, from the impossibility of choosing one's identifications. This means that, besides the evidence of injustices caused by social inequalities – related to social positions as well as to possible discrimination – there is also the more treacherous danger of permanent and unjustified attention towards a 'difference' that can easily become a negative reified label and a form of conditioning of everyday behaviour.

In our interviews, the children of immigrants claim not only more equality of rights and recognition of their difference; they also claim autonomy, recognition of their individual merits and their capacity for mediation. Thus, they claim full involvement in Italian society, to be called to prove abilities and talents as individuals, and to have the opportunity to shape their future in a situation of equal opportunity. To be accepted as an equal does not mean merely being admitted, assimilated and conforming, but nor does it mean being recognized solely as the member of an ethnic minority with reified cultural differences.

We have summed up these attitudes in the reference to a quest for justness, where justice and equality, justification and accountability of one's difference, and fitness and harmony with the context are connected and overlap in daily practices and identifications. This is what it is a stake and offers a better definition of the challenge facing the present generation of children of immigrants. Certainly, our insistence on the concepts of generation, active minority or on the idea of justness is not a way of encouraging an uncritical exaltation of personal opportunities and skills, nor of embracing a conciliatory vision which suppresses the dimensions of conflict and domination – far from it. It is a way of proposing an analytical viewpoint able to point out the existence of new processes of identification and belonging, activated by these young people, as a significant and privileged place for understanding how, and in which direction, contemporary society is changing.

Notes

Introduction

1. Autochthonous literally means 'native to the soil'; more generally, it means 'native to the place where found', 'member of an indigenous people'. We use 'autochthonous' to refer to children of Italian parents who are considered, and consider themselves, as 'naturally' part of the Italian society.

1 The Future of Immigrants' Children in a Globalized World

1. According to Karl Mannheim the generation location refers to 'individuals who belong to the same generation, who share the same year of birth, are endowed to that extent, with a common location in the historical dimension of the social process' (1952: 290). 'Members of a generation are similarly located first of all in so far as they all are exposed to the same phase of the collective process [...] they are in a position to experience the same events and data' (1952: 297).
2. The concept of generation has been widely used, but analytically explored by few sociologists, unsurprisingly this concept became important during the 1950s with the studies of Mannheim (1952/1923), Eisenstadt (1956) and Raymond Williams (1958) themselves part of a generation of sociologists who had witnessed two world wars, the Holocaust, the Russian revolution, the end of colonialism and other major social changes.
3. According to Mannheim 'the generation unit represents a much more concrete bond [...] those groups within the same actual generation which work up the material or their common experiences in different specific ways constitutes separate generation units' (1952: 304).

2 Framing Contexts and Actors

1. The first study carried out between 2003 and 2005 involved adolescents attending Italian upper secondary schools in Milan (Bosisio et al. 2005). High schools in Italy are *lyceum* (academic schools), technical schools and vocational schools. This first study involved mainly students from *lyceum*. A second piece of research (2006–8) involved students enrolled in high schools (technical and vocational) in the wider urban area of Milan (Leonini and Rebughini 2010; Rebughini 2011). A third study (2007–9) involved young people attending *lyceum*, technical and vocational schools in Milan (Colombo, 2010a, 2010b; Colombo et al. 2011). Overall, all our

interviewees were high school students: 33.5 per cent were students in *lyceum*; 24.4 per cent in technical schools; and 42.1 per cent were students in vocational schools.

2. Among our interviewees – following the classical classification of Portes and Rumbaut (2001) – the second generation represents 21.1 per cent of the panel; the immigrants' children arrived in Italy in their early childhood, before they were 6 years old: 14.7 per cent; those arrived between 6 and 13 years old: 42.1 per cent; and finally the immigrants' children arrived in Italy after they were 13 years old: 27.2 per cent.

3. About half of the parents of the children interviewed have a high school diploma and a quarter of them have a university degree.

4. The adjective 'marginal' intends to signal, on the one hand, that immigrants have to face the autochthonous reluctance to accept them as entitled to a relatively comfortable and secure social position; on the other hand, with reference to the idea of 'marginal man' introduced by Robert Park (1928), that their simultaneously belonging to at least two different socio-cultural networks allows them to develop a specific critical and detached point of view which is open to change. A large amount of sociological thought has insisted on the idea of marginality as potential for social innovation, and the idea of a 'new marginal middle class' may be useful in suggesting the formation of a specific *social location* based on the shared thought of being entitled to a fully recognized (also if not yet achieved) position in the society in which one lives (Bagnasco 2008; Allasino and Eve 2008).

5. Between 1876 and 1976 nearly 28 million Italians went abroad, almost half of them crossed the Atlantic. However, contrary to the Irish experience, emigration in Italy has not been considered a fundamental part of the nation building process.

6. On the one hand, Italy started to attract illegal immigration more than other European countries due to the difficulty of controlling its extensive borders and because of the size of its informal economy (Zincone 2006). On the other hand, the formulation of immigration laws has followed the perception of migrants as simply a temporary workforce, and regulated their entry accordingly.

7. The specific features of the Italian situation cannot be understood without considering the pull factors that characterized both the industrial and post-industrial Italian socio-economic structure and the welfare state model. First, the growing proportion of small and medium-sized enterprises in the 1980s, and the simultaneous expansion of the informal economy needed the low-cost immigrant workforce. Second, the character of the 'family-based' welfare system helped reinforce this immigration trend, because family networks retain a strong role in the provision of basic care services within Italian society. With the loosening of family ties and the increase in female participation in the labour force, some compensatory support was needed: immigrant housekeepers, baby-sitters and care-workers became indispensable to millions of Italian families (Sciortino 2004).

8. Especially after Romania joined the UE in 2007 Romanians have become the largest national community (1 million) followed by Albanians (586,000), Moroccans (575,000) Chinese (233,000). Concerning religion, most of these immigrants – around 50 per cent out of all non-EU immigrants – declare themselves to be Christians (70% of them being Catholics). Muslims amount to 37 per cent (ISTAT 2011).

9. The *North League for the Independence of Padania* is a separatist and regionalist Italian political party (cfr. Diamanti 1995; Tambini 2001a; Gold 2003; Biorcio 2010) that made a particularly intense use of racist and xenophobic propaganda (cf. Sniderman et al. 2000; European Commission Against Racism and Intolerance 2002, 2006, 2012).

10. Half of them are under 7 years old. The 13–17-year-old teenagers currently represent 23 per cent of these minors. In the main cities of the Northern regions, where migrants are more concentrated, almost one newborn out of every four had one or both immigrant parents. Around 70 per cent of the children of immigrants live in the Northern regions of the country; in the Southern regions they are more numerous in Sicily.

11. The percentage of foreign-born minors attending Italian schools is growing steadily. In 1983/84 there were only 6104 pupils without Italian citizenship in Italian schools (0.06% of the total); ten years later (1993/94) there were 37,478 (0.4%); but in 2009 the number rose to 700,000. Today foreign students represent 7 per cent of the national scholastic population. This concerns a non-homogeneous growth over the entire national territory. The foreign pupils are concentrated especially in the North: 65 per cent, against 25 per cent in the Centre, and just 10 per cent in the South. However, even the peaks of their presence do not correspond to ethnic concentrations because of the highly differentiated composition of the foreign students.

12. According to the latest statistics (ISTAT 2011) 79 per cent of pupils with immigrant parents are enrolled in professional (41%) and technical schools (38%); whereas only 19 per cent are enrolled in *lyceum* (against 40% of Italian students). However, as the presence of students with foreign parents but who were born in Italy becomes more significant in *lyceum*, it is likely that the presence of children of immigrants will grow in *lyceum* and universities in the near future.

13. Around 40 per cent of the foreign students present such difficulties, and usually they are older than their Italian schoolmates. These students normally attend short-term courses in professional education and vocational training and sometimes the lack of external support can make it impossible for them to reach the final qualification (Besozzi et al. 2009).

14. More information can be found in the special issue of the Italian Journal of Sociology of Education 4(1) 2010: www.ijse.eu/index.php/ijse/issue/archive.

15. Second generation girls are less fatalist than boys, more oriented towards the success of their studies, more ambitious about their future, which

they imagine to be very different compared to the life of their mothers. It is well known, today in the most important Western countries, scholastic success is greater among females than among males. In Italy too, the numbers of females with diplomas and degrees are higher than those of males and the scores are also higher. Girls with immigrant parents are following this tendency, because of personal ambitions but also because of a higher supervision by parents and community. Such controls are usually weaker for boys (Ravecca 2009).

3   A Specific Generational Location

1. For the concept of 'misrecognition' and its relevance in the current debate on multiculturalism, social justice and the construction of Self, see Taylor 1992; Honneth 1995; Fraser and Honneth 2003; Thompson and Yar 2011.
2. When we use the terms 'culture' and 'way of life' in italics we refer to the ordinary, mundane meanings used by our interviewees; we do not use them as analytical tools.

4   Multiple Belonging

1. We are mainly interested in the cultural dimension of citizenship, that is how it is represented, experienced and acted by young people, rather than in its mere normative formulations. For a cultural, dynamic and active idea of citizenship see: Stevenson 2001; Benhabib 2004; Isin and Nielsen 2008; Pawley 2008. For representations of citizenship among young people see: Hall et al. 1999; Lister et al. 2003; Hussain and Bagguley 2005; Benedicto and Morales 2007; Miller-Idriss 2006; Hart 2009; Colombo 2010b.
2. They have just one year to submit their application (they must be between 18 and 19); they must prove they have been living in Italy without interruption; moreover, their parents had to be legally recognized at the moment of the child's birth and have remained so for the entire period until the coming of age of the son or the daughter (Ministero dell'Interno 2007). This latter requirement is particularly penalizing for children who end up paying for the 'faults' of their parents. Around half of the foreigners who currently hold an official residence permit have prior experience of irregular migration status. Moreover, it is quite common that parents decide to raise their children in the country of origin, at least for a short period of time, due to the long hours and harsh working conditions in Italy that do not allow them to take care of their children adequately, or because, by entrusting their children to relatives in their country of origin, they want their kids to learn their native language and traditions.
3. In the period 2007–10 there were around 40,000 new citizens each year, meaning that less than 1 per cent of regular migrants became citizens in

these years. Half of them had obtained citizenship by marrying an Italian (Ministero dell'Interno 2009, 2010).

5　Complex Identifications

1. See Portes 1996; Portes and Rumbaut 2001; Zéphir 2001; Levit and Waters 2002; Crul and Vermeulen 2003; Kasinitz et al. 2004; Saint-Blancat 2004; Zhou and Xiong 2005; Aparicio 2007; Fangen 2007; Massey and Sanchez 2007; Shah 2007; Räthzel 2008; Levitt 2009; Crul and Schneider 2010; Song 2010.
2. This is particularly evident with research using data reduction techniques or theoretically interested in constructing categories, so that it is possible to collocate all the different empirical forms of identification into a single table in which each case fits only one cell: 'One's cultural identity can be primarily *ethnic*, based in one's ethnic group, primarily *national*, based in the national society, or *bicultural*, based on a balancing or blending of the two cultures. If youth are unable to resolve the cultural identity issues that they face, they may exhibit identity *diffusion*' (Berry et al. 2006: 5).
3. For a critical introduction to the concept, see Collins 1990; West and Fenstermaker 1995; Anthias 2002b; Yuval-Davis 2006b, 2007, 2011; Nash 2008; Bilge 2010; Choo and Ferree 2010; Dhamoon 2011; Purkayastha 2012.

6　Children of Immigrants in Search of Justness

1. If we look at the etymology of the word, justness means both the quality or the state of being just, fair, equitable, right and the correctness of one's adjustment to a situation, according to its rules, constraints, opportunities and standards. Particularly, in Greek etymology justness concerns the practical harmony with the natural and right equilibrium of things; it is subjective and immanent.
2. If philosophy is engaged in the discussion of the normative and abstract status of justice – what justice should be, how it should be defined and with which procedures it should be applied – sociology has worked mainly on the empirical definitions and practices of the idea of justice. Thus, justice is not a transcendent truth, it is instead a contextualized interpretation for which social actors can 'feel in justness'. What the sociological research of Boltansky and Thévenot (2006) and later of François Dubet (2006) has shown is that in general there is a plural and contradictory definition of justice. The concern is not with the transcendent a priori of justice, but more with its representation and interpretation. Social actors produce normative ideas of justice, of what is legitimized and justified, and these ideas are not homogeneous.

References

Alba, R. D. and Nee, V. (1997) 'Rethinking Assimilation Theory for a New Era of Immigration', *International Migration Review*, 31(4): 826–74.

Alba, R. D. and Nee, V. (2003) *Remaking the American Mainstream: Assimilation and Contemporary Immigration*, Cambridge, MA: Harvard University Press.

Allasino, E. and Eve, M. (2008) 'Ceto medio negato? Fenomeni migratori e nuove questioni', in A. Bagnasco (ed.) *Ceto medio: Perché e come occuparsene*, Bologna: Il Mulino.

Ambrosini, M. (2001) *La Fatica di Integrarsi: Immigrati e Lavoro in Italia*, Bologna: Il Mulino.

Ambrosini, M. (2011) 'Surviving Underground: Irregular Migrants, Italian Families, Invisible Welfare', *International Journal of Social Welfare*, doi: 10.1111/j.1468-2397.2011.00837.x.

Ambrosini, M. and Queirolo Palmas, L. (2005) (eds) *I Latinos alla Scoperta dell'Europa, Nuove Migrazioni e Spazi di Cittadinanza*, Milano: FrancoAngeli.

Amin, A. (2002) 'Ethnicity and the Multicultural City: Living with Diversity', *Environment and Planning A*, 34(6): 959–80.

Andall, J. M. (2002) 'Second Generation Attitude? African-Italians in Milan', *Journal of Ethnic and Migration Studies*, 28(3): 389–407.

Andall, J. and Dukan, D. (2005) (eds) *Italian Colonialism. Legacy and Memory*, Bern: Peter Lang.

Anthias, F. (2001) 'New Hybridities, Old Concepts: The Limits of "Culture"', *Ethnic and Racial Studies*, (24)4: 619–41.

Anthias, F. (2002a) 'Where do I Belong? Narrating Collective Identity and Translocational Positionality', *Ethnicities*, 2(4): 491–514.

Anthias, F. (2002b) 'Beyond Feminism and Multiculturalism: Locating Difference and the Politics of Location', *Women's Studies International Forum*, 25(3): 275–86.

Anthias, F. (2006) 'Belonging in a Globalising and Unequal World: rethinking translocations', in N. Yuval-Davis, K. Kannabiran and U. M. Vieten (eds), *The Situated Politics of Belonging*, London: Sage.

Anthias, F. and Lloyd, C. (2002) *Rethinking Anti-Racism: From Theory to Practice*, London and New York: Routledge.

Antonsich, M. (2010) 'Searching for Belonging – An Analytical Framework', *Geography Compass*, 4(6): 644–59.

Aparicio, A. (2007) 'Contesting Race and Power: Second-Generation Dominican Youth in the New Gotham', *City & Society*, 19(2): 179–201.

Appadurai, A. (1996) *Modernity at Large: Cultural Dimensions of Globalization*, Minneapolis-London: University of Minnesota Press.

Appadurai, A. (2004) 'The Capacity to Aspire: Culture and the Terms of Recognition' in V. Rao and M. Walton (eds) *Culture and Public Action*, Stanford: Stanford University Press.

Appadurai, A. (2006) *Fear of Small Number: An Essay on the Geography of Anger*, Durham: Duke University Press.

Back, L. (1996) *New Ethnicities and Urban Culture*, London: UCL Press.

Bagnasco, A. (2008) (eds) *Ceto medio. Perché e come occuparsene*, Bologna: Il Mulino.

Baldassar, L. and Pesman, R. (2005) *From Paesani to Global Italians: Veneto Migrants in Australia*, Perth: University of Western Australia.

Baldwin-Edwards, M. and Arango, J. (1999) (eds.) *Immigrants and the Informal Economy in Southern Europe*, London: Frank Cass.

Balibar, E. (1988) 'Propositions on Citizenship', *Ethics*, 98(4): 723–30.

Ballard, R. (1994) 'Introduction: The Emergence of Desh Pardesh', in R. Ballard (ed.), *Desh Pardesh: The South Asian Presence in Britain*, London: Hurst & Company, London.

Banfield, E. C. (1958) *The Moral Basis of a Backward Society*, Glencoe: The Free Press.

Bauböck, R. and Guiraudon V. (2009) 'Introduction: Realignments of Citizenship: Reassessing Rights in the Age of Plural Membership and Multi-Level Governance', *Citizenship Studies*, 13(5): 439–50.

Bauman, Z. (2001) *Community: Seeking Safety in an Insecure World*, Cambridge: Polity Press.

Baumann, G. (1996) *Contesting Culture. Discourses of Identity in Multi-Ethnic London*, Cambridge: Cambridge University Press.

Baumann, G. (1997) 'Dominant and Demotic Discourses of Culture: Their Relevance to Multi-Ethnic Alliances', in P. Werbner and T. Moodod (eds) *Debating Cultural Hybridity. Multi-Cultural Identities and the Politics of Anti-Racism*, London: Zed.

Baumann, G. (1999) *The Multicultural Riddle*, New York and London: Routledge.

Beck, U. (2002) 'The Cosmopolitan Society and Its Enemies', *Theory, Culture & Society*, 19(1–2): 17–44.

Beck, U. (2006) *Cosmopolitan Vision*, Cambridge: Polity Press.

Beck, U. and Sznaider, N. (2006) 'Unpacking Cosmopolitanism for the Social Sciences: A Research Agenda', *The British Journal of Sociology*, 57(1): 1–23.

Benedicto, J. and Morales, M. L. (2007) 'Becoming a Citizen', *European Societies*, 9(4): 601–22.

Benhabib, S. (2002) *The Claims of Culture: Equality and Diversity in the Global Era*, Princeton: Princeton University Press.

Benhabib, S. (2004) *The Rights of Others: Aliens, Residents and Citizens*, Cambridge: Cambridge University Press.

Berry, J. W., Phinney, J. S., Sam, D. L. and Vedder, P. (2006) (eds) *Immigrant Youth in Cultural Transition. Acculturation, Identity and Adaptation Across National Contexts*, Mahwah, NJ: Lawrence Erlbaum Associates.

Besozzi, E., Colombo, M. and Santagati, M. (2009) *Giovani Stranieri, Nuovi Cittadini. Le Strategie di una Generazione Ponte*, Milano: FrancoAngeli.

Bhabha, H. K. (1994) *The Location of Culture*, London: Routledge.

Bilge, S. (2010) 'Beyond Subordination vs. Resistance: An Intersectional Approach to the Agency of Veiled Muslim Women', *Journal of Intercultural Studies*, 31(1): 9–28.

Biorcio, R. (2010) *La rivincita del Nord: La Lega dalla contestazione al governo*, Roma-Bari: Laterza.

Body-Gendrot, S. and Withol de Wenden, C. (2007) *Sortir des banlieues*, Paris: Autrement.

Boltanski, L. and Thévenot, L. (1991) *De la Justification: Les Economies de la Grandeur*, Paris: Gallimard. English Translation (2006) *On Justification. Economies of Worth*, Princeton: Princeton University Press.

Boltanski, L. and Chiapello, E. (2005) *The New Spirit of Capitalism*, London: Verso.

Bosisio, R., Colombo, E., Leonini, L. and Rebughini, P. (2005) *Stranieri & Italiani: Una Ricerca tra gli Adolescenti Figli di Immigranti nelle Scuole Superiori*, Roma: Donzelli.

Boubeker, A. (2003) *Les mondes de l'ethnicité*, Paris: Balland.

Boucher, M. and Lapeyronnie, D. (2010) (eds) *Les internés du ghetto. Ethnographie des confrontations violentes dans une cité impopulaire*, Paris: L'Harmattan.

Bourdieu, P. (1980) 'La jeunesse n'est qu'un mot', in Bourdieu, P. *Questions de Sociologie*, Paris: Ed. de Minuit.

Brubaker, R. (2001) 'The return of assimilation', *Ethnic and Racial Studies*, 24(4): 531–48.

Brubaker, R., Loveman, M. and Stamatov, P. (2004) 'Ethnicity as Cognition', *Theory and Society*, 33(1): 31–64.

Butcher, M. (2004) 'Universal Processes of Cultural Change: Reflections on the Identity Strategies of Indian and Australian Youth', *Journal of Intercultural Studies*, 25(3): 215–31.

Butcher, M. (2008) 'FOB Boys, VCs and Habibs: Using Language to Navigate Difference and Belonging in Cultural Diverse Sydney', *Journal of Ethnic and Migration Studies*, 34(3): 371–87.

Butcher, M. (2011) *Managing Cultural Change: Reclaiming Synchronicity in a Mobile World*, Farnham: Ashgate.

Caglar, A. S. (1997) 'Hyphenated Identity and the Limits of "Culture"', in T. Modood and P. Werbner (eds) *The Politics of Multiculturalism in the New Europe*, London: Zed Books.

Carrillo Rowe, A. (2005) 'Be Longing: Toward a Feminist Politics of Relation', *NWSA Journal*, 17(2): 15–46.

Caritas (2010) *Dossier Statistico Immigrazione Caritas-Migrantes 2010*, Roma: Edizioni Idos.

Castells, M. (2009) *Communication Power*, Oxford and New York: Oxford University Press.

Child, I. L. (1943) *Italian or American? The Second Generation in Conflict*, New Haven: Yale University Press.

Choo, H. Y. and Ferree M. M. (2010) 'Practicing Intersectionality in Sociological Research: A Critical Analysis of Inclusions, Interactions, and Institutions in the Study of Inequalities', *Sociological Theory*, 28(2): 129–49.

Collins, P. H. (1990) *Black Feminist Thought: Knowledge, Consciousness, and the Politics of Empowerment*, Boston: Unwin Hyman.

Colombo, E. (2010a) 'Crossing Differences: How Young Children of Immigrants Keep Everyday Multiculturalism Alive', *Journal of Intercultural Studies*, 31(5): 455–70.

Colombo, E. (2010b) 'Changing Citizenship: Everyday Representations of Membership, Belonging and Identification among Italian Senior Secondary School Students', *Italian Journal of Sociology of Education*, 4(1): 129–53.

Colombo, E., Domaneschi, L. and Marchetti, C. (2011) 'Citizenship and Multiple Belonging. Representations of Inclusion, Identification and Participation among Children of Immigrants in Italy', *Journal of Modern Italian Studies*, 16(3): 334–47.

Colombo, E., Leonini, L. and Rebughini, P. (2009) 'Different But Not Stranger: Everyday Collective Identification among Adolescent Children of Immigrants in Italy', *Journal of Ethnic and Migration Studies*, 35(1): 37–59.

Colombo, E. and Semi, G. (2007) *Multiculturalismo quotidiano: Le pratiche della differenza*, Milano: Franco Angeli.

Crul, M. and Vermeulen, H. (2003) 'The Second Generation in Europe', *International Migration Review*, 37(4): 965–86.

Crul, M. and Schneider, J. (2009) *The Second Generation in Europe: Education and the Transition to the Labour Market*, London: OSI.

Crul, M. and Schneider, J. (2010) 'Comparative Integration Context Theory: Participation and Belonging in New Diverse European Cities, *Ethnic and Racial Studies*, 33(7): 1249–68.

Dean, H. and Melrose, M. (1999) *Poverty, Riches and Social Citizenship*, Basingstoke: Macmillan.

De Certeau, M. (1990) *L'invention du quotidien. I. Arts de faire*, Paris: Gallimard.

Delanty, G. (2000) *Citizenship in a Global Age*, Buckingham: Open University Press.

Dalla Zuanna, G., Farina, P. and Strozza, S. (2009) *Nuovi Italiani. I giovani immigrati cambieranno il nostro paese?* Bologna: Il Mulino.

Dhamoon, R.K. (2011) 'Considerations on Mainstreaming Intersectionality', *Political Research Quarterly*, 64(1): 230–43.

Diamanti, I. (1995) *La Lega. Geografia, storia e sociologia di un nuovo soggetto politico*, Roma: Donzelli.

Domaneschi, L. and Rebughini, P. (2009) 'Le scelte di consumo dei giovani figli di migranti. Tra inclusione, esclusione e risorse di identificazione', in L. Bovone and C. Lunghi (eds) *Consumi ai margini*, Roma: Donzelli.

Dubet, F. and Lapeyronnie, D. (1992) *Les quartiers d'exil*, Paris: Seuil.

Dubet, F. (2004) *L'école des chances: Qu'est-ce qu'une école juste?*, Paris: Seuil.

Dubet, F. (2006) *Injustices: L'Expérience des Inegalités au Travail*, Paris: Seuil.

Edmunds, J. and Turner, B. S. (2002) *Generations, Culture and Society*, London: Open University Press.

Eisenstadt, S. N. (1956) *From Generation to Generation*, New York: The Free Press.

Elias, N. and Lemish, D. (2009) 'Spinning the Web of Identity: the Roles of the Internet in the Lives of Immigrant Adolescents', *New Media & Society*, 11(4): 533–51.

Espiritu, Y. L. (1992) *Asian American Panethnicity*, Philadelphia: Temple University Press.

Eurobarometer, (2009) http://ec.europa.eu/public_opinion/archives/eb/eb71/eb71_it_en_exec.pdf.

European Commission Against Racism and Intolerance (2002) *Second Report on Italy*, http://hudoc.ecri.coe.int/XMLEcri/ENGLISH/Cycle_02/02_ CbC_eng/02-cbc-italy-eng.pdf.

European Commission Against Racism and Intolerance (2006) *Third Report on Italy*, http://hudoc.ecri.coe.int/XMLEcri/ENGLISH/Cycle_03/03_CbC_eng/ ITA-CbC-III-2006-19-ENG.pdf.

European Commission Against Racism and Intolerance (2012) *ECRI Report on Italy. Fourth Monitoring Cycle*, http://www.coe.int/t/dghl/monitoring/ecri/ Country-by-country/Italy/ITA-CbC-IV-2012-002-ENG.pdf.

Eve, M. (2010) 'Integrating via networks: foreigners and others', *Ethnic and Racial Studies*, 33(7): 1231–48.

Faist, T. (2000) *The Volume and Dynamics of International Migration and Transnational Spaces*, Oxford: Oxford University Press.

Faist, T. (2009) 'Diversity – a New Mode of Incorporation?', *Ethnic and Racial Studies*, 32(1): 171–90.

Fangen, K. (2007) 'Breaking Up the Different Constituting Part of Ethnicity: The Case of Young Somalis in Norway', *Acta Sociologica*, 50(4): 401–14.

Fanon, F. (1963) *The Wretched of the Earth*, New York: Grove.

Fanon, F. (1966) *Black Skin, White Masks*, New York: Grove.

Favaro, G. and Omenetto, C. (1998) *Bambine e Bambini di qui e d'Altrove*, Milano: Guerini e Associati.

Featherstone, M. (2002) 'Cosmopolis: An Introduction', *Theory, Culture & Society*, 19(1–2): 1–16.

Fraser, N. (2009) *Scales of Justice: Reimagining Political Space in a Globalizing World*, New York: Columbia University Press.

Fraser, N. and Honneth, A. (2003) *Redistribution or Recognition: A Political Philosophical Exchange*, London: Verso.

Frisina, A. (2010) 'Young Muslims' Everyday Tactics and Strategies: Resisting Islamophobia, Negotiating Italianness, Becoming Citizens', *Journal of Intercultural Studies*, 31(5): 557–72.

Gans, H. J. (1979) 'Symbolic Ethnicity: The Future of Ethnic Groups and Culture in America', *Ethnic and Racial Studies*, 2(1): 1–20.

Gans, H. J. (1992) 'Second-generation Decline: Scenarios for the Economic and Ethic Futures of the Post-1965 American Immigrants', *Ethnic and Racial Studies*, 15(2): 173–92.

Gans, H. J. (1997) 'Toward a Reconciliation of "Assimilation" and "Pluralism": The Interplay of Acculturation and Ethnic Retention', *International Migration Review*, 31(4): 875–92.

Giddens, A. (1990) *The Consequences of Modernity*, Stanford: Stanford University Press.

Gilroy, P. (1987) *There Ain't No Black in the Union Jack: The Cultural Politics of Race and Nation*, London: Hutchinson.

Gilroy, P. (1993) *The Black Atlantic. Modernity and Double Consciousness*, London: Verso.

Glick Schiller, N., Basch, H. and Szanton Blanc, C. (1992) (eds) *Toward a Transnational Perspective on Migration*, New York: New York Academy of Sciences.

Goffman, E. (1956) 'The Nature of Deference and Demeanor', *American Anthropologist*, 58(3): 473–502.

Gold, T. W. (2003) *The Lega Nord and Contemporary Politics in Italy*, Basingstoke: Palgrave Macmillan.

Gordon, M. M. (1966) *Assimilation in American Life*, New York: Oxford University Press.

Habermas, J. (1999) *Wahrheit und Rechtfertigung: Philosophische Aufsätze*, Frankfurt am Main: Suhrkamp. English Translation (2003) *Truth and Justification*, Cambridge MA: MIT Press.

Hage, G. (2010) 'The Affective Politics of Racial Mis-interpellation', *Theory, Culture & Society*, 27(7–8): 112–29.

Hall, S. (1989) 'New Ethnicities', in K. Mercer (ed.) *ICA Documents 7: Black Film, British Cinema*, London: Institute of Contemporary Arts.

Hall, S., Critcher, C., Jefferson, T, Clarke, J. N. and Roberts, B. (1978) *Policing the Crisis: Mugging, the State and Law and Order*, Basingstoke: Macmillan.

Hall, T., Coffey, A. and Williamson, H. (1999) 'Self, Space and Place: Youth Identities and Citizenship', *British Journal of Sociology of Education*, 20(4): 501–13.

Hammack, P. L. (2010) 'Narrating Hyphenated Selves: Intergroup Contact and Configurations of Identity among Young Palestinian Citizens of Israel', *International Journal of Intercultural Relations*, 34(4): 368–85.

Hannerz, U. (1996) *Transnational Connections: Culture, People, Places*, London and New York: Routledge.

Harris, A. (2010) 'Young People, Everyday Civic Life and the Limits of Social Cohesion', *Journal of Intercultural Studies*, 31(5): 573–89.

Hart, S. (2009) 'The "Problem" with Youth: Young People, Citizenship and the Community', *Citizenship Studies*, 13(6): 641–57.

Honneth, A. (1995) *The Struggle for Recognition*, Cambridge: Polity.

Hussain, Y. and Bagguley, P. (2005) 'Citizenship, Ethnicity and Identity: British Pakistanis after the 2001 "Riots"', *Sociology*, 39(3): 407–25.

Isin, E. F. and Nielsen, G. M. (2008) (eds) *Acts of Citizenship*, London and New York: Zed Books.

Isin, E. F. and Turner, B. S. (2002) *Handbook of Citizenship Studies*, London: Sage.

ISTAT (2011) 'La popolazione straniera residente in Italia', http://www.istat.it/it/archivio/39726.

Jiménez, T. R. (2010) 'Affiliative Ethnic Identity: A More Elastic Link between Ethnic Ancestry and Culture', *Ethnic and Racial Studies*, 33(10): 1756–75.

Joppke, C. (2007a) 'Transformation of Citizenship: Status, Rights, Identity', *Citizenship Studies*, 11(1): 37–48.

Joppke, C. (2007b) 'Transformation of Immigrant Integration; Civic Integration and Antidiscrimination in the Netherlands, France and Germany', *World Politics*, 59(2): 243–73.

Khanna, N. (2011) 'Ethnicity and Race as "Symbolic": The Use of Ethnic and Racial Symbols in Asserting a Biracial Identity', *Ethnic and Racial Studies*, 34(6): 1049–67.

Kasinitz, P., Mollenkopf, J. H. and Waters, M. C. (2004) (eds) *Becoming New Yorkers: Ethnographies of the New York Second Generation*, New York: Russell Sage Foundation.

Kasinitz, P., Mollenkopf, J. H., Waters, M. C. and Holdaway, J. (2008) *Inheriting the City. The Children of Immigrants Come of Age*, New York: Russell Sage Foundation.

Keith, M. and Cross, M. (1993) *Racism, the City and the State*, London: Routledge.

Kendall, G., Woodward, I. and Skrbis, Z. (2009) *The Sociology of Cosmopolitanism*, Basingstoke: Palgrave Macmillan.

Kennedy, D. M. and Bailey, T. A. (2010) *The American Spirit: Volume II. Since the 1865*, Boston: Wadsworth Cengage Learning.

Kibria, N. (2002) *Becoming Asian American. Second-Generation Chinese and Korean American Identities*, Baltimore: The Johns Hopkins University Press.

Kivisto, P. (2001) 'Theorizing Transnational Immigration: A Critical View of Current Efforts', *Ethnic and Racial Studies*, 24(4): 549–77.

Kivisto, P. (2006) *Multiculturalism in Global Society*, Oxford: Blackwell Publishing.

Lamont, M., Camic, C. and Gross, N. (2011) (eds) *Social Knowledge in the Making*, Chicago: University of Chicago Press.

Landau, L. B. and Freemantle, I. (2010) 'Tactical Cosmopolitanism and Idioms of Belonging: Insertion and Self-Exclusion in Johannesburg', *Journal of Ethnic and Migration Studies*, 36(3): 375–90.

Lapeyronnie, D. (2008) *Ghetto urbain: Ségrégation, violence, pauvreté en France aujourd'hui*, Paris: Laffont.

Lash, S. (1999) *Another Modernity: A Different Rationality*, Oxford: Blackwell.

Leonini, L. and Rebughini, P. (2010) (eds) *Legami di Nuova Generazione: Relazioni Famigliari e Pratiche di Consumo tra i Giovani Discendenti di Migranti*, Bologna: Il Mulino.

Levitt, P. (2009) 'Roots and Routes: Understanding the Lives of the Second Generation Transnationally', *Journal of Ethnic and Migration Studies*, 35(7): 1225–42.

Levitt, P. and Glick Schiller, N. (2004) 'Conceptualizing Simultaneity: A Transnational Social Field Perspective on Society', *International Migration Review*, 38(3): 1002–39.

Levitt, P. and Waters, M. C. (2002) (eds) *The Changing Face of Home. The Transnational Lives of the Second Generation*, New York: Russell Sage Foundation.

Lister, R., Smith, N., Middleton, S. and Cox, L. (2003) 'Young People Talk about Citizenship: Empirical Perspectives on Theoretical and Political Debate', *Citizenship Studies*, 7(2): 235–53.

Livingstone, S. (2002) *Young People and New Media: Children and the Changing Media Environment*, London: Sage.

Mannheim, K. (1952) 'The Problem of Generations', in K. Mannheim (ed.) *Essays on the Sociology of Knowledge*, London: Routledge & Kegan Paul Ltd.

Martuccelli, D. (2010) *La Société Singulariste*, Paris: Armand Colin.

Marshall, T. H. (1964) *Class, Citizenship and Social Development: Essays by T. H. Marshall*, New York: Anchor Books.

Massey, D. S. and Sanchez, M. R. (2007) 'Latino and American Identities as Perceived by Immigrants', *Qualitative Sociology*, 30(1): 81–107.

Melucci, A. (1996a) *Challenging Codes: Collective Action in the Information Age,* Cambridge: Cambridge University Press.

Melucci, A. (1996b) *The Playing Self: Person and Meaning in the Planetary Society,* Cambridge: Cambridge University Press.

Ministero dell'Interno (2007) *Primo rapporto sugli immigrati in Italia,* http://www.interno.it/mininterno/export/sites/default/it/assets/files/15/0673_Rapporto_immigrazione_BARBAGLI.pdf.

Ministero dell'Interno (2009) *L'immigrazione in Italia tra identità e pluralismo culturale,* http://www.interno.it/mininterno/export/sites/default/it/assets/files/17/0995_immigrazione_Italia_Indice_rev5.pdf.

Ministero dell'Interno (2010) *Cittadinanza,* http://www.interno.it/mininterno/export/sites/default/it/temi/cittadinanza.

Miller-Idriss, C. (2006) 'Everyday Understanding of Citizenship in Germany', *Citizenship Studies,* 10(5): 541–70.

Moscovici, S. (1979) *Psychologie des minorités actives,* Paris: PUF.

Nash, J. C. (2008) 'Re-Thinking Intersectionality', *Feminist Review,* 89(1): 1–15.

Noble, G. (2009) 'Everyday Cosmopolitanism and the Labour of Intercultural Community', in A. Wise and S. Velayutham (eds) *Everyday Multiculturalism,* Basingstoke: Palgrave Macmillan.

Noble, G., Poynting, S. and Tabar, P. (1999) 'Youth, Ethnicity and the Mapping of Identities: Strategic Essentialism and Strategic Hybridity among Male Arabic-Speaking Youth in South-Western Sydney', *Communal/plural,* 7(1): 29–44.

Nussbaum, M. and Sen, A. (1993) *The Quality of Life,* Oxford: Clarendon Press.

Okamura, J. (1981) 'Situational Ethnicity', *Ethnic and Racial Studies,* 4(4): 452–65.

Ong, A. (1999) *Flexible Citizenship. The Cultural Logic of Transnationalism,* Durham: Duke University Press.

Park, R. E. (1928) 'Human Migration and the Marginal Man', *American Journal of Sociology,* 33(6): 881–93.

Park, R. E. (1950) *Race and Culture,* Glencoe Hill: Free Press.

Pawley, L. (2008) 'Cultural Citizenship', *Sociology Compass,* 2(2): 594–608.

Payet, J.-P. (2002) 'Ségrégation scolaire: état des lieux, perspectives d'action', *Les Cahiers du CR-DSU,* 36: 39–40.

Perry, P. (2001) 'White Means Never having to Say you're Ethnic: White Youth and the Construction of "Cultureless" Identities', *Journal of Contemporary Ethnography,* 30(1): 56–91.

Pilcher, J. (1994) 'Mannheim's Sociology of Generations: An Undervalued Legacy', *The British Journal of Sociology,* 45(3) 481–95.

Portes, A. (ed.) (1996) *The New Second Generation,* New York: Russell Sage Foundation.

Portes, A., Fernández-Kelly, P. and Haller, W. (2009) 'The Adaptation of the Immigrant Second Generation in America: A Theoretical Overview and Recent Evidence', *Journal of Ethnic and Migration Studies,* 35(7): 1077–104.

Portes, A. and Rumbaut, R. G. (2001) *Legacies. The Story of the Immigrant Second Generation,* Berkeley: University of California Press.

Poynting, S., Noble, S., Tabar, P. and Collins, J. (2004) *Bin Laden in the Suburbs: Criminalising the Arab Other,* Sydney: Institute of Criminology.

Pugliese, E. (2006) *L'Italia tra migrazioni internazionali e migrazioni interne*, Bologna: Il Mulino.

Purkayastha, B. (2005) *Negotiating Ethnicity. Second-Generation South Asian Americans Traverse a Transnational World*, New Brunswick: Rutgers University Press.

Purkayastha, B. (2012) 'Intersectionality in a Transnational World', *Gender & Society*, 26(1): 55–66.

Queirolo Palmas, L. (2006) *Prove di Seconde Generazioni*, Milano: FrancoAngeli.

Räthzel, N. (2008) (ed.) *Finding the Way Home*, Göttingen: V&R unipress.

Räthzel, N. (2010) 'The Injuries of the Margins and the Restorative Power of the Political: How Young People with Migrant Background Create their Capacity to Act', *Journal of Intercultural Studies*, 31(5): 541–55.

Ravecca, A. (2009) *Studiare nonostante: capitale sociale e successo scolastico degli studenti di origine immigrata nella scuola superiore*, Milano: FrancoAngeli.

Rawls, J. (1971) *A Theory of Justice*, Harvard: Harvard University Press.

Rebughini, P. (1999) 'Réflexions sur la violence juvénile. Un regard comparatif sur la situation française et italienne', *Recherches Sociologiques*, 30(1): 139–56.

Rebughini, P. (2010) 'Critique and Social Movements: Looking beyond Contingency and Normativity', *European Journal of Social Theory*, 13(4): 459–79.

Rebughini, P. (2011) 'Consommation et cultures de la différence chez les jeunes descendants d'immigrés: le cas italien' *Revue Européenne des Migrations Internationales*, 27 (2): 101–16.

Rex, J. (1996) *Ethnic Minorities in the Modern Nation State*, Basingstoke: Macmillan.

Riccio, B. (2008) *Migrazioni Transnazionali dall'Africa*, Torino: UTET.

Riccio, B. and Russo, M. (2011) 'Everyday Practised Citizenship and the Challenges of Representation: Second-Generation Associations in Bologna', *Journal of Modern Italian Studies*, 16(3): 360–72.

Rich, P. (1986) *Race and Empire in British Politics*, Cambridge: Cambridge University Press.

Said, E. W. (2001) (G. Wisvanathan, ed.) *Power, Politics and Culture: Interviews with Edward W. Said*, New York: Pantheon Books.

Saint-Blancat, C. (2004) 'La transmission de l'Islam auprès des nouvelles générations de la diaspora', *Social Compass*, 51(2): 235–47.

Sassen, S. (1998) *Globalization and its Discontents: Essays on the New Mobility of People and Money*, New York: The New Press.

Sayad, A. (1999) *La double absence: Des illusions de l'émigré aux souffrances de l'immigré*, Paris: Seuil.

Scheibelhofer, P. (2007) 'His-Stories of Belonging: Young Second-Generation Turkish Men in Austria', *Journal of Intercultural Studies*, 28(3): 317–30.

Sciortino, G. (2004) 'Immigration in a Mediterranean Welfare State: The Italian Experience in a Comparative Perspective', *Journal of Comparative Policy Analysis* 6: 111–28.

Sciortino, G. and Colombo, A. (2004) 'The Flows and the Flood: The Public Discourse on Immigration in Italy, 1969–2001', *Journal of Modern Italian Studies*, 9(1): 94–113.

Semi G., Colombo, E., Camozzi, I. and Frisina, A. (2009) 'Practices of Difference: Analysing Multiculturalism in Everyday Life', in A. Wise and S. Velayutham (eds) *Everyday Multiculturalism*, Basingstoke: Palgrave Macmillan.

Sennett, R. (2008) *The Craftsman*, New Haven: Yale University Press.

Shah, B. (2007) 'Being Young, Female and Laotian: Ethnicity as Social Capital at the Intersection of Gender, Generation, "Race" and Age', *Ethnic and Racial Studies*, 30(1): 28–50.

Skrbiš, Z., Baldassar, L. and Poynting, S. (2007) 'Introduction – Negotiating Belonging: Migration and Generation', *Journal of Intercultural Studies*, 28(3): 261–9.

Skrobanek, J. (2009) 'Perceived Discrimination, Ethnic Identity and the (Re-) Ethnicisation of Youth with a Turkish Ethnic Background in Germany', *Journal of Ethnic and Migration Studies*, 35(4): 535–54.

Smith, M. P. and Guarnizo, L. E. (1998) (eds) *Transnationalism from Below*, New Brunswick: Transaction Publishers.

Sniderman, P. M., Peri, P., de Figueiredo, R. J. P. and Piazza, T. (2000) *The Outsider: Prejudice and Politics in Italy*, Princeton: Princeton University Press.

Solomos J. and Beyon, J. (1987) (eds) *The Roots of Urban Unrest*, Oxford: Pergamon Press.

Solomos, J. and Back, L. (1995) *Race, Politics and Social Change*, London: Routledge.

Somerville, K. (2008) 'Transnational Belonging among Second Generation Youth: Identity in a Globalized World', *Journal of Social Science*, Special Volume n. 10: 23–33.

Song, M. (2003) *Choosing Ethnic Identity*, Cambridge: Polity Press.

Song, M. (2010) 'What Happens after Segmented Assimilation? An Exploration of Intermarriage and "Mixed Race" Young People in Britain', *Ethnic and Racial Studies*, 33(7): 1194–213.

Soysal, Y. (1994) *Limits of Citizenship: Migrants and Postnational Membership in Europe*, Chicago: University of Chicago Press.

Spanò, A. (2011) (ed.) *Esistere, coesistere, resistere*, Milano: FrancoAngeli.

Spivak, G. C. (S. Harasym, ed.) (1990) *The Post-colonial Critic: Interviews, Strategies, Dialogues*, New York & London: Routledge.

Spivak, G. C. (1999) *A Critique of Postcolonial Reason: Toward a History of Vanishing Present*, Harvard: Harvard University Press.

Stanczak, G.C. (2006) 'Strategic Ethnicity: The Construction of Multi-Racial/ Multi-Ethnic Religious Community', *Ethnic and Racial Studies*, 29(5): 856–81.

Stevenson, N. (ed.) (2001) *Culture and Citizenship*, London: Sage.

Suárez-Orozco, M. (2001) 'Global shifts: US Migration and the cultural impact of demographic change' in J. S. Little and R. K. Triest (eds) *Seismic Shifts: The Economic Impact of Demographic Change*, Boston: Federal Reserve Bank of Boston Conference Series No. 46: 179–88.

Tambini, D. (2001a) *Nationalism in Italian Politics: The Stories of the Northern League 1980–2000*, London and New York: Routledge.

Tambini, D. (2001b) 'Post-National Citizenship', *Ethnic and Racial Studies*, 24(2): 195–217.

Taylor, C. (1992) *Multiculturalism and the Politics of Recognition*, Princeton: Princeton University Press.

Thompson, S. and Yar, M. (2011) (eds.) *The Politics of Misrecognition*, Farnham: Ashgate.

Tomlinson, J. (1999) *Globalisation and Culture*, Chicago: University of Chicago Press.

Touraine, A. (1984) *Le Retour de l'Acteur*, Paris: Fayard.

Touraine, A. (1997) *Pourrons nous vivre ensemble? Egaux et différents*, Paris: Fayard.

Valtolina G. and Marazzi, A. (2006) *Appartenenze multiple: L'esperienza dell'immigrazione nelle nuove generazioni*, Milano: FrancoAngeli.

Vasquez, J. M. (2010) 'Blurred Borders for some but not "Others": Racialization, "Flexible Ethnicity", Gender and Third-Generation Mexican American Identity', *Sociological Perspectives*, 53(1): 45–71.

Vertovec, S. (1999) 'Conceiving and Researching Transnationalism', *Ethnic and Racial Studies*, 22(2): 447–62.

Vertovec, S. (2004) 'Migrant Transnationalism and Modes of Transformation', *International Migration Review*, 38(3): 970–1001.

Warikoo, N. (2005) 'Gender and Ethnic Identity among Second-generation Indo-Caribbeans', *Ethnic and Racial Studies*, 28(5): 803–31.

Waters, M. C. (1990), *Ethnic Options: Choosing Identities in America*, Berkeley: University of California Press.

Werbner, P. (1997) 'Essentialising Essentialism, Essentialising Silence: Ambivalence and Multiplicity in the Constructions of Racism and Ethnicity', in P. Werbner and T. Moodod (eds) *Debating Cultural Hybridity: Multi-Cultural Identities and the Politics of Anti-Racism*, London: Zed.

Werbner, P. (2005) 'The Translocation of Culture: "Community Cohesion" and the Force of Multiculturalism in History', *The Sociological Review*, 53(4): 745–68.

Werbner, P. and Anwar, M. (1991) *Black and Ethnic Leaderships in Britain: The cultural Dimensions of Political Action*, London and New York: Routledge.

Wessendorf, S. (2007) 'Roots-Migrants: Transnationalism and "Return" among Second-generation Italians in Switzerland', *Journal of Ethnic and Migration Studies*, 33(7): 1083–102.

Wessendorf, S. (2010) 'Local Attachments and Transnational Everyday Lives: Second-Generation Italians in Switzerland', *Global Networks*, 10(3): 365–82.

West, C. and Fenstermaker, S. (1995) 'Doing Difference', *Gender & Society*, 9(1): 8–37.

Wieviorka, M. (1996) (eds) *Une société fragmentée? Le multiculturalisme en débat*, Paris: La Découverte.

Wieviorka, M. (1999) (eds) *Violence en France*, Paris: Seuil.

Wieviorka, M. (2008) 'L'intégration: un concept en difficulté', *Cahiers Internationaux de Sociologie*, 75: 221–40.

Williams, R. (1958) *Culture and Society*, London: Harper and Row.

Wise, A. and Velayutham, S. (eds) (2009) *Everyday Multiculturalism*, Basingstoke: Palgrave Macmillan.

Withol de Wenden, C. (2008) *La Globalisation Humaine*, Paris: PUF.
Yeğenoğlu, M. (2005) 'Cosmopolitanism and Nationalism in a Globalized World', *Ethnic and Racial Studies*, 28(1): 103–31.
Yuval-Davis, N. (2006a) 'Belonging and the Politics of Belonging', *Patterns of Prejudice*, 40(3): 197–214.
Yuval-Davis, N. (2006b) 'Intersectionality and Feminist Politics', *European Journal of Women's Studies*, 13(3): 193–209.
Yuval-Davis, N. (2007) 'Intersectionality, Citizenship and Contemporary Politics of Belonging', *Critical Review of International Social and Political Philosophy*, 10(4): 561–74.
Yuval-Davis, N. (2011) *The Politics of Belonging: Intersectional Contestations*, London: Sage.
Yuval-Davis, N., Kannabiran, K. and Vieten, U. M. (2006) *The Situated Politics of Belonging*, London: Sage.
Zéphir, F. (2001) *Trends in Ethnic Identification among Second-Generation Haitian Immigrants in New York City*, Westport, CT: Bergin & Garvey.
Zhou, M. and Xiong, Y.S. (2005) 'The Multifaceted American Experiences of the Children of Asian Immigrants: Lessons for Segmented Assimilation', *Ethnic and Racial Studies*, 28(6): 1119–52.
Zincone, G. (2006) 'The Making of Policies: Immigration and Immigrants in Italy,' *Journal of Ethnic and Migration Studies*, 32(3): 347–75.
Zinn, D. L. (2011) '"Loud and clear": The G2 Second Generations Network in Italy', *Journal of Modern Italian Studies*, 16(3): 373–85.
Zukin, S. (2010) *Naked City: The Death and Life of Authentic Urban Places*, Oxford: Oxford University Press.

Index